EMPRESS OF REVOLT

Neema G.W.

About the author *Neema G.W.*

In a world rich with the echoes of history and vibrant heritage, Neema G.W emerges as a unique voice, weaving the past with the present and tradition with modern insight. Born in Kenya and later honed by the disciplines of nursing in Germany, Neema stands at the nexus of neurology, psychiatry, and profound storytelling. Her journey - from an avid young reader, finding solace in book reading and writing short stories amidst the tumults of adolescence, to declaring her future authorship within the sterile environ-ment of medical school - reflects a steadfast dream undiminished by any barrier.

Neema's writing is deeply rooted in her Mijikenda heritage, drawing inspiration from the resilient figure of Me-Katilili wa Menza, to shine a light on historical narratives long overshadowed.

Her pilgrimage to Kenya, immersing herself in the wisdom of elders, marked the beginning of a renewed storytelling endeavor - imbuing her narratives with the soul of Mijikenda culture - influenced by luminaries such as John Grisham and Maya Angelou, her literary work nonetheless centers on the enriching tales of Me-Katilili, blending personal lineage with broader human experiences.

Her ambition extends beyond storytelling; it is a mission to encapsulate the rich tableau of African legends and fables, safeguarding these tales for posterity.

Neema invites readers on a captivating journey through the landscapes of imagination and the essence of cultural heritage. She offers a retreat from the rapid pace of modern life, encouraging a dive into the depth of stories that have not only shaped her vision but also poised to inspire exploration and discovery in others.

Join Neema in traversing the realms of thought and the rich heritage of the Mijikenda, where the vibrancy of African stories awaits to unfold.

https://neemagw.com

Facebook: @neema.gw   Twitter: @neemagw

Instagram: @neema.g.w   Pinterest: @neemagw

EMPRESS
OF
REVOLT

Me~Katilili's fight for the motherland's soul

A thrilling factual novel. True story.

Author: Neema G.W.

1st Paperback Edition 04/2024

Published by:

GoWriters Media, D-81375 Munich (Germany), Eichenstr. 28 b

https://www.gowriters.media

Author: Neema G.W. c/o GoWriters Media

ISBN: 978-3-911370-10-3

DEDICATION

This book is dedicated to our distinguished forebears and all eminent ancestors, especially to the invincible Me-Katilili, and to all the valiant freedom fighters who courageously battled for Africa's freedom.

It is also a tribute to my father, M. Gakweli W., who made every effort to provide me, an African girl, with the finest education within his means.

HEARTFELT APPRECIATION

In this journey, the warmth and unwavering support of my family and friends have been my lighthouse in the storm. Your support, encouragement, and endless patience transcend words and fill me with an indescribable sense of gratitude.

I extend my deepest appreciation to the elders of the sacred *Kayas*, notably Justice Joseph Mwarandu, Baya Mitstanze, Mwanyae, Kazungu wa Hawe-Risa and the lineage of Me-Katilili. Their selfless generosity in sharing invaluable insights has been a cornerstone of this endeavor.

A heartfelt acknowledgment to Mrs. Agnes Thoya, who graciously guided me through the hidden treasures of the remaining Giriama villages.

My gratitude also embraces those whose vision birthed *Kiuyeuye* and the community-centric MADCA (Malindi District Cultural Association), Justice Joseph Mwarandu and Stanslous Kahindi Kiraga.

To Christian Weiss, mere words fall short of expressing my immense gratitude. You have been an inspiration, urging me to aim beyond the stars. Your support is out of this world! The nights spent in pursuit of knowledge and ideas, our "bat" nights, were invaluable. Your brilliant mind grasped Me-Katilili's narrative with ease, providing me with all the necessary information with agility and readiness. Your generous spirit illuminates the darkest corners, and for that, I am eternally grateful.

To my phenomenal mother Nkanzingo, a fighter, who embarks victorious in all battles of life. Thank you for fighting for me.

To my extraordinarily gifted son, Sadiq Gakweli, I see the vastness of the universe reflected in your eyes. You embody potential and promise. I see you, my son, shining bright with endless possibilities.

Last but not least, to my adventurous nieces, Daiya and Aziza, continue to explore without limits. A magnificent world awaits your footsteps. Soar high.

DISCLAIMER

This book is a creative retelling of the life and struggles of Me-Katilili wa Menza, a renowned freedom fighter who played a pivotal role in resisting colonial rule. The narrative within these pages seeks to honor her legacy and the indomitable spirit of all those who stood beside her during those turbulent times.

In our endeavor to present a cohesive and respectful narrative, we have made certain adjustments to the historical account. Some names have been changed to protect the dignity and privacy of individuals who might otherwise find their portrayals in a diminutive, dehumanizing, or embarrassing light. This decision was made out of respect for the descendants of these figures and the communities involved, ensuring that their ancestors are remembered with honor and integrity.

Additionally, please be aware that some events have been creatively sculptured to more vividly capture the essence of the era and the monumental struggles faced by Me-Katilili wa Menza and her contemporaries. These adaptations were crafted with the utmost respect for historical accuracy, aiming to fill the gaps where historical records may be sparse or contradictory.

It is important to note that the information presented in this book is drawn from a wide array of sources, encompassing oral narratives passed down through generations and various documented reports. Given the nature of these sources, there are instances where accounts differ or contradict one another. Our narrative seeks to navigate these complexities, offering a portrayal that respects the multifaceted nature of history and the many voices that contribute to it.

By engaging with this book, readers embark on a journey through a creatively reimagined past that, while not strictly adhering to every historical detail, strives to convey the profound impact of Me-Katilili wa Menza's fight for freedom.

Our goal is to inspire reflection on the sacrifices made for the liberties we enjoy today and to celebrate the enduring legacy of those who dared to resist oppression.

We invite you to read this account with an open heart and mind, embracing the spirit of resilience and courage that defines the remarkable story of Me-Katilili wa Menza.

CONTENT

The Ancient World of the Mijikenda

Before the chronicles of history were etched in the annals of time, there existed a world where the spirit of humanity danced with the rhythm of the earth. This was the land of the Mijikenda, nestled along the lush eastern coast of Africa, a place where the echoes of the past whispered through the dense forests of the sacred *Kayas*. Here, in this cradle of civilization, the Mijikenda thrived under the canopy of equatorial skies, their lives a harmonious blend of tradition, spirituality, and communal integrity.

The governance of the Mijikenda was a testament to their sophisticated societal structure. It was presided over by a council of elders and chiefs, who guided their people with wisdom and foresight. Their economy flourished through agriculture, hunting, and trade, and their markets were a bustling nexus of cultural exchange.

The heart of their faith pulsed with a deep reverence for *Mulungu*, the supreme God, and a veneration for the ancestors, whose spirits safeguarded their communities.

The arrival of foreign influences since late 15th century

However, the tranquility of this society was destined to be shattered by the sails of foreign ships on the horizon.

The arrival of Vasco da Gama in the late 15th century heralded the beginning of an era of external influence and domination. The Portuguese, with their fortresses and firepower, were but the first in a series of foreign powers that would seek to claim dominion over the East African coast.

Mombasa and Zanzibar became focal points of conflict and cultural exchange, as the Portuguese were supplanted by the Omani Arabs in the late 17th century, who left an indelible mark on the region through the spread of Islam and the integration of Omani customs into the local culture.

In the early 19th century, the Omanis had moved their capital city from Oman to Zanzibar, from where they controlled the Kenyan coastal area as well.

Eventually the British took over the control in the late 19th century by claiming Kenya as protectorate and later as colony.

The cultural fusion of East Africa was further enriched by the arrival of foreign traders and immigrants: Persians, Indians, Chinese, Spaniards, Turks, Italians, Germans, and French - each adding new threads to the fabric of local society.

The Kiswahili language, a linguistic melding of Bantu, Arabic, Persian, and later European languages, emerged as a lingua franca, binding the diverse peoples of the coast into a unique Swahili culture.

The shadow of the slave trade (16th-19th century)

Yet, this era of cultural synthesis was darkened by the shadow of the slave trade, a scourge that bled the continent for centuries. Zanzibar, particularly under Sultan Sayyid Bargash bin Said al-Busaidi, became the heart of this grim commerce, serving the demands of markets from the Arabian Peninsula to the Americas. This dark turning point coincided with the aftermath of Christopher Columbus's voyages, which had unveiled the 'New World' to European ambitions.

The indigenous peoples, once the masters of their lands, found themselves caught in a vortex of exploitation and resistance. The local populations soon confronted this grim reality as Arab slave traders like Hamad bin Muhammad anchored themselves in places like Zanzibar, transforming these locales into pivotal markets. Zanzibar, in particular, emerged as a crucial hub, catering to the demands of the Arabian Peninsula, Iran, Britain, and the Americas. What began as a quest for prosperity morphed into an era of unbridled greed, where the pursuit of wealth eclipsed the value of human life.

Resistance and defiance (early 20th century)

It was within this turbulent historical tapestry that Me-Katilili wa Menza, a woman of the Giriama, rose as a beacon of defiance against colonial subjugation. Her revolt was not just a battle against the British encroachment but a stand for the dignity, independence, and cultural heritage of her people.

The British - under the monarch of Queen Victoria, then her son King Edward VII - in their quest to impose control, not only undermined the local economy through the manipulation of trade, notably the ivory trade, but also sought to alienate the Mijikenda from their lands, introducing foreign crops and seizing vast tracts for rubber plantations.

Legacy of resilience and freedom

The resilience of the Mijikenda, their refusal to succumb to the forces of colonialism, and the spirit of Me-Katilili wa Menza, resonate through history as a testament to the enduring strength of a people fighting for their freedom and identity. From the sacred *Kayas* to the bustling markets of Mombasa and the courtrooms where battles for justice were fought, the story of the Mijikenda is one of courage, resistance, and the unbreakable bond between a people and their land.

As we journey through the pages of this tale, we traverse the pathways of time, from the ancient days of prosperity and peace through the tumult of invasion and resistance to the dawn of a new era marked by the legacy of those who fought with unwavering spirit.

This is not just the story of Me-Katilili wa Menza or the Mijikenda; it is the saga of human resilience against the tide of history, a narrative that echoes the timeless struggle for freedom, dignity, and the right to forge one's destiny.

MAP OF AFRICA

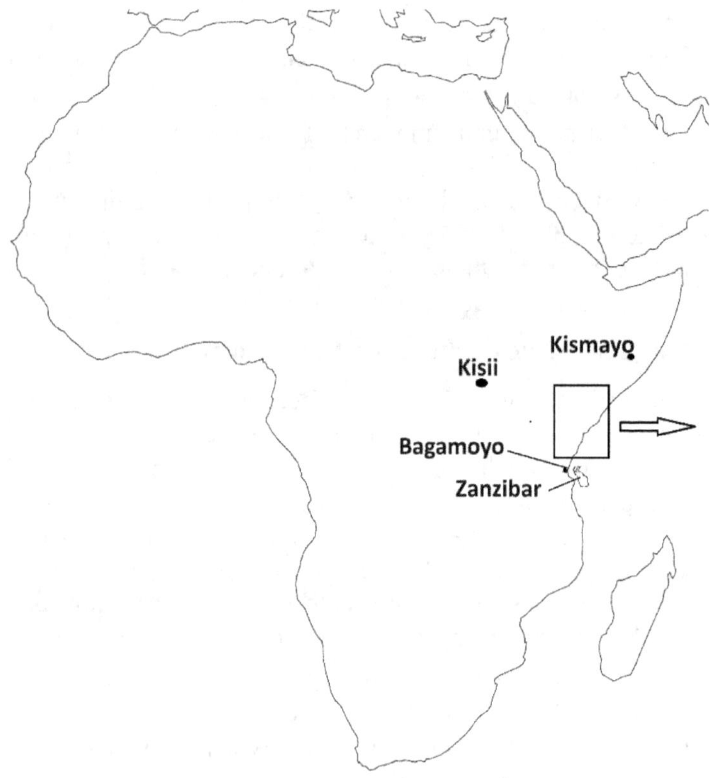

Source: https://www.freeworldmaps.net/printable/africa/blank.png

HIST. MAP OF EASTERN KENYA

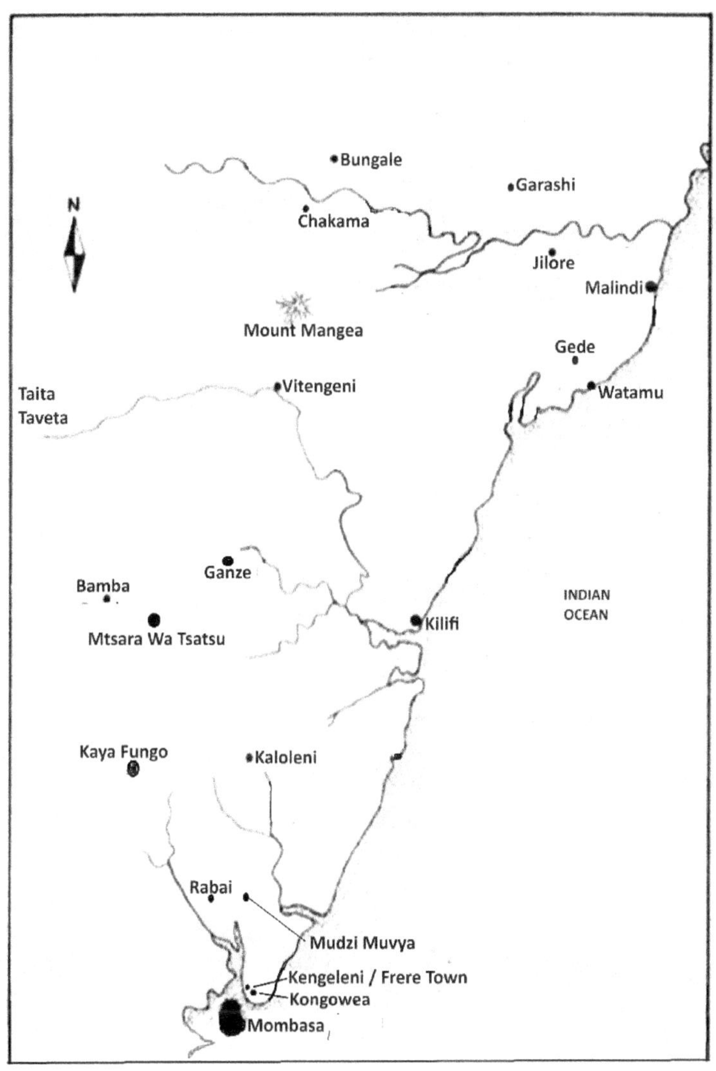

GLOSSARY

Me-Katilili ("Mother of Katilili) aka **Mekatilili** resp. **Mekatilili Wa Menza** – a fearless Giriama woman warrior.

Mijikenda ("the Nine Tribes") are a nine related Bantu ethnic groups (tribes) inhabiting the coast of Kenya, in an area stretching from Tanzania in the south to the border near Somalia in the north: Chonyi, Kambe, Duruma, Kauma, Ribe, Rabai, Jibana, **Giriama**, and Digo.

Agiriama: The people of the Giriama subtribe.

chifudu: A spiritual dance performed in times of grief.

chigoda: Traditional three-legged stool.

hando: Traditional white skirt of the Giriama.

Kaya (home or village) Kayas are the homesteads of the Mijikendas. The **sacred _Kaya_ forests** are abandoned Kayas, still held as ancestral sites for rituals and prayers to date.

khanga or *leso*: thin cotton fabric with colored design, wrapped around the body, used mainly for women's clothing.

kisuthu: Khanga with a specific pattern.

Kiswahili: The language of the Swahili,

Mulungu: The creator and supreme being.

Swahili: An ethnic group in coastal East Africa, culturally and linguistically distinct, with a mix of African and Araba heritage.

vikoi: Traditional clothes worn by men, colorful garment wrapped around the waist.

CHAPTER 1

The Prophecy

In this corner of the globe, the concept of time, as recorded in written form, did not exist. Yet, the passage of days and years was marked by the rhythm of the natural world: the changing seasons, the daily journey of the sun from dawn till dusk, and the cyclical phases of the moon, from full to new and back again. Life was woven with ordinary and extraordinary moments, with each event and observation part of a larger, timeless tapestry. Only centuries later, historians estimated these events to have unfolded around the year 1300, roughly five centuries before the pivotal moment.

As twilight descended on one particular evening, the sun's last rays vanished behind a thickening veil of clouds. This night unfurled a blanket of darkness more profound than any before. The air, charged with the electricity of anticipation, trembled as the soft murmurings of an approaching storm began to thread through the *Kaya*'s lush canopy, hinting at the tumult that lay ahead.

The Mijikenda, whose lives were deeply entwined with the rhythms of the earth and sky, sensed the change, a tension that hummed in the earth's bones, a prelude to the storm's song.

As night deepened, the heavens themselves seemed to brood with unrest. The once-clear sky, a mosaic of innumerable stars, was gradually obscured by menacing clouds that rolled in from the Indian Ocean, vast and relentless. They amassed an impenetrable fortress of vapor above the community, swallowing the moon's silvery glow and casting the village into shadows. The air grew heavy, pregnant with the scent of rain, that unique aroma that speaks of rejuvenated earth and awakened life, yet also whispered forebodings of the fury about to be unleashed. An elder of one of the homesteads blew a distinctive horn, calling for attention among all *Kaya* villages.

"A storm is coming; a storm is coming! Stay in your housings and do not come out until the storm is over," called an elder in a deep, clear voice. These announcements were messages to be passed over from homestead to homestead until every *Kaya* was informed. The homesteads prepared themselves; they proofed their thatched roofs, checking for leakage possibilities. They put their livestock in a safe shelter, and people were seen hurriedly bringing items like pottery, weavers, foodstuffs, and breweries into the housing to prevent them from impending destruction. Eventually, each family closed their palm-tree-woven doors.

The first herald of the storm was the wind, a serenade that grew into a howl. It danced through the village, a wild, untamed spirit, caressing the thatched roofs of the huts, rustling the leaves of the baobab and palm trees that stood as silent sentinels over the people. The Mijikenda listened, their hearts beating with the wind's crescendo as it spoke of power, majesty, and the raw beauty of nature's might.

Then came the lightning, a spectral ballet of light that fractured the night's canvas, illuminating the village in stark, fleeting moments of daylight. Each flash was a snapshot of a world held momentarily in thrall: children's faces wide with wonder, elder's eyes reflecting the wisdom of those who have seen the skies ablaze before, and the fierce, protective lines of warriors' stances as they watched over their families.

Thunder roared, a primal chorus that echoed the ancestors' voices, rumbling through the village and vibrating in the souls of the Mijikenda. It spoke of the ages, the cycles of life and death, and the eternal dance between the earth and the heavens. The community felt it together, a shared pulse, a reminder of their smallness in the face of nature's grandeur and their unity in its embrace.

And then, with a suddenness that took breaths away, the rain descended. It was not a gentle shower but a deluge, a torrential outpouring of the skies' pent-up sorrow and joy. It rattled on the roofs, drummed on the ground, and washed over everything in a cleansing flood. Streams formed, rivers burst their banks, and the earth drank greedily, reviving under the rain's caress.

In the heart of the storm, the Mijikenda stood resilient, a community bound by the threads of tradition, respect for nature, and an unbreakable connection to their ancestors. In the storm's fury, they found strength - in its beauty, a reminder of the delicate balance of life.

As the storm passed, leaving behind a world refreshed and a sky of unparalleled clarity, the Mijikenda knew they would remember this night. It was a testament to the enduring bond between them and the elemental forces that shaped their lives, a night when the earth and sky had spoken with thunderous voices, and they had listened, humbled yet unbroken, beneath the vast African sky.

Day broke. The skies were crystal clear as the sun rose with a refreshing charm. These *Kayas* were communities known for their unity and strength. It was expected, after disturbing events, that the natives went to check on each other. After the storm, they went to see if anyone was missing or if any housing had been destroyed. No one went missing or got hurt, and no relevant destruction occurred. Relieved, the people of the *Kayas* set out under the flourishing hue of the rising sun, going about their usual businesses. Among the villagers, a group of five women, bound by the daily chore of fetching water, shared stories and dreams as they walked to the pond to fetch water. Habitually, their voices interact, singing and laughter fill the air.

However, they heard a distant baby's cry as they approached the riverbank on this particular day. Amidst the reeds, they found a baby swaddled in a blue cloth as fine as any they had seen. The traditional indigo clothing, *Musimbiji*, symbolized power, divination, and prophecy. Bewildered and concerned, they looked around, but no one was in sight. Amidst all odds, the baby was found nicely wrapped and dry after the ground-tearing storm. The immense pond, an arm of the river Galana, known to them as a giver of life, had presented them with a new life in the most unexpected way.

With the baby cradled gently, the women returned to the village, the news of their discovery spreading like wildfire. Villagers gathered, each curious to see the child that had appeared from nowhere. Despite inquiries and messengers sent everywhere, no one came to claim the baby. No woman in the village or neighboring areas was missing a child or had been recently pregnant to be missing a child, nor had been recently pregnant.

Among the women, Kadzo stood out. She had yearned for a child for years without the blessing of becoming a mother. Seeing the baby, Kadzo felt a connection that she could not explain. With the elders' blessing, she adopted the child as her own. The villages came together for a naming ceremony, a vibrant celebration of life and community. They named her Mepoho, meaning "whisper of the wind," for she had come to them as gently and unexpectedly as a breeze.

Mepoho grew under Kadzo's loving care, her intelligence and wisdom becoming apparent early on. She observed the world with a keen eye, learning from the stories and experiences shared within the village. As she grew, her advice, though from a young voice, held depth and insight that belied her age, earning her respect among the villagers.

By the time Mepoho reached adulthood, her words were not just heard but sought after. Her transition to a prophet was seamless, her visions and prophecies guiding the *Kayas* through seasons of drought and plenty alike. Every prophecy she uttered came to pass, cementing her place as a revered figure in the *Kayas* and beyond.

Mepoho's guidance transformed the *Kayas* in ways both small and significant. Under her influence, the *Kayas* thrived, navigating the challenges of their world with grace and wisdom that seemed to emanate from the very earth they walked upon. Mepoho spent a lot of time discovering spirituality and nature. She would go to the sacred *Kaya* forests and stay there for days. Around her mid-age, Mepoho was a chosen diviner and prophetess. Through spiritual dances, Mepoho would call in the spirits to foretell upcoming events. She would use spiritual intervention to predict droughts, famine, and heavy rains that would cause floods. Hence, Mepoho used these foresights to protect the Mijikenda people.

Mepoho came from a sacred *Kaya* forest one afternoon, looking concerned and worn out. She demanded that the people of the *Kaya* she lived in perform a spiritual dance, the *Chifudu* dance. She revealed she had a crucial message to the Mijikenda community. Amidst the vigorous beating drums, the *kayamba*; a tray-shaped percussion instrument, bullhorns, flutes, and profound singing, Mepoho sat on her traditional *chigoda* chair in the middle of the crowd, swaying with an inner rhythm. A medicine man was sprinkling a concoction of herbs on her and uttering sacred words. Mepoho got carried away by intense spiritual music.

In this state, she had a vision. Shaken and terrified, she sprung up in shock. Panting between weeps and gazing toward the sky, she gasped, "My people, I saw the future, which is devastating! People will come with very pale skin and hair, like sisal fibers. They will bring vessels in the sky, on water, and land. These pale people will smoke a strange plant. Young girls will give birth to young babies ... When these things come to pass, they will destroy our culture, we will be displaced, and they will take away our land."

Mstanganyiko Market, Kilifi Town, Kenya

Under the rich bounty of the season, the four eldest siblings of the Menza family embarked, their arms laden with the earth's generosity: corn, mangoes dripping with the promise of sweetness, coconuts rugged and brimming with milk, an orchestra of spices and herbs exuding fragrant melodies, and baskets pulsating with the vitality of live chickens. Their parents, full of caution and love, initially hesitated. Yet, besieged by the relentless pleas of their adventurous progeny and trusting in the keenness of their young minds, they yielded. They offered their blessings, a mosaic of lessons, warnings, and guidance, hoping these intangible gifts would safeguard their children in the bustling world of trade.

Before the first whispers of dawn teased the horizon, the Menza homestead awoke, pulsing with a silent anticipation. In the soft glow of early morning, Me-Nzai and Menza moved with purpose, their hands both steady and gentle as they equipped their offspring for the journey ahead. Each item packed was a symbol of love and survival, a testament to their hopes and fears. Their hearts, a medley of emotions, weighed heavy with the gravity of farewell. Yet, it was hope that shimmered in their eyes as they whispered their goodbyes, each word a silent prayer for the safety and success of their children in the world beyond their loving embrace.

With the thrill of anticipation, Kithi, Nzai, Harre, and their sister Munyazi began their journey from the heart of Bamba as the first whispers of dawn caressed the earth. Their path, guided by the symphony of the awakening wild, led them to the vibrant embrace of Mtsanganyiko's market. They arrived at the bustling coastal marketplace as the sun cast a golden hue over the vibrant tapestries and colorful stalls. The market was brimming with the scents of exotic spices, fresh fruits, herbs, and the salty tang of the sea. All alive with the vibrant thrums of commerce.

Munyazi, a warrior in spirit, her quick wit matched only by her swiftness with a spear, was bartering for spices, her laughter a familiar melody in the clamor of the market. Nzai and Hare, were nearby, examining the craftsmanship of a local blacksmith, their robust laughter mingling with the metallic clangs of the forge. After observing the artisans for a while, Kithi navigated through the dense crowd, his eyes reflecting a world known for its harsh beauty and merciless truths.

Kithi, a young African man, with youthful energy and bright, inquisitive eyes, maneuvered the throngs of traders and locals. He was in his prime, his skin the color of the rich earth that nurtured his village, his muscles honed from years of helping his family tend their land.

In an instant, the tranquility of the marketplace was shattered. The air turned electric, charged with a palpable dread that sliced through the bustling atmosphere. Shouts erupted, piercing the hum of everyday life like a knife through silk.

"Run! Run, the Arabs are here!" The market exploded into pandemonium, voices raised in terror, as every soul scrambled for refuge. Arab slave traders, infamous embodiments of ruthlessness, stormed into the square, their presence an ominous storm cloud over the sunlit day. Their cold and methodical gaze swept across the crowd, a chilling shadow that darkened the land. At their forefront stood a figure of menace - a leader marked by a sinister scar trailing down his cheek, his stature towering, his aura commanding fear and obedience. The once vibrant marketplace descended into a nightmare of screams and desperate struggles for escape. With a predator's precision, the leader locked eyes on Kithi, an unsuspecting youth among the throng. With a mere gesture, he unleashed his minions.

Kithi's world turned chaotic in the blink of an eye. The traders' cruel embrace engulfed him before he could grasp the gravity of his fate. They seized him with a ferocity that left no room for resistance, his arms twisted cruelly behind him, their grip as unforgiving as iron clamps. The sharp pain bore into his flesh, a cruel reminder of his imminent doom.

Amid the chaos, Kithi's voice rose in a desperate plea, his heart wrenching with fear and despair. "Save me, mama, save me!" he cried out, his call for salvation echoing through the turmoil, a poignant cry that seemed to reach for the very heavens yet drowned in the cacophony of a world turned upside down.

Munyazi, quick as a flash, darted towards him, her other two brothers close behind. She screamed, her voice a mix of rage and despair, as she lunged towards the traders, her brothers Nzai and Harre, at her side. But they were no match for the slave traders who, with ruthless force and cold threats, held them at bay. Munyazi, a fierce spirit with eyes as sharp as the edge of a spear, witnessed the horror unfold. Fiercely determined, she lunged forward, trying to grab her brother Kithi. Her fierce determination was met with a harsh blow that sent her reeling, her vision blurring with tears of rage and helplessness. The siblings' efforts were like waves crashing futilely against an unyielding cliff.

Bound in chains, robbed of his freedom, Kithi's heart raced with fear and shock. Pounded against his ribcage, each beat a drum of panic and sorrow. He was dragged mercilessly through the sandy streets, past the familiar stalls and faces, now blurred through his tears. Each step took him further from everything he knew and loved. The traders, unmoved by his plight, hauled him onto a waiting ship, a dark vessel that reeked of despair and sorrow. Its dark hull was a foreboding shadow against the setting sun.

The ship's deck was a canvas of despair, crowded with other captives. Each is a story of a life interrupted. Their faces etched with stories of shattered lives and stolen freedoms. Older men with eyes that spoke of wisdom and long years. Young women whose dreams were as shuttered as their spirits, and children too young to understand the depth of their predicament. They were bound together, their chains a cruel parody of unity, a mosaic of human suffering. Everyone a tale of a home lost, a family torn apart, an identity ripped off.

As night fell, the ship set sail and began its ominous journey, sailing away from the shores of Africa. The horizon swallowed the last glimpse of Kithis's homeland. Once a symbol of freedom and adventure, the ocean was now an endless expanse of captivity. The night fell, and with it, a heavy silence among captives, each lost in their thoughts of home, and families left behind. The steady beat of the waves caressing the hull was a cruel lullaby for the captives. Kithi, amidst his fear and despair, looked up at the blanket of stars overhead, the same stars that once shone over his home, now a beacon of a distant, untouchable past.

In the moon's pale glow, lying in his chains, staring at the stars, Kithi's thoughts drifted to his family, their faces a lingering comfort in his chains' cold, unfeeling grip. In the comfort of his mind, he heard Munyazi's laughter and storytelling, Nzai's strength and jokes, and Harre's quick wit and wisdom. His heart ached when he thought of his dear, warm-hearted mother, his sedulous father, and his cheeky brother, Mwarandu. Will he ever see them again? How will he fight to go back to his family? He looked down in despair at his chained wrists and ankles. The darkness of the night seemed to mirror the abyss that now lay in Kithi's heart, a once vibrant soul, now cast into the depths of an uncertain and harrowing future. In his heart, a vow formed – to survive, to return, to fight. The night air was cold, but it fueled the fire of resolve in Kithi's heart.

The ship, a specter in the moonlight, sailed on, its cargo of broken dreams and resilient spirits moving towards an uncertain fate. Kithi, amidst the sea of despair, held onto a glimmer of hope, a beacon in the dark, guiding him through the Chains of the Tide.

CHAPTER 2

The family of Munyazi (young Me-Katilili)

"Yours," Kithi announced, his voice brimming with the vibrant delight characteristic of childhood. His eyes sparkled with a hint of mischief as he gently nudged his older brother, Nzai, with a clay cow - a charming testament to their shared imagination, guided by their father's hand just the day before. Swift as a breeze, he scampered off, seeking sanctuary behind the steadfast figure of their mother. This playful exchange, affectionately known as 'who's milking the cow,' transcended mere play. It wove a fabric of joy, a tribute to the purity that flowed like a river through the heart of their home. The one caught holding the cow at the end of the game was tasked with rising at dawn to assist in milking the real cows, a chore each child playfully sought to eschew. Meanwhile, Harre, another brother, concealed himself behind the robust silhouette of a large mortar and pestle.

Me-Nzai, the matriarch of this lively ensemble, presided under the emerald canopy of a mango tree, its limbs stretched wide as if to embrace the family it watched over. Her abode, a symphony of meticulous care and natural beauty, stood proudly beside her. "No, Kithi, no hiding behind me; I have to work," she cautioned, her voice a blend of affection and gentle reproof. Her hands, skilled everyday artisans, danced through the task of peeling *cassava* (Maniok), each movement a testament to years of nurturing and toil. Yet, her eyes, those windows to a soul steeped in maternal love, wandered frequently to the tableau of her children's play. Their laughter, a melody that painted the air with hues of joy, was occasionally underscored by the soft thud of youthful endeavor, be it against the earth or the makeshift fortresses of log piles.

Me-Nzai, ever the sentinel of safety, had woven a rainbow of warnings around the rougher edges of their play, especially near the logs that were the foundation of dreams yet to be built. But the children, in their bubble of adventure, skirted the edges of caution, lost in the thrill of their own making.

A sudden stumble, a momentary eclipse of joy - Kithi, the strong-spirited second son, was trapped by an aerial root, his expression a tableau of shock and budding distress. In that fleeting glance shared with his mother, a silent conversation of concern and anticipated admonition passed between them. "I don't want to see anyone crying. I've repeatedly warned you over your silly, dangerous games!" Me-Nzai's voice, a mixture of worry and love, reached out to her children. Yet, deep and unwavering, beneath the stern veneer lay a river of affection.

Kithi, with a resilience born of youthful exuberance, and Mwarandu, the youngest and font of mischief - who had recently conjured laughter and gasped by bestowing a live frog upon the terracotta pot's unsuspecting waters could not contain their amusement. Their laughter, a beacon of light, resonated through the homestead, touching even Me-Nzai's heart. Her eyes, alight with amusement and a mother's tender exasperation, danced over her children. Mwarandu's antics, though a source of sudden surprise, were woven into the framework of their daily lives, adding color to every day, reminding Me-Nzai of the vibrant spirits she had nurtured.

Me-Nzai returned to her task, methodically peeling and slicing the cassava harvested several sunrises ago. She laid out the cut pieces on expansive winnowers crafted from straw and palm leaves, a process vital for their preservation. Her instructions to the children were clear: they were to keep a respectful distance from the mats, a directive stemming from both a place of care and a practical need to protect the cassava from their playful havoc.

As she engaged in this routine, a part of her mind wandered to the life growing within her. Whether the new arrival would be a boy, or a girl preoccupied her thoughts. She harbored a deep desire for a daughter this time, envisioning their bond and the traditions she would pass on. Me-Nzai longed to impart the Mijikenda primary female education to her daughter, teaching her the virtues of politeness, helpfulness, and the essential skills of homemaking, cooking, and basic medicinal knowledge. She imagined sharing the rich history of their heritage through stories told by her grandmother - tales of great migrations, humorous folktales with moral lessons, all shared in the intimate setting of evening gatherings after dinner.

Yet, for all her dreams of a daughter, Me-Nzai held an unwavering love for her sons. Their presence had elevated Menza's standing in the village, earning him respect and a place among the council of elders. But the desire for a daughter remained, fueled by dreams of making her little skirts from the finest cotton, adorning her hair with intricate braids and beads, and teaching her the art of pottery. Me-Nzai was renowned in her *Kaya* for her pottery skills, a craft she had honed under the tutelage of her great-aunt since childhood.

Her sons, while dearly loved, were known for their playful negligence, especially when sent to fetch water from the stream. Their adventures often led to less than trustworthy water, a consequence of their penchant for games over the responsibility of their chore. Despite this, their homestead's family bonds, and daily life rhythm painted a picture of unity, tradition, and the perpetual cycle of learning and growth. In this environment, Me-Nzai thrived, a matriarch deeply rooted in her culture and the love for her family, ever hopeful for the future and the potential arrival of a daughter to share in the legacy of her lineage.

The air was heavy with the scent of earth and ripening mangoes as the quiet hum of daily life unfolded beneath the expansive sky. The rhythmic sound of Me-Nzai's cassava peeling was momentarily broken by a familiar call, "Enyeeee..." – a traditional greeting signaling a visitor's respect for the household they were entering. Me-Nzai's hands stilled, a soft smile gracing her lips as she recognized the voice, a heartwarming sound of community and friendship.

"Eeeeh…" Me-Nzai responded, her voice carrying the lightness of welcomed interruption. Turning to her left, she saw the silhouette of Sayo, her closest friend and neighbor, approaching. Their bond was more than just proximity; it was a connection woven through shared experiences and mutual support.

"Wa Mwakiringi, how have you felt today?" Sayo inquired, using the customary address that denoted Me-Nzai's affiliation with her clan. It was a term of respect, acknowledging Me-Nzai's place within the community and her adopted lineage. And casually, she was known as Me-Nzai, meaning mother to Nzai. It was common for the Mijikenda women to acquire the pronoun Me fondly, meaning mother of, and then accompany it with the name of their first child.

"I am well, just so exhausted. I don't know why this baby is taking their time to come and see the world," Me-Nzai replied, her voice laced with the weariness and anticipation that marked the final days of pregnancy. Her hands rested momentarily on her swollen belly, a universal gesture of maternal connection.

"Aaah, Me-Nzai, I think it is a girl. They say girls take longer," Sayo chimed in, her voice a mixture of wisdom and wishful thinking. Her observation meant reassurance and sparked a flicker of hope within Me-Nzai. The possibility that *Mulungu* (the supreme god) might soon fulfill her deep yearning for a daughter stirred a whirlwind of emotions within her – eager anticipation, the dread of potential disappointment, and a profound craving for a shift in the family dynamic.

"And the way you look more beautiful even as you are this heavy… it means it is a girl," Sayo added, her compliment flowing effortlessly, a testament to the bond of sisterhood that thrived among the women of their community.

Me-Nzai sighed, a sound that carried the weight of her hopes and the fear of them being unmet. The legacy of the Milalani lineage, emphasizing sons as heirs and protectors, loomed large in her thoughts. Yet, as they continued chatting, exchanging news and light-hearted gossip, Me-Nzai felt profound gratitude for Sayo. Her neighbor had become an anchor, especially since Me-Nzai's sister moved to the Digo sub-tribe of the Mijikenda after her marriage. Sayo seemed to have stepped in when she needed a close sister.

"What did the midwife tell you..." The sound of distress abruptly cut off Sayo's question. Kithi, Me-Nzai's third son, came running towards them, tears streaming down his face, his cries slicing through the afternoon's calm. "Mama, my eye, mama, my eye, there's sand in my eye." His small body collided with his mother, the urgency of his pain rendering him oblivious to the delicate state of her pregnancy.

"Oh, careful, you might hurt the baby," Me-Nzai exclaimed, her maternal instincts kicking in as she attempted to soothe her son while protecting the life within her. Once busy with the day's chores, her hands now gently cradled Kithi's face, trying to assess the damage without exacerbating his discomfort.

"Mameee here, here..." Kithi whimpered, his small fingers rubbing at his left eye, inadvertently pushing the grains of sand deeper. Me-Nzai's heart ached at the sight of her child in pain, a reminder of the constant balancing act of motherhood - the need to protect, soothe, and teach all wrapped into one.

At that moment, the complexities of life in their homestead were laid bare. The joys, the worries, the anticipation of new life, and the everyday challenges of raising a family in a world where tradition and modernity intertwined were all part of Me-Nzai's journey. As she comforted Kithi, her thoughts drifted to the baby yet to be born, the dreams she harbored for her children, and the legacy she hoped to build with Menza. The presence of Sayo, a friend who had become family, underscored the importance of community - a network of support that nurtured and sustained them through the cycles of life.

From the Digo subtribe to their kins' ears

In the fading days of a season past, within the confines of Golini, Kwale - a hamlet nestled among the Digo lineage of the Mijikenda - under a canvas of twilight skies painted with the last whispers of sunlight, the earth graciously bestowed its riches. Fields of maize unfurled across the horizon, a vivid mosaic of gold and emerald marking harvest time. During this bountiful period, Nimahongo, a revered seer of the Digo subtribe, sensed an ethereal commotion. The spirits convened, their voices a hushed murmur, carrying premonition of what was yet to come. Despite the darkness that had enveloped her physical sight, her spiritual eyes remained unclouded, slicing through the barriers separating the tangible from the unseen. She stood as a conduit between realms, her insight unveiling mysteries veiled to the mortal gaze.

Summoning her most trusted messengers, Nimahongo entrusted them with a message of paramount importance, a revelation that would alter the course of history for the Mijikenda.

"Venture forth," she instructed, her voice resonating with the weight of prophecy, "to the far reaches of our kin. Let not a single community among the nine remain untouched by this news. From the Digo to the Jibana, from the Giriama to the Kauma, carry forth my words."

And so, with the urgency of the wind itself, nine messengers set forth, each bearing the weight of destiny. They went to the Digo, Giriama, Chonyi, Duruma, Rabai, Ribe, Kambe, Kauma, and Jibana, their feet swift and their resolve unwavering.

Nimahongo's message was clear: a harbinger of change and a call to unity in the face of the unknown.

"Tell our people," Nimahongo commanded, her voice imbued with a power that belied her physical blindness, "that the great upheaval draws near. Vast sea vessels, like behemoths of the deep, and iron serpents that stretch across the land, herald their approach. The skies, too, shall be torn asunder by iron birds, strangers to our lands and harbingers of change. Yet, fear not, for amidst this turmoil, *Mulungu*, our Supreme God, in His infinite wisdom, has foreseen the birth of a savior. This warrior shall rise, born upon our soil, nurtured by the waters of a river as briny as our tears."

Her words, steeped in the lore of ancient prophecies, spoke of Mepoho's visions and Nimunyumba's foretelling, echoing the fears and hopes of generations. "This warrior," she continued, a mystical fervor lacing her words, "shall stand as a bulwark against the invaders, against those who ride upon the waves and cast shadows over our lands. Heed the signs, for the prophecies of old unfold before us this day."

In a sacred *Kaya* forest, where the spirits of ancestors lingered and the air thrummed with unseen power, the council of elders absorbed her words. The message, imbued with urgency and hope, was a beacon in the gathering darkness, a promise of resistance and redemption in the face of impending invasion.

As the messengers disseminated the prophecy throughout the nine subtribes, the land held its breath, awaiting the fulfillment of Nimahongo's words. The pale-skinned foreign invaders with hair like sisal, arrived on the tides of destiny, their ships casting long shadows over Malindi, Mombasa, and Zanzibar. They brought with them the clangor of change, erecting stone edifices that pierced the sky, and imposing their will upon the people of the land.

The promised leader symbolized not just the prospect of victory in battle, but the rekindling of a spirit that no invader could extinguish - the indomitable heart of the Mijikenda, enduring like the ancient groves that whispered of endurance, resistance, and the hope of a dawn yet to come.

As the late afternoon sun hung high in the sky, its intense rays casting elongated shadows that seemed to dance gently against the vibrant backdrop, the village of Bamba was alive with the harmonious buzz of daily life. The bright and sunny afternoon was adorned with white, fluffy clouds drifting slowly across the azure sky while birds glided past the horizon, their squawks and rickrack sounds filling the air with a sense of freedom and joy. A gentle wind caressed the faces of the villagers, bringing a refreshing respite from the sun's warmth. Everyone in the Giriama *Kayas* appreciated the weather, starkly contrasting the previous season's harshness. This season was a blessing, rich in harvest and thriving livestock, a testament to the abundance of nature's generosity.

As the day waned, men, having returned from their daily ventures of hunting or farming, gathered in small groups, immersing themselves in import discussions or simply enjoying their traditional palm wines, known as *uchi wa mnazi*. Their laughter and voices melded with the tales of young men recounting adventurous experiences and shared history. Elsewhere, the melodic voices of young women and girls carried through the air, narrating the day's events, and singing songs passed down through generations. The village was a hive of activity, with women busily preparing the evening meals in their half-open-air kitchens, the aroma of cooking food promising a hearty end to the day.

However, as sunset neared, a sudden shift in the atmosphere sent ripples of unease through the village. The once gentle wind transformed into a howling force, palm trees bending and swaying as if in a frenzied dance. Dry palm leaves detached and fluttered to the ground, rustling as they landed, while dust clouds rose, blurring the once clear skies. The animals, too, sensed the change; dogs barked in alarm, chickens squawked in distress, and livestock stirred restlessly in their enclosures. The village was gripped by a sense of foreboding as the weather turned with an abruptness witnessed never before.

Amidst the growing chaos, a religious specialist, eyes turned skyward, muttered incantations, seeking guidance and assurance from the heavens. Turning to the council of elders, he proclaimed with a solemnity that commanded silence, "Alumeee, we are going to receive a very significant guest. The heavens have spoken. A message from *Mulungu*, the Supreme God." Heavy with implication, his words hung in the air, a forecast of something momentous on the horizon.

The storm that ensued was unlike any the villagers had experienced. Rain poured down with a ferocity that seemed intent on reclaiming the earth itself, the wind howled from all directions, and the sky was rent with the roar of thunder and the searing flash of lightning. The people of Bamba and those in neighboring *Kayas* took shelter, protecting their families and belongings as best they could against nature's tumultuous display.

The birth of Munyazi, the young Me-Katilili

Mid 1800s. Amid this maelstrom, a different kind of storm was brewing within the walls of Menza's homestead in the heart of Mtswara Wa Tsatsu. Me-Nzai, his wife, had fallen into labor. The air in their home was thick with tension and anticipation as the well-reputed midwife and Sayo, Me-Nzai's steadfast neighbor, attended to her. Sweat beaded Me-Nzai's brow, and tears born of pain and fear streaked her cheeks. The ordeal of childbirth was intense, and as the hours dragged on, Me-Nzai's strength waned. Yet, her resolve never faltered through the storm outside and the turmoil within. Guided by the midwife's experienced hands and encouraged by Sayo's unwavering support, Me-Nzai pushed beyond the limits of her endurance.

When a newborn's cries finally pierced the air, a profound sense of relief washed over Me-Nzai. Lying back, exhausted yet elated, she listened as the midwife announced, "The baby is fine and healthy. It's a beautiful baby girl." Tears of joy, pure and unbidden, streamed down Me-Nzai's face as she held her daughter for the first time. Her heart's longing, hopes, and dreams that she harbored for so long were embodied in the tiny form cradled in her arms. "Finally," she thought, her heart swelling with love and gratitude. She whispered prayers of thanks to the ancestors and *Mulungu*, the supreme God, for the precious gift of her daughter.

The precise moment of Munyazi's emergence into the world remains veiled in the mists of history, with educated guesses placing her birth within the heart of the nineteenth century - a time teeming with momentous shifts and resonant with historical consequence.

Upon meeting his daughter, Menza was overcome with a profound sense of pride and joy. He chose the name Munyazi for her in honor of his favorite aunt, a woman of strength and grace who had been a guiding light in his life. Following tradition, he ritually spoke words of affirmation into Munyazi's ear, 'holding the ear', blessing her with their ancestors' wisdom, strength, and courage. The next day, Menza slaughtered a goat, and a feast was held to celebrate Munyazi's arrival, a fitting welcome for the significant guest heralded by the storm, a new life destined into the rich heritage of their community's history.

The storm that had raged outside mirrored the tumultuous journey Me-Nzai had endured to bring Munyazi into the world. Yet, as the storm passed and calm returned to the village of Bamba, the significance of what had transpired within the walls of Menza's homestead was not lost on those who had witnessed it. Munyazi's birth, amidst the chaos of nature's fury, symbolized life's persistent strength and resilience.

As the first light of dawn crept across the sky, painting the horizon in hues of gold and crimson, the village of the ancient Mijikenda stirred to life. It was a day unlike any other, for a child born under the veil of night would be announced to the world. The air hummed with anticipation, for the villagers had long awaited the birth of a boy destined to be a warrior who would lead them against the invaders threatening their land.

Elder Kalama, a figure of respect and wisdom within the community, stood at the center of the village. His presence commanded silence, and all eyes turned to him as the sun's first rays touched the earth. The moment came to unveil the future of the Mijikenda, a revelation that had been whispered among the leaves of the sacred forest and danced upon the winds of fate.

"Children of the soil, bearers of our ancestors' spirit," Elder Kalama began, his voice strong and clear, "the night has bestowed upon us a gift, a beacon of hope. The child born under the starlit sky is here to be woven into the fabric of our destiny."

The villagers, clad in their finest clothing – the men colorful *vikoi*, the women *kisuthu*, and white *handos* - leaned in closer. Others, adorned with beads that reflected the morning light, leaned in closer. Their hearts beat in unison, a rhythmic echo of their collective hope for a boy.

"Her name," Kalama continued, pausing for a breath that drew the entire village into a moment of shared suspense, "is Munyazi. Munyazi wa Menza."

A murmur rippled through the crowd, like the gentle waves of the Indian Ocean kissing the shores of their homeland. "Munyazi - a girl?" In that instant, the air seemed to shift, laden with the weight of unspoken thoughts and veiled disappointment. Yet, the Mijikenda were people of resilience and grace, masked their feelings with practiced ease.

Sensing the undercurrent of their collective sentiment, Elder Kalama raised his hands for silence. "Let us remember that the spirits of our ancestors guide our paths. Munyazi, lightning, will carve her own journey through the skies of our history. Today, we embrace her with our traditions, with gifts that signify our love and hopes for her future."

And so, the ceremony unfolded as it had for generations, but with a whisper of change carried on the breeze. Villagers came forth, one by one, to present their offerings to Munyazi. They brought clothing woven from the softest fibers of the baobab tree, each piece dyed with vibrant colors, telling stories of the Mijikenda's connection to the land. Poultry, symbols of nourishment and community, clucked and fluttered, their presence promising sustenance and life. Firewood gathered from the best-known groves and spoke of warmth and the flame of spirit that Munyazi would carry within her heart. Beads, each a testament to the beauty and craftsmanship of the Mijikenda, shimmered in the morning light, encircling Munyazi in the wealth of her people's love and hopes.

As the ceremony drew to a close, elder Kalama spoke once more, his words carrying the wisdom of ages. "Today, we have welcomed Munyazi into our midst, not as the warrior we anticipated, but as a beacon of change. Let us not be blinded by our expectations, for the spirits remind us that strength comes in many forms. Munyazi's path is yet to be revealed, and it is our duty to support her and nurture her light so that it may guide us through the challenges to come."

The village echoed with chants and songs, celebrating life and the unbreakable bonds of community. Munyazi, cradled in the arms of her mother, Me-Nzai, gazed out with eyes wide and curious, unaware of the role destiny had carved for her. Though faced with the unexpected, the Mijikenda found strength in their traditions and the promise of tomorrow.

The Gratitude Ritual

Menza, Munyazi's father, stood at the riverbank of Sabaki in the pale light of dawn, alongside three of the village's most respected elders. Their task was of great significance - a pilgrimage to the sacred *Kaya* Fungo to offer thanks for the blessings bestowed upon their village, most recently the birth of Munyazi. The air was thick with the scent of morning dew and the unspoken reverence for the journey ahead.

Each man carried with him a piece of their gratitude: a white goat, symbolizing purity and innocence; pottery, crafted with the skill passed down through generations, to hold the waters of life; and valuable stones, glistening under the early sun, representing the enduring strength of their people.

They pushed their canoe into the Sabaki River, the waters whispering ancient secrets as they paddled harmoniously. The river, a lifeline to their community, carried them with gentle assurance, winding towards the heart of the sacred forest. The sun climbed higher, casting a kaleidoscope of light through the canopy of trees that lined the riverbanks.

After a time that seemed both fleeting and eternal, they reached where the river kissed the forest's edge. Here, they descended, their feet sinking softly into the earth that whispered of ages past. The forest of *Kaya* Fungo loomed before them, a guardian of history and tradition, its trees reaching towards the heavens, their roots entwined with the very soul of the earth.

As they ventured into the forest, the atmosphere shifted. The air was alive with the symphony of the jungle - the distant call of birds hidden within the foliage, the rustle of leaves stirred by unseen creatures, and the gentle murmur of the wind as it danced through the trees. The light here was dappled, a play of shadow and illumination that painted the forest floor in patterns of mystique and wonder.

The elders moved with purpose yet with the caution of those who tread on sacred ground. Their eyes wide, they beheld trees that soared to unimaginable heights, their trunks so broad that it would take many men to encircle them. The forest seemed to breathe around them; each exhale a whisper of the ancients who had once walked these paths.

The deeper they ventured, the more the forest seemed to close in around them, a cocoon of green that held them in its embrace. The air grew thicker, charged with a palpable sense of anticipation. And then, they saw the boundary of *Kaya* Fungo marked by trees adorned with red and white clothing, fluttering like silent sentinels at the unseen threshold.

Menza and the elders halted, their hearts beating a rhythm of respect and awe. They called out traditional words of pre-notification and peace, "*Similani azhere, similani atumia*," their voices carrying through the trees, offering their intentions to the spirits that watched over this sacred place.

The forest held its breath, the silence a canvas for the moment unfolding. And then, from the shadows of the trees, a figure emerged. A man of middle age, his presence commanding yet serene, adorned with deep blue cloth wrapped around his waist and another draped over his neck, revealing a chest that bore the marks of his journey through life.

In his hand, he held a conch, its spirals a testament to the mysteries of the sea and the cycles of existence. With deliberate grace, he lifted the conch to his lips and blew three times, the sound echoing through the forest, a call to the spirits, an acknowledgment of the men who had come in peace and reverence.

He swayed his right hand in a welcome gesture, an invitation to enter the heart of *Kaya* Fungo. Menza and the elders, understanding the significance of this moment, stepped forward, their offerings in hand, crossing the boundary into a realm where the mundane and the divine intertwined. In an abrupt gesture, he ordered them to stop. Startled, they glanced at each other, not sure what was expected of them. He requested them to remove their shoes.

The man in a deep blue cloth led them deeper into the forest, where the trees seemed to part before them, revealing a clearing bathed in a light that seemed not of this world. Here, at the center of *Kaya* Fungo, they were to make their offerings, to lay down the symbols of their gratitude and hopes before the unseen forces that guided their fate. Ahead was a ground covered with mats woven from dried coconut palm leaves, spread under a tree with long stretching brunches. At the foot of this tree was a shrine; two other spiritual leaders sat on the traditional *chigoda* stools.

"*Similani,*" the diviner announced a greeting, breaking the silence in the air. It was customary to direct these greetings not only to those who were physically there but also to the ancestors and the good spirits.

"*Haaiii*" Menza, his companions, and the other spiritual leaders responded.

The diviner would repeat the greeting several times as if to get full attention from every being, physical or otherwise. He continued to speak words of praise and gratitude to *Mulungu,* the supreme God, the creator of all beings.

"We have guests here who have come to speak with us. They have brought precious gifts and glad tidings."

The diviner placed himself between the two spiritual leaders and offered stools facing them. He reached out beside his seat, pulled out a white shawl, and threw it around his nape, letting the white fabric hang on his front, covering his bare chest with a striking contrast.

As they prepared to present their gifts, the air around them stirred, a gentle breeze carrying whispers of those who had stood in this very spot through the ages. The white goat bleated softly, a sound that carried the weight of the moment, echoing off the ancient trees that stood as silent witnesses to the ceremony.

The pottery had filled with water from the sacred spring that bubbled at the edge of the clearing, its contents shimmering with the reflection of the sky above. The valuable stones were placed with reverence upon an altar of earth and root, their surfaces catching the light, casting prisms of color across the faces of the men who had brought them. The diviner, with a solemn grace, presented the guard with palm wine, its rich aroma mingling with the air of anticipation. He then carefully poured a libation upon the hallowed earth of the *Kaya*, the sacred ground vibrating with the echoes of ancestral spirits. As he whispered invocations, calling out names of their forebears, his voice a gentle murmur blending with the wind, there was a sacred communion between the present and the ethereal realm. The wine seeped into the earth, a silent testament to the ancestors' acceptance. Observing this sacred absorption, the diviner, his eyes reflecting the depth of centuries-old wisdom, proclaimed with a resonant authority, "Our ancestors are pleased, we may continue." This affirmation, steeped in tradition, echoed around them, a clear beacon that they were under the watchful gaze and protection of their forebears.

As the ceremony reached its crescendo, the diviner spoke words of blessing, his voice resonating with the power of the land and the sea, invoking the protection and prosperity of the village and its newest member, Munyazi. The conch sounded once more, a final seal on the offerings and prayers, sending them on the wings of the wind to the ears of the ancestors.

The journey back through the forest and down the Sabaki River was one of reflection. The elders carried with them not just the physical remnants of their pilgrimage but a deepened connection to the forces that shaped their world. They returned to the village as bearers of a story, a testament to the power of faith, tradition, and the unbreakable bond between the people and the sacred lands they called home.

In the days that followed, the villagers spoke of Munyazi's ceremony with a sense of wonder. In the face of their initial disappointment, they discovered a deeper understanding of their own resilience and adaptability. They realized the true warrior they sought was not one of physical prowess but of spirit and unity.

CHAPTER 3

Port of London, Britain, in the mid-1800s

In the same epoch that saw Munyazi's entrance into the world, albeit across the vast stretches of Earth; in Britain, the atmosphere at the Port of London was laden with a palpable sense of anticipation and the heavy scent of salt and tar. It was a scene of orchestrated chaos where British traders and sailors moved with purpose, their actions dictated by years of seafaring tradition. The ship, The Queen's Endeavour, sat majestically at the dock, its masts reaching towards the grey, early morning sky. Families and friends of the crew lined the quayside, their faces a mix of pride, excitement, and underlying concern.

Captain Theodore, a seasoned sailor with a gaze as sharp as the north wind, oversaw the final preparations. His crew, including William, Arthur, Oliver, and Barney, hustled across the deck, securing crates and barrels that contained provisions and trade goods for their ambitious journey to the east coast of Africa. Their goal was clear: to explore uncharted territories and return with gold, ivory, spices, and a variety of other lucrative goods.

Sir Herbert, the leading explorer and trader among them, stood near the helm, his eyes scanning the horizon. He had considerable experience in both navigation and trade, having made several voyages to distant lands. His presence on this expedition lent the endeavor an air of authority and confidence.

As the time for departure neared, Captain Theodore climbed atop a barrel to address his crew and the small crowd that had gathered.

"Men," he began, his voice carrying over the crowd's murmur, "Today, we embark on a journey that will take us to the very edges of the known world. Our mission is not without risk, but I have faith in each and every one of you. Together, we shall navigate the treacherous waters, face the unknown, and return with riches that will secure our fortunes and honor for generations to come."

A cheer erupted from the crew, echoed by the supportive cries of their loved ones. The captain then turned to Sir Herbert, nodding respectfully.

"Sir Herbert, would you care to share a few words on our course and the winds we'll harness to carry us forth?" Captain Theodore requested.

Sir Herbert stepped forward, his eyes gleaming with the thrill of the adventure ahead.

"Gentlemen, our route will take us around the Cape of Good Hope, utilizing the trade winds to speed our journey. The seas can be unpredictable, but we shall make good time with careful navigation and a keen eye on the skies. Our destination holds the promise of wealth beyond measure, but it is not without its dangers. We must remain vigilant, work as a united crew, and trust Captain Theodore's leadership." He then looked towards the crowd, his voice firm yet reassuring.

"To our families and friends, I say this: your faith in us fuels our courage. We carry your hopes with us as much as we carry our dreams of discovery and prosperity. We shall return, bearing the fruits of our labor and tales of the wondrous lands beyond."

With the speeches concluded, the crew sprang into action. "Set the masts! Hoist the sails!" Captain Theodore commanded, his voice now all business. The sailors scurried up the rigging, unfurling the sails as the wind began to catch them, billowing outwards with promise. Oliver took his position at the helm, his hands steady on the wheel, while William and Arthur coordinated the crew on deck, securing every line with practiced efficiency.

The crowd's cheers and waves became a vibrant backdrop as the ship began to ease away from the dock. Handkerchiefs fluttered in the wind, and shouts of "Godspeed!" and "Return safely!" filled the air.

Barney, the youngest sailor, stood at the ship's bow, looking back at the receding figures. He felt a mix of exhilaration and a pang of homesickness, but the adventure ahead was the dream of a lifetime. Turning his gaze forward, he whispered to himself, "To Africa and beyond."

Below deck, in the captain's quarters, Theodore and Sir Herbert poured over maps and charts, discussing their strategy for navigating the African coast and identifying potential trading posts.

"Our first stop will be along the Gold Coast," Sir Herbert suggested, pointing to a section of the map. "The locals are willing to trade, and if we establish a good rapport, we can secure a steady supply of gold and ivory."

Captain Theodore nodded in agreement. "And the spices," he added, "we must not forget the spices. The demand in London is high, and a good cargo can fetch a king's ransom."

Their conversation continued, combining strategy, speculation, and shared experiences from past voyages. They spoke of the winds, the currents, and the best times to sail. They discussed the crew's strengths and how to best utilize each man's skills. The path forward was riddled with obstacles, but their resolve was unwavering.

As The Queen's Endeavour sailed forth, cutting through the waves with grace and determination, it carried more than just men and goods. It carried the hopes of a nation eager for expansion, the dreams of explorers seeking the unknown, and the promise of adventure that has called to sailors throughout history. The journey to the east coast of Africa was just the beginning, but it was a chapter that each man aboard would remember for the rest of his days.

Arriving at Mombasa port

The crew of the Queen's Endeavour gathered on the deck as the ship anchored in the port of Mombasa, the golden light of the late afternoon sun casting long shadows across the wooden planks. The moment was one of vivid reflection, a pause in the whirlwind of their arrival to honor those who had not survived the journey.

Captain Theodore, his usually commanding presence softened by grief, addressed his crew with a solemnity that matched the occasion. "We stand here, on the brink of new horizons, not as conquerors, but as humble guests of this vast continent. Yet, our hearts are heavy, for not all who embarked on this voyage with us are here to witness its culmination." He paused, allowing his gaze to sweep over his crew, each man bearing the weight of loss in his own way. "We remember our fallen comrades - brave souls who sought adventure and purpose but found their journeys cut short. Let their memories guide us as we tread these unfamiliar lands. Let us honor them not just in word, but indeed."

Sir Herbert, ever the articulate diplomat, stepped forward. "In the annals of history," he began, his voice steady and clear, "it is often the destination that is remembered, but the journey, with all its trials and tribulations, truly shapes us. Our fallen brethren have paid the ultimate price in pursuit of the noble exploration endeavor. Our duty is to ensure that their sacrifice was not in vain."

A silence fell over the crew, a collective moment of remembrance for those who had succumbed to disease and hardship. William, the seasoned sailor, removed his hat, his weathered face marked by lines of sorrow and respect. "To our comrades," he said, his voice a whisper carried away by the sea breeze.

Arthur and Oliver, standing side by side, shared a look of understanding. Like the rest, they had felt the sting of loss, the pain of saying goodbye to those they had come to regard as family. Oliver, the youngest among them, felt a lump in his throat. "May they find calm seas and favorable winds," he added, his voice barely audible.

They concluded the memorial with a moment of silence, the sound of the waves against the hull serving as a gentle reminder of the journey's end and the beginning of their endeavor in Mombasa. As the sun descended beyond the horizon, enveloping the sky in a spectacular canvas of orange and red, a revitalized sense of mission gripped the crew aboard the Queen's Endeavour. Captain Theodore turned to his men, his expression one of resolve. "Let us carry their dreams forward in every step we take, negotiation we enter, and new friendship we forge. We are here only for trade or exploration but to build bridges between worlds. We shall retire early this evening, and disembark the ship at sunrise, to begin our mission here. Any questions?"

Several crew members voiced inquiries regarding the upcoming meeting with the Sheikh and expressed concerns about the local population's attitude toward outsiders, seeking advice on precautions to observe. Sir Herbert, alongside Captain Theodore, shared insights from their seasoned voyages. "The eastern seaboard of the continent generally welcomes new arrivals with open arms, fostering a harmonious existence among most," Sir Herbert elucidated. "Nonetheless, it's prudent to remain vigilant and cautious at every step," he added.

At the end of their assembly, the crew members agreed to meet on the deck the next morning.

"Good night brave hearts. May the stars guide thee to thy berths with gentle winds at thy back. Rest well, for on morrow, we shall disembark at dawn's first light. Goodspeed, and keep watch over us all" Captain Theodore bade the crew members.

With that, the crew dispersed, each man carrying with him the memory of those lost and the determination to make their journey meaningful.

By dawn, the vibrant heart of Mombasa pulsed with life, a cacophony of sounds, and a kaleidoscope of colors greeting the crew as they made their first steps into the bustling port. The air was thick with the scent of spices - cinnamon, cardamom, and cloves - each whiff carrying stories from distant lands. The sun, bathed the city in golden light, casting long shadows that danced on the cobblestone streets. Their journey, fraught with peril and promise, was already reshaping their understanding of the world and their place within it. With its bustling streets and vibrant spirit, Mombasa had offered them a glimpse into the vastness of human existence - as complex as it was beautiful. The aura sunbathed the surroundings in tranquil, warm tones over the docks as The Queen's Endeavour crew prepared to meet the emissaries of Mubarak bin Rashid al-Mazrui, the Omani governor of Mombasa. The air, still laden with the day's heat, carried the anticipation of the forthcoming encounter.

The crew's interaction with the locals offered a glimpse into Mombasa's daily life. Despite the language barrier, smiles and gestures bridged the gap, creating moments of connection that transcended words. A local merchant, intrigued by their interest, offered them samples of fresh tropical fruits and nuts, each flavor a testament to the richness of the land.

Watching his crew immerse themselves in the local culture, Captain Theodore felt a surge of pride. "This," he thought, "is the essence of exploration. Not just the discovery of new lands, but the meeting of minds and hearts."

Sir Herbert, ever the diplomat, was engaged in a conversation with a group of local elders. His intent was clear - to understand the nuances of Mombasa's society, governance, and people. The exchange was marked by mutual respect and a shared desire for understanding, bridging the gap between their worlds.

As the day peaked, the crew made their way through the maze of streets, each turn revealing new wonders. The architecture, a blend of Swahili, Arabic and Portuguese influences, told the city's history in its walls. The call to Islamic prayer echoed through the air, a reminder of the spiritual fabric that wove the community together. They finally arrived at the front of the outer bailey of Mubarak bin Rashid's residence.

Standing tall and composed, Captain Theodore adjusted his jacket, the symbol of his command and responsibility. Beside him, Sir Herbert, embodying the essence of British diplomacy, wore an expression of keen interest and readiness. The crew lined up with a sense of decorum, their faces a mix of curiosity and resolve.

The emissaries, a trio of dignified figures clad in traditional robes of rich colors and intricate designs, approached with measured steps. Their leader, a man of notable stature with an air of authority, extended a hand in greeting. "Captain Theodore, Sir Herbert, we welcome you to Mombasa on behalf of Mubarak bin Rashid," he announced, his voice carrying a warm timbre.

Captain Theodore responded with a firm handshake, his voice steady. "We are honored by your welcome. Our journey has been long, but the sight of your city has lifted our spirits. We look forward to fruitful discussions with Sheikh Isa."

Sir Herbert, stepping forward, added, "Indeed, the reputation of Mombasa's hospitality precedes it. We are eager to learn more about your culture and to explore the possibilities of mutual benefit."

The emissaries, pleased with the respectful tone of the greeting, gestured towards the city. "Mubarak bin Rashid has prepared a welcome befitting our esteemed guests. If you follow us, we shall escort you to the palace."

Captain Theodore, leading his crew with a blend of curiosity and caution, observed the city with the keen eyes of a navigator accustomed to deciphering unknown waters. "There's a story behind every corner," he remarked quietly to Sir Herbert, who walked by his side, his gaze absorbing the details of the surrounding architecture and the people who called this city home. The emissaries, knowledgeable and proud of their heritage, shared insights and anecdotes, painting a vivid picture of Mombasa's rich cultural tapestry.

As they approached the palace, the streets became quieter, the air cooler as the shadows of the tall buildings offered respite from the sun's gaze. Sensing the visitors' growing anticipation, the emissaries began to share stories of Sheikh Isa's rule - how he navigated leadership challenges, fostering peace and prosperity in a time of change.

 The residence's grand entrance was a grandeur of Swahili architecture on full display. Intricate wooden carvings adorned the doors, and the walls, built from coral stone and painted in chalk stood as a testament to the ingenuity and skill of its artisans. The bailey was flanked by towering palms opening into a courtyard where the air was perfumed with the scent of blooming jasmine. Water, the source of life, flowed gently in a central fountain, its sound a soothing backdrop to the buzz of whispered conversations and the rustle of silk robes. Their surroundings' opulence and grandeur enveloped the British delegation as the guard led them through the palace's corridors. Tapestries of vibrant hues adorned the walls, each telling tales of battles won, alliances forged, and the prosperity those victories had brought to the land.

The envoy meets Mubarak bin Rashid

The captain and his British delegation were led through the palace's ornately decorated halls, each more impressive than the last. The air was scented with frankincense, adding to the sense of entering a different world where history, culture, and diplomacy intertwined. As they awaited their audience with Mubarak bin Rashid (the crew members exchanged glances, each reflecting on the journey that had brought them here. The initial encounter with the emissaries had set the tone for what promised to be a meeting of significant consequence, not just for The Queen's Endeavour crew but for the future relations between Britain and the vibrant city of Mombasa -including the east coast of Africa.

His mind racing with questions and observations, Sir Herbert leaned in toward Captain Theodore, whispering, "This meeting, this moment, it's more than a mere exchange of pleasantries and goods. We're stepping into a narrative that's been unfolding for centuries. I daresay our part in this story could shape the future of our relations with this remarkable land."

Captain Theodore nodded, his expression one of solemn agreement. "Let's proceed with the respect and the dignity this occasion demands. Today, our actions could be a turning point, not just for us, but for the future generations."

As they were finally ushered into Mubarak bin Rashid's residence, the air seemed still, and anticipation hung heavy. The meeting, set against the backdrop of Mombasa's ancient grandeur, was not just a diplomatic encounter but a confluence of cultures, each with its dreams, aspirations, and, perhaps, apprehensions about the unknown future ahead.

As the evening sun vanished beneath the horizon, casting a soft golden light through the latticed windows of Mubarak bin Rashid's residence. The British delegation was ushered into a grand dining hall. The room was a spectacle of opulence and grandeur, with lofty ceilings supported by intricately carved columns and walls adorned with tapestries that depicted the rich history of Mombasa and its people. The palace's servants set a long table at the center of the room. They covered the table with fine cotton and laden with various dishes that promised a culinary journey unlike any Sir Herbert and his companions had ever experienced.

Mubarak bin Rashid, resplendent in his robes of the finest linen adorned with gold embroidery, greeted each of his guests with a warmth that belied the formal setting. "Welcome, friends from afar," he began, his voice carrying the assurance of a leader well-versed in diplomacy. "Tonight, we feast not only in honor of your safe arrival but in the spirit of friendship and mutual respect that we hope to build between our peoples."

Taking his cue from the governor's gracious welcome, Sir Herbert replied, "Your Highness, we are humbled by your hospitality and the opportunity to partake in the rich traditions of your culture. We sincerely wish that this evening marks the beginning of a fruitful and enduring partnership."

As they took their seats, Captain Theodore, William, Arthur, and Oliver were introduced to a culinary landscape that was as diverse as flavorful. The dishes served were a testament to the region's abundance and its pivotal role in the spice trade. Platters of succulent meats, seasoned with spices that Sir Herbert could only guess at, were accompanied by an array of fruits and vegetables that painted a vibrant palette on the ceramic plates. Throughout the meal, The governor shared stories of Mombasa's history, its triumphs, and challenges, offering insights into the complexities of trade, politics, and culture that defined the region. His knowledge and wisdom commanded attention; even Captain Theodore, a man of few words, was engrossed in the conversation.

With his innate curiosity, Sir Herbert engaged the Sheikh in discussions about the local cuisine, admiring the flavors and techniques that delighted their palates. "The way food can unite people, transcending boundaries and creating a common ground, is truly remarkable," he noted.

The dialogue that ensued was broader than pleasantries and culinary exchanges. It ventured into diplomacy and shared interests, with Captain Theodore outlining the potential for trade and cooperation. Listening intently, Sheikh Isa acknowledged the benefits such an alliance could bring, emphasizing the importance of respecting traditions and ensuring mutual benefits.

As the evening progressed, the conversation delved deeper into the aspirations and challenges faced by both parties. The contentious issue of the slave trade was approached with sensitivity and a shared desire for progress. Sheikh Isa expressed his vision for a future where prosperity could be achieved through trade and innovation rather than exploiting human lives.

The dinner, marked by a blend of respect, insight, and the underlying drive to forge a meaningful relationship, concluded with a sense of accomplishment and anticipation. Sir Herbert and Captain Theodore exchanged glances as they rose from the table, recognizing the significance of the evening's discussions.

By the time they finished the meeting, it was too late to return to their Ship. They were offered guest quarters. As they retired to their quarters, the air scented with frankincense and the night sounds of Mombasa filtering through the windows, the members of The Queen's Endeavour reflected on the journey that had brought them here. The evening had satisfied their appetites and nourished their spirits, opening their minds to the possibilities ahead in this land of contrast and convergence.

The following morning, under the clear blue sky of Mombasa, Captain Theodore, Sir Herbert, and Mubarak bin Rashid resumed their formal discussions. This time, the setting was the palace's opulent reception room, where sunlight filtered through intricate latticework, casting patterns of light and shadow across the richly adorned carpets.

Captain Theodore initiated the dialogue, demonstrating the authority of his position and the gravitas of the mission he represented. "Governor, we come to you with the highest respect for your leadership and the prosperity of Mombasa. Our voyage here, fraught with challenges, was undertaken to establish a beneficial trade route for our peoples."

With his diplomatic finesse, Sir Herbert added to Theodore's points by highlighting the potential for cultural and technological exchange. "Beyond the exchange of goods, we believe there is immense value in sharing knowledge, from navigation techniques to agricultural practices. Such exchanges, we hope, will foster not only economic growth but also mutual understanding and respect."

Mubarak bin Rashid, listening intently, expressed his appreciation for their honesty. "Your journey here speaks volumes of your commitment. Also, Mombasa stands at a crossroads, looking towards a future where prosperity does not come at the cost of our values or freedom. We seek partners who understand this vision."

The discussion then turned to the specifics of the proposed trade agreements. Captain Theodore outlined The Queen's Endeavour's goods - cotton, silk, beads, gunpowder, and weapons - highlighting their quality and the benefits they could offer the local market. In return, they sought gold, ivory, coffee, tea, and spices, which were highly valued in Britain.

Sir Herbert took the opportunity to address the contentious issue of the slave trade, which weighed heavily on his conscience. "We are aware of the complexities surrounding this trade. We hope that, together, we can find a path forward that respects the dignity of all individuals and aligns with our shared ideals of progress and humanity."

Mubarak bin Rashid, his expression contemplative, acknowledged the gravity of the topic. "The slave trade has long been a scourge upon this land, driven by external demands. We hope to build an economy that relies on the wealth of resources and the ingenuity of our people. However, there has been a high demand here lately since the western coasts of the continent seem to have run out of supplies."

"We've come to understand that His Highness Sayyid Majid bin Said al Busaidi of Zanzibar finds himself in a tight spot, grappling with the demands of implementing the anti-slavery legislation. Could we have your esteemed perspective on this challenging situation, You understand?" Sir Herbert asked, ensuring his words tread lightly on the sensitive issue at hand.

While challenging, the negotiations were conducted with a spirit of openness and a shared desire for a fair and lasting partnership. Points of contention were met with a willingness to understand the other's perspective, and compromises were reached with the future benefits of both parties in mind.

As the meeting came to a close, Sheikh Isa invited the British delegation to explore more of Mombasa and its surroundings to understand the land and its people better. "Seeing Mombasa through your own eyes," he said, "will reveal more than any negotiation could. We welcome you as potential trade partners, guests, and friends."

Captain Theodore and Sir Herbert accepted the invitation with gratitude, recognizing the value of experiencing Mombasa's culture and daily life firsthand. The meeting marked the beginning of what was promised to be a complex yet rewarding relationship; one built on mutual respect and the recognition of each other's humanity.

As they left the reception room, the air filled with the sounds of Mombasa coming to life in the morning, and the scents of cloves, ginger, and cinnamon lingered in the air. The British delegation felt optimistic, believing many challenges were ahead. They were convinced that the foundations laid during these discussions offered hope for a partnership to bring about change, progress, and a better future for both their peoples.

As they made their way back through the bustling streets, Sir Herbert observed keenly, fascinated by the intricate designs of the Swahili doors, each carved with motifs that spoke of trade, travel, and the cosmopolitan essence of Mombasa. "Remarkable," he mused aloud, "how these doors are not just barriers but invitations to understand the rich heritage of this place."

Oliver could hardly contain his enthusiasm as children ran alongside their procession. Their laughter was a universal language that needed no translation. He exchanged smiles and playful gestures with them, feeling a connection that transcended the vast distances he had traveled from his homeland.

William and Arthur, seasoned by their experiences yet open to the newness of this adventure, engaged with the local merchants they passed. William's interest in the goods on display - a mix of local crafts, spices, and textiles- sparked conversations, albeit broken by the language barrier, rich in mutual respect and the unspoken acknowledgment of their shared humanity.

CHAPTER 4

Munyazi wa Menza (the young Me-Katilili)

Northward, a distance from the vibrant port of Mombasa, lies Bamba; a lush village where the air thrums with the whispers of the ancestors. Munyazi wa Menza thrived, embodying her people's spirit and resilience. Her presence was a vivid brushstroke on the canvas of her world, a testament to the deep-rooted strength and beauty of the Mijikenda. A living testament to grace, power, and profound wisdom that resonates with the soul of the earth itself.

Her skin, a luminous hue of chocolate brown, radiated the warmth and vitality of the land that had cradled countless generations before her. This radiant complexion spoke volumes of her lineage's resilience, echoing the enduring beauty of the terrain that sustained her people. Adorned with intricate braids, Munyazi's strong black hair flowed like the rivers of her homeland - each braid a symbol of the rich cultural heritage she carries with pride. Artfully composed braids are not merely a hairstyle but a declaration of identity, woven with the same precision and care she brought to every facet of her life.

Munyazi's features capture the essence of her spirit: her face, striking and unforgettable, was an open book of her innermost emotions. Her eyes, dark pools of brown, sparkling with intelligence and a profound depth of understanding, could draw others into the breadth of her vision. These eyes illuminated her expressive face, telling tales of joy, resilience, hope, and the weight of wisdom gleaned from a life deeply connected to her community and the natural world. The proud arc of her pointed nose, a hallmark of her African heritage, and her elongated neck, poised with the elegance of the lush Mijikenda's most graceful creatures, that further accentuated her striking appearance.

When Munyazi smiled, the world around her lightened up in response. Her wide and welcoming smile revealed a set of impeccably arranged teeth whose brilliance rivals the morning sun reflecting off the dew-laden foliage. This smile, so genuine and pure, had the power to disarm the weariest of hearts, radiating warmth and inviting kinship. She moved with an innate and mesmerizing grace. Her confident yet unassuming gait suggested a deep-rooted connection to the earth with every step she took. In motion, whether walking or running, she embodied the untamed beauty of her surroundings - her movements fluid like the wind, conveyed strength, freedom, and the sheer joy of existence.

Her voice, a precise and charismatic instrument, carried the weight of her stories, beliefs, and dreams. With every word she spoke, Munyazi captivated her audience, drawing them into a world where wisdom dances on the edge of her tongue and her message resonates with the clarity of a bell. Whether interacting with her mates, or imparting ancient lore, her speech was a melody that binds, uplifts, and inspires.

One of numerous Arab incursions

At the tender threshold of puberty for Munyazi, a series of raids on several Mijikenda villages occurred. The tranquility of Mijikenda villages was shattered. On this afternoon, a village in Rabai experienced the ominous thunder of hooves and the chilling clash of weapons. The Omani Arabs, mounted on their formidable horses, descended upon the Rabai village like a storm of fury and steel. Adorned in their traditional robes, they were a fearsome sight, their weapons glinting menacingly under the African sun - a stark contrast to the simple tools and homemade weapons of the Mijikenda.

The Arabs' swords were curved and sharp, designed for swift, lethal strikes, while their rifles, a technology yet alien to the Mijikenda, promised death from a distance. The villagers armed only with spears, bows, arrows, and the courage in their hearts, found themselves outmatched in this sudden, brutal encounter.

As the invaders charged through the village, chaos erupted. Men, women, and children scrambled for safety, their screams piercing the air, a cacophony of despair and terror. The Omani Arabs, driven by a relentless quest for captives and plunder, spared no one who dared resist. Their swords cut through the air, striking down the defenders of the village, while those who could not flee fast enough were seized, their futures condemned to the chains of slavery.

The air was thick with the scent of fear and the acrid smell of gunpowder as shots rang out, claiming lives with ruthless efficiency. The ground, once a place of community and celebration, was now marred by the stains of blood and the bodies of the fallen.

Amidst this turmoil, Karisa, a young light spirited young man was tending to his family's livestock in the fields, tending to the numerous beasts that belonged to his family. These fields, a gentle rise of land kissing the outskirts of the village in Rabai, served as his place of duty. Karisa was not a stranger to Munyazi's brothers; their bonds were forged in the innocence of childhood and tempered through the shared trials of Mijikenda rites of passage. With Nzai and Harre, he shared a brotherhood deeper than blood, their camaraderie blossoming into an unbreakable alliance. Karisa was celebrated, not just for his natural affinity with the livestock under his care, but also for his unmatched precision with a bow and arrow, a skill that won him admiration everywhere.

The herd that grazed under his watchful eye was a testament to his family's wealth in livestock, a pride that resonated through the plains of Rabai. His home was a haven of resilience and warmth, woven by the presence of his mother - a survivor of a raid in her youth, a testament to her strength - and a stepfather whose kindness filled the spaces of their dwelling. Alongside his siblings, Karisa's life in a village near Rabai was a harmonious blend of tradition, love, and the echoes of a past that shaped their present.

From his herding spot, the distant sounds of the attack reached him, a foreboding echo that quickened his pulse. Cautiously, he edged closer, moving through the underbrush with the stealth of a shadow until the horrific tableau of the invasion lay before him.

From his vantage point, Karisa witnessed the cruelty of the Omani Arabs, his heart pounding with a mixture of fear and rage. As he watched his people being rounded up, chained, and led away, a fierce determination took hold. Together with Nzai and Harre, they had recently completed their rite of passage into manhood. Karisa, known for his unmatched skill with a bow and arrow, knew this moment called for action, however reckless it might seem.

With a steady hand and a silent prayer to his ancestors, Karisa nocked an arrow to his bow, aiming with precision honed through years of practice. The moment stretched, suspended in time, before he released the arrow, watching it fly true to its target - an Omani Arab leading the charge. The invader fell from his horse, a silent testament to Karisa's deadly accuracy.

The arrow's impact sowed a momentary confusion among the Arabs, their formation disrupted by the unexpected assault. Panic and rage painted their faces as they scanned the bushes, seeking the source of this defiance. The captives, sensing a fleeting chance for escape, pulled at their chains, and made desperate, chaotic attempts to flee. Tragically, the Arabs reacted with swift violence, their rifles speaking in deadly whispers that cut down those who dared to seek freedom.

Realizing his position was compromised, Karisa made the split-second decision to flee. As the three remaining Arabs spurred their horses towards his hiding place, he sprang from the bushes, his heart racing as he dashed for the safety of the forest. The sounds of pursuit filled the air, a terrifying symphony that urged him to push his body beyond its limits.

Karisa's flight through the underbrush was a desperate bid for survival, branches whipping at his face, thorns tearing at his clothes. His lungs burned with the effort, but the fear of capture - or worse, death - propelled him forward, a specter fleeing through the shadows of the trees.

The Omani Arabs, enraged by the audacity of the attack and the loss of one of their own, pursued Karisa with relentless determination. Their shouts filled the forest, a menacing promise of retribution that echoed off the trees, mingling with the sounds of the natural world now disrupted by this intrusion of violence.

Driven by a primal instinct to survive and protect his people, Karisa knew the odds were against him. The realization that he could not outrun the mounted invaders for long weighed heavily on his mind. Yet, the spirit of the Mijikenda warrior within him refused to succumb to despair, fueling his legs with a strength he scarcely knew he possessed.

As he ran, Karisa's thoughts raced back to his village, to the faces of his family and friends now trapped in the clutches of the invaders. His heart ached with the knowledge of their suffering and with the uncertainty of what fate awaited them in the cruel grasp of slavery.

The chase continued, a deadly game of cat and mouse through the dense foliage of the forest, until Karisa, realizing he could not evade his pursuers indefinitely, began to look for a place to make his stand. His mind worked feverishly, crafting a plan out of desperation and the slim hope that he might turn the tide of this fateful encounter.

In the unforgiving grip of the Omani Arabs, Karisa found himself trapped in a nightmare from which there was no awakening. The savagery of his captors knew no bounds; they unleashed a torrent of brutality upon him, their whips carving tales of agony across his bare chest and back. As the lashes descended, each strike was a thunderous declaration of their disdain, leaving behind a canvas of open wounds that spoke volumes of his torment.

Amidst this maelstrom of pain, their voices cut through, taunting him in a language alien and harsh. "Where is your God? Show us where your God is," they demanded in Arabic, their words laden with scorn. Karisa, trembling from the assault, could only muster a weak gesture towards his village, now consumed by flames, a beacon of despair in the dying light.

"Idiot, fool!" one of the Arabs bellowed, his hand connecting with Karisa's face in a deafening slap that sent him spiraling into darkness. When consciousness mercifully returned, it brought with it no respite from his ordeal. Another captor, his command of Kiswahili broken and barely intelligible, pressed him further. *"Mungu, api Mungu wako?"* The confusion that clouded Karisa's mind deepened at the question. *"Mungu Kaya apiiii?"* the Arab screamed, demanding the sacred *Kaya* forest's location, piercing the fog of Karisa's torment.

With every fiber of his being screaming in protest, Karisa uttered a defiant "Nooo." Yet, defiance was met with further cruelty, the Arabs torturing him to the brink of endurance. Broken, both in spirit and body, Karisa pointed towards a path concealed behind the bush, betraying the sacred to his tormentors. Shackled, a chain around his neck and hands, he was forced to lead them to the sacred *Kaya* forest, a sanctuary of his people now threatened by the encroaching darkness of invasion.

Upon their arrival, they encountered three elders - two men and a woman - who stood as guardians of the sacred grove. One of the men, driven by a primal instinct for survival, vanished into the deeper recesses of the forest, leaving his companions to face the invaders' wrath. Dismounting their horses with predatory grace, the Arabs approached, seizing the remaining elders by their hair locks and forcing them onto their knees with contemptuous ease.

"Where is your God!" they demanded, their voices a blasphemous echo in the sanctity of the sacred *Kaya* forest. Karisa defeated and kneeling, could only turn away as the invaders executed their heinous act, slitting the throats of the two *Kaya* elders. Blood, warm and damning, splattered onto him, a visceral testament to the sacrilege committed upon sacred ground.

At that moment, something within Karisa fractured irreparably. The physical pain that wracked his body paled in comparison to the desolation that engulfed his soul. Witnessing the defilement of the sacred and the merciless slaughter of the elders, he felt an emptiness so profound it threatened to consume him. The forest, once a bastion of peace and spiritual sanctuary, had been defiled by the violence of the invaders, its sanctity shattered by the screams of the dying and the silence of the dead.

The Arabs, emboldened by their vile act, turned their gaze upon Karisa, their eyes alight with the fervor of conquest and the satisfaction of having crushed the spirit of one more defender of the land. But in their arrogance, they failed to recognize the resilience of the human spirit, the indomitable will that clings to the faintest glimmer of hope even in the darkest times.

Though broken, Karisa was not defeated. The blood of the elders, mingled with his own, became a solemn pact - a vow that their sacrifice would not be in vain, that their deaths would be avenged. In the depths of his despair, he found a resolve as unyielding as the ancient trees that stood witness to the atrocity.

The journey back from the sacred *Kaya* forest, with the Arabs leading him away in chains, was a blur of pain and grief. Yet, within Karisa, a plan began to take shape, born of necessity and fueled by the desire for retribution. He understood the monumental task that lay before him, the need to rally his people, to awaken the dormant fury of the Mijikenda, and to drive out the invaders who sought to desecrate their lands and enslave their people.

As the shores approached, where the Arabs would ship him away to an unknown fate, Karisa's mind raced with the possibilities of escape, of resistance, and of the restoration of his people's freedom and dignity. The memory of the elders' sacrifice, the sight of his village in flames, and the pain of his wounds forged within his warrior's heart. A memory that would not rest until justice is served.

Mourning with Rabai

As the first light of dawn pierced the horizon, the women of Bamba, Ganze, and surrounding hamlets began their solemn pilgrimage to a village nestled in the heart of Rabai. Heavy with the scent of impending rain, the air was saturated with tangible grief, enveloping them like a dense fog. They advanced in a procession shrouded in silence, their footsteps echoing the sorrow that gripped their hearts, their voices mournful melodies that fluttered through the morning breeze. Some allowed their tears to flow freely, carving paths down their cheeks, merging with the earth beneath their feet, while others muttered curses, their words laced with anger and despair, directed at the marauders who had cast a shadow of destruction over their kin in Rabai.

The night before had been marked by an urgent summons, as bullhorns, conch and drums resonated through the Mijikenda lands, carrying the harrowing news of a brutal assault on one of their own - a village within the Rabai enclave, a fragment of the Mijikenda community. The raiders left behind a devastating trail - homes reduced to ashes, innocent lives extinguished, two guardians of faith ruthlessly slain before the sanctity of the

Kaya forest altar, and amongst the chaos, young Karisa, a shepherd, along with many others, were captured, their freedom stolen, destined for a life of bondage. The air was thick with mourning, and the women, under the guidance of Me-Nzai, a revered figure within the *Chifudu* dance ensemble, felt an overwhelming urge to unite and express their solidarity with the stricken souls of Rabai. *Chifudu*, a spiritual dance performed in times of grief, brought together the religious women of the Mikushekushe organization - a beacon of strength for the Mijikenda women - and other mourners as they embarked on their journey in the veil of twilight. Me-Nzai, the heart of the *Chifudu* and mother to Munyazi, set forth on this daunting trek to Rabai, undeterred by the relentless blaze of the tropical sun.

As the sun reached its zenith, they reached their destination, casting stark shadows upon the ruins. The remnants of once vibrant homes stood as silent testaments to the atrocity, the air still ripe with the acrid scent of charred thatch and timber. The raw cries of the bereaved pierced the heavy silence, a somber welcome to the mourners. Their arrival was a bittersweet sight, their presence a symbol of unity and shared sorrow. The women, their spirits intertwined with those of Rabai, began their sacred *Chifudu*, their movements a poignant expression of empathy, their songs a catharsis for the collective grief that enveloped them. As they danced, the boundary between them and the villagers blurred, their shared loss forging them into resilience, their mourning not just an act of remembrance but a defiant stand against the darkness that sought to divide them.

Me-Nzai and her group, their faces streaked with tears, began to hum and sing as they moved rhythmically, offering their dance as a tribute to the lives lost and as a balm for the grieving souls. That afternoon, a mass funeral was held. The community came together to bury their dead – men, women, and children – a short distance from the ruins of their village. In the aftermath, yet another village was abandoned, becoming a ghost town, a silent testament to the horrors of the raid.

A meeting in sacred *Kaya* Mudzi Muvya

The gravity of the circumstances necessitated swift action, leading to the organization of a meeting within the hallowed confines of the Mudzi Muvya sacred *Kaya* forest on the same day. This assembly saw the attendance of the Mijikenda government's entire hierarchy, spanning from the common folk to kings and chiefs to esteemed elders. These venerable figures, draped in traditional attire that both signified their rank and paid homage to their cultural heritage, commanded respect. Despite their senior years, they radiated a sense of vigor and skill, drawing all eyes to them with their authoritative presence.

The meeting began with traditional rituals performed at the shrine, aimed at casting a curse on the assailants, seeking protection from further harm, and appealing for peace from *Mulungu*, the supreme God. The diviners called upon the ancestors, invoking their spirits in a ceremony that bridged the gap between the living and the dead - the ritual creating an intense feeling of unity and shared purpose.

As the sun dipped lower, casting elongated shadows through the Mudzi Muvya sacred *Kaya* forest, the circle of elders deepened their discussion, their voices a blend of concern and determination. Each elder, in turn, shared their wisdom, proposing strategies to fortify their defenses, enhance the prowess of their warriors, refine their weaponry and tactics, and ultimately expel the invaders from their lands permanently.

The air was thick with the gravity of their situation yet charged with a unity of purpose. "In times past, we thrived as one, undivided. We must dissolve our sub-tribal lines and come together as a singular, formidable community, as our ancestors did," one elder voiced firmly, his gaze sweeping across the attentive faces.

Another stood, his voice resonant with authority, "Central to our unity is leadership. We must rally under one king, a leader for all the Mijikenda, to guide us through this disruption."

A third chimed in, adding a note of pragmatism, "Our strength lies in our warriors. It is imperative that we bolster our army, ensuring they are unmatched in skill and resolve."

The conversation took a strategic turn as another elder suggested, "We should extend our reach to the Swahili people for armaments. Their proximity and dealings with the Arabs could prove advantageous in securing what we need."

However, this proposal was met with immediate contention. "No, I disagree," interjected an elder sternly, silencing the murmurs of agreement. "Engaging openly with the Swahili people might inadvertently reveal our intentions to the Arabs. Our movements, our plans, must be cloaked in discretion. We cannot afford to lead our adversaries right to our doorstep."

The air was charged with anticipation as Chirau, king of the Digo subtribe of Mijikenda, cleared his throat, signaling the start of his address. He spoke with a firm yet sad tone, lamenting the loss of lives and the repeated attacks on their villages. His words, simple yet profound, resonated with everyone present.

"Snakes get killed easily due to their disunity," he began, his gaze sweeping over the crowd, making each individual feel personally addressed. He emphasized the need for unity and strength in the face of adversity, urging his people to stand together to protect their communities and put an end to the invasions. "My brothers, my sisters, we are losing count of the number of villages attacked and certainly the number of lives lost! Our tribe is vanishing before our eyes!" The congregation agreed.

The discussion continued, each contribution building upon the last, weaving a carpet of strategy and solidarity. Through their dialogue, a vision of a united, indomitable Mijikenda emerged, ready to face the challenges ahead with wisdom, courage, and an unwavering commitment to their people's freedom and way of life. They unanimously agreed that the Mijikenda were united and would stand together in times of adversity.

As the meeting came to a close, the attendees left the sacred *Kaya*, their spirits buoyed by the words of the kings, chiefs, and elders. They muttered liturgical words and spat into a large pot as they exited the sacred forest, a symbolic act meant to seal their vows and commitments made during the meeting. The community, united in their grief and resolve, left the sacred *Kaya* Forest with a renewed sense of purpose. They were determined to overcome the challenges they faced and protect their people from further harm.

Munyazi's early diligence

Back in Bamba, in Menza's homestead, the dawn greets Munyazi with a yard that whispers for attention. She begins by sweeping the compound, her movements as rhythmic and practiced as a dance passed down through generations. The dust and leaves gathered overnight were swiped away, leaving the earth refreshed and welcoming. Next, she turned her attention to the pots, their clay surfaces stained with the remnants of yesterday's meals. With care and diligence, she cleaned them until they shone, ready to be filled again with the day's sustenance.

In a Mijikenda household, every family member contributes significantly, and their responsibilities fit together seamlessly to forge a strong bond of unity and resilience. Munyazi, though the eldest daughter, finds herself as the junior to her five brothers. It falls upon her shoulders to oversee the well-being of her family in her mother's absence. Her steadfast commitment and affection position her as the linchpin of their familial harmony, her actions serving as a pillar of strength and care. Through Munyazi, the Mijikenda traditions are vibrantly kept alive, acting as the rhythmic pulse that safeguards the continuity of their cultural legacy and cements the familial bond.

Her chores continue with a journey to the forest's edge, where she collects firewood, her arms embracing the bundles that will warm her home and cook their food. The stream calls to her next, its waters calm and clear, a natural mirror reflecting the sky above. Here, she does the laundry, the rhythmic sound of clothes against stones mingling with the stream's gentle babble. Her hands move purposefully, washing away the dirt and grime, preparing the garments to embrace her family again.

As the sun begins its descent, Munyazi returns home, her thoughts turning to the evening meal. She prepares a feast that is a testament to her skill and heritage - plantain, green vegetables, and dried fish, all simmered in a rich coconut cream. The aroma fills the homestead, a scent as comforting as a hug, promising nourishment and joy.

Munyazi's little stepsister, too young to shoulder the heavier burdens, flits about the compound as she prepared a meal. Her laughter, a melody amidst the day's labor, blends with the shouts and giggles of their neighbor's children. Munyazi watches over her, a guardian and mentor, occasionally calling her to assist with simpler tasks, instilling in her the values of their ancestors, one small chore at a time.

The brothers, each with their role, contribute to the family's well-being. Mwarandu, with the strength and determination of his ancestors, plows the farm, turning the earth to reveal its fertile heart. Kithi, patient and meticulous, battles the weeds that threaten their crops, ensuring their fields remain a testament to their hard work. Nzai, adventurous and bold, ventures into the wilderness with his age mates, hunting for game that will supplement their meals and clothe them. With the courage of a lion, Harre pursues warrior training, preparing to defend their home and honor.

Me-Nzai came back home exhausted and distraught. Her aching feet bore a collection of the dusty paths she and other women had walked and danced *Chifudu*, the funeral dance, the entire day. Me-Nzai was grateful for Munyazi, the eldest female offspring whose role transcends mere responsibility. With her mother absent, the weight of the homestead's well-being rests squarely on her capable shoulders. Her days are a symphony of chores, each task a verse in the song of her family's survival and comfort.

As twilight enveloped their homestead, the family settled onto a mat, their bodies forming a circle that was a testament to their unity and enduring bonds. However, This evening, the air was thick with an uncharacteristic hush, a palpable tension that seemed to mute the usual chatter and laughter accompanying their meals. The raids in Rabai, a specter of violence and fear that loomed over their community, cast a long shadow over the gathering. Yet, amidst this somber backdrop, there was a flicker of gratitude - a shared relief that, despite the turmoil that raged outside their village, they were together, safe within the sanctuary of their home. This sense of security was a luxury, they knew, in these tumultuous times when peace was as fleeting as the setting sun.

Dinner passed with unusual solemnity. The ritual of sharing the day's events, usually a time of animated conversation and communal reflection, was subdued. Eyes flicked with unspoken questions and hearts heavy with anticipation. All awaited the voice of Me-Nzai, their matriarch, whose experience that day bore the weight of untold stories. Munyazi's brothers found themselves profoundly shaken and enveloped in sorrow over the departure of their friend, a bond so deep it mirrored that of family. Although Munyazi had never met Karisa in person, she felt a sense of familiarity with him, nurtured by the lively and passionate stories her brothers shared about their adventures together.

Menza, their father, broke the silence with words of appreciation, his voice, a warm embrace in the cool evening air. "You have cooked very well, my daughter," he praised, his words directed at Munyazi, whose culinary skills had given them this moment of solace.

"Yes, she is an excellent cook. My husband, what do you expect when she has learned from the best?" Me-Nzai responded, her voice tinged with pride. Her words were not just praise for Munyazi's skills, but a reflection of the legacy of knowledge and tradition passed down through generations. They were a testament to their resilience and the ability to find moments of joy and pride even in the darkest times.

With dinner concluded, the time came for Me-Nzai to share her ordeal, the narrative of a day marked by horror and bravery. The raid in Rabai was not just an event; it was a moment that had shaken the very foundations of their community. She recounted the story of Karisa, a young man whose courage had briefly turned the tide, his actions a beacon of resistance in the face of overwhelming darkness. All were awed at the symbol of youthful bravery, whose defiance in the face of adversity illuminated the darkness. His subsequent capture and the forced betrayal he was coerced into, leading the invaders to their sacred *Kaya*, were a blow to him and all of Mijikenda. The brutality that followed, the desecration of the *Kaya*, was an affront to their ancestral spirits, a wound that would take long to heal - a tale of bravery overshadowed by treachery, leaving a scar on the collective soul of the Mijikenda.

Through Me-Nzai's narrative, the family was transported to the heart of the conflict, feeling each moment of fear and each act of bravery as if they had been there themselves. It was a tale of devastation and terror but also of the resilience and courage that defined their people. In her recounting, Me-Nzai conveyed the events of the day and instilled in her children a sense of their heritage, the strength and unity that had always been their most significant defense against the storms that sought to break them.

After their parents and youngest siblings retired to bed, Munyazi and her older brothers discussed the fateful event of the Rabai raids. It became a part of their collective memory, a reminder of the fragility of peace and the enduring strength of family. It was a solemn reminder that in a world where darkness loomed large, their light - the light of unity, love, and resilience - would always shine brighter.

Munyazi stood before her brothers, her voice carrying weight and conviction that seemed to echo through the heart of the earth beneath them. "Listen, my brothers," she began, each word deliberate, imbued with a resolve that pierced the veil of silence that had fallen over them. The brothers, caught in a web of unease and anticipation, exchanged glances, their thoughts a whirlwind of questions and uncertainties. Yet, Munyazi allowed the silence to linger, her message a slow, penetrating force that sought to reach the depths of their beings. They remained seated outside in the lingering warmth of the evening, a symbolic circle of unity and contemplation.

As she paced before them, her movements were measured, her gaze intense and unwavering, challenging each brother to grasp the gravity of her words. A palpable tension filled the air, a testament to Munyazi's frustration and the simmering anger that underscored her plea for change. "This land is ours, and that could have been us! We are all living in constant fear!" she declared with escalating fervor. "We are left with but one choice.; to act."

Kithi, caught in a moment of introspection by the dimming light of the fireplace, voiced the despair that haunted them all. "The intruders wield weapons of speed and death," he said, his voice reflecting their collective despondency.

"Indeed, they possess formidable weapons, but we are armed with strengths that transcend the physical," Munyazi countered, her assurance a beacon in the fog of their doubts.

"Our warriors are crafting a monumental weapon capable of unleashing a volley of arrows in a single breath. They are also perfecting the art of the burning spear," Harre announced, his voice laced with the pride of a warrior in the making.

"That sounds promising; we must act swiftly!" Kithi interjected, his spirit buoyed by the prospect of resistance.

Their conversation evolved into a strategic discourse on potential armaments and tactics, a brainstorming session of hope and determination. Yet, as Munyazi poignantly noted, "We have yet to find a definitive answer. We cannot always be on the run, hiding in the bushes with no permanent housing. It is frustrating! How shall we prevent these invaders from encroaching upon our lands?"

A heavy silence fell, the weight of her inquiry grounding them in a solemn moment of realization. Their beloved Mijikenda lands were under siege, their sacred *Kayas* desecrated by the ceaseless brutality of the invaders.

"We must stand united as the Mijikenda," Munyazi persisted, her voice now embodying a calm yet indomitable will. "Alone, a single finger cannot crush lice, but together, our strength is unassailable. Our ancestors have bestowed upon us the stewardship of this land. It falls upon us, each one, to defend its sanctity, to restore the harmony that has been shattered."

Inspired by Munyazi's unwavering spirit, her brothers felt a surge of resolve awaken within them. Her vision of unity and defiance ignited a flame of hope, a guiding light amidst the shadows of their trials.

"We will stand as one: one family, one village, one community, united in purpose," Munyazi proclaimed, her eyes sweeping over her brothers, who now regarded her with a renewed sense of purpose and determination. Clasping her forehead in a moment of solemn contemplation, she added, "The invaders may boast their weapons and their legions, but we inherit the strength of our forebears, the wisdom of our land, and the justice of our cause."

Nzai, the eldest among the siblings, was the first to rise, and his stature was a physical manifestation of the resolve that burned within him. "Munyazi is right," he declared, his voice deep and resonant, echoing the depth of his conviction. "We must not let fear govern our existence. The moment has come for us to seize control of our fate, to demonstrate that we are not mere bystanders in the saga of our land." The intensity in his deep brown eyes flickered with a restrained and potent fury, a visual testament to his inner turmoil and steadfast determination.

Inspired by Nzai's stance, one after another, her brothers stood, each amplifying the sentiment he had voiced. Their voices merged into a mighty chorus of defiance and hope, resonating with the strength of their shared resolve. Munyazi, encircled by this brotherhood of warriors, felt a profound shift in the air. It was as though the currents of history were being redirected, heralding the dawn of a new era for them.

As they engaged in strategic planning, the essence of their Mijikenda ancestors seemed to permeate the space, a palpable presence that lent their resolution a sacred sanction and guidance. It was a moment of profound connection, bridging the past with the present, empowering them with the wisdom and bravery of generations that had walked the land before them.

Munyazi and her brothers were acutely aware of the daunting path ahead. They understood that the journey would be strewn with obstacles and trials. Yet, fortified by the enduring legacy of their ancestors and the unbreakable bond of their unity, they embraced the future with an unwavering spirit. They were not just prepared to face the forthcoming challenges; they were determined to overcome them, carrying forward the torch of their heritage and defending the sanctity of their homeland with every fiber of their being.

The return without Kithi

The following season, Nzai, the eldest, led the somber procession, his usually bright eyes dulled by the scenes he could not unsee. Harre walked close behind, anger simmering beneath his calm exterior, fists clenched at his sides. Mwarandu, the youngest brother, trailed, his steps uncertain, eyes on the ground, lost in a haze of confusion and fear. Munyazi walked alongside her siblings, her heart a maelstrom of sorrow and resolve.

As they approached their home, the scent of the surrounding sacred *Kayas* Forests did little to ease the heaviness in their hearts. Their mother, Me-Nzai, emerged from the homestead, her expression turning from anticipation to dread as she read the silent anguish in her children's eyes.

"What has happened? Where is Kithi?" Me-Nzai's voice trembled, piercing the thick silence that enveloped them.

Nzai stepped forward, his voice barely above a whisper, "Mother, Kithi...he was taken. The slavers..." He could not finish, the words choking him as the reality of what he was sharing sunk in.

Me-Nzai's knees buckled, her wails of grief cutting through the still air, reaching out to the heavens in a raw, haunting cry. Menza, their father, rushed to her side, his grief etched deep in the lines of his face, but he remained silent, his arm around Me-Nzai a meager comfort against the tidal wave of despair that had struck them.

In the days that followed, the homestead seemed shrouded in perpetual dusk, and the laughter and warmth that once filled their home were distant memories. Me-Nzai, driven by a desperate need for hope, sought out the diviners within the sacred confines of the *Kayas* Forest, her heart clinging to any thread of possibility that Kithi might still be alive.

Shrouded in mystery and reverence, the diviners welcomed her with solemn faces. "Kithi lives," they confirmed after a series of rituals, "but his path is one of great suffering and danger."

Me-Nzai's heart, momentarily lifted by the knowledge of Kithi's survival, plummeted back into despair. "What can we do? How can we bring him back to us?" she pleaded, her voice a blend of hope and agony.

"The excursion ahead is fraught with peril," the diviners warned. "It will require a strength and unity unlike any before."

With this knowledge, Me-Nzai returned to her family, and her resolve hardened. The news of Kithi's survival ignited a flicker of hope within the Menza family, a beacon in the overwhelming darkness.

Menza, wrestling with his challenges, found solace in the resolve of his wife and children. "We must stand together," he declared one evening, his voice steady for the first time since Kithi's capture. "For Kithi, for each other. We will face this darkness and bring our son home."

And so, amidst their grief, a plan began to take shape. Munyazi, her brothers, and their parents, each carrying their pain, found strength in their unity. The village rallied around them, offering support in myriad forms. The once-dimmed communal fires began to flicker with a renewed sense of purpose as stories of Kithi's bravery and the family's resolve spread like wildfire.

In the Giriama *Kayas* Forest, under the cover of night, the Munyazi family, alongside a few brave souls from the village, gathered to embark on their quest. The air was charged with a palpable sense of determination and hope.

"We do this for Kithi, for all those taken from us," Munyazi spoke, her voice resonant in the silent night. "May the spirits of our ancestors guide us and protect us."

Her brothers nodded - their faces set in grim determination. Menza placed a hand on Me-Nzai's shoulder, and their shared look was one of unspoken understanding and love.

Searching for Kithi

As the Menza family ventured into the enveloping darkness of the forest, their hearts were laden with a collective purpose. This resolve bound them tighter than the shadows looming around them. They knew this journey would be the crucible through which their courage, their unwavering faith in one another, and their determination to confront the encroaching darkness would be tested to their very cores.

The way forward was shrouded in uncertainty, a path beset with perils both seen and unforeseen. Yet, the bond they shared, forged in the fires of adversity and love for Kithi - and one another - served as their beacon. They were a family, tempest-tossed yet indomitable, stepping into the night with a collective gaze fixed on the faint, hopeful glow that danced on the distant horizon.

As the first light of dawn painted the sacred *Kayas* Forest in hues of gold, the Munyazi family arrived at the clearing of the diviner. The solemn sound of a conch being blown twice cut through the morning air was a signal that was both an announcement and an invitation. The diviner, an enigmatic figure and imposing, welcomed them with the words, "Similani, similani tsona." the greetings to the living and the ancestors, and spirits.

"Haai," they responded in unison, a chorus of voices intertwined with hope and desperation.

They spoke a prayer to *Mulungu,* the supreme God.

"We seek your wisdom," Menza implored, his plea heavy with the burden of a father's anguish.

With ritualistic solemnity, the diviner prepared his sacred tools - a coconut shell filled with cowrie shells and diminutive bones. He cast these artifacts upon the earth, his murmurs weaving through the silence, a litany of ancient chants. "The trail you tread is fraught with danger," he intoned, his gaze piercing into Menza's soul. "Yet, the strength of your bond shines brightly. Trust in this light." Once more, he consulted the shells and bones, seeking signs and portents. "Good tidings - Kithi lives," he revealed, igniting a spark of relief that coursed through each of them.

"Where is he?" the question burst forth from their collective breath.

The diviner, communing with the unseen, cast his gaze skyward, his breath carrying his words to the heavens before consulting the shells once again. The family watched every movement, every silence heavy with meaning. Finally, he spoke, his voice barely above a whisper, "He drifts upon one of the three great oceans, far from the embrace of land."

Munyazi's resolve hardened, her declaration ringing with a steely determination. "We will bring Kithi home," she vowed, her voice a testament to the strength that adversity had wrought within her.

The parents united in their resolve, affirmed, "We call upon the aid of our ancestors, and God, *Mulungu*, in our quest." With a plan to return bearing a cow and three bottles of seawater as offerings, they left the sacred *Kaya*, a symbol of their commitment and faith.

As they retraced their steps through the forest, Munyazi voiced a newfound aspiration, "When I am older, I wish to become a diviner. I will use my gifts to combat the invaders, to return our people home." It was a promise, not just to her family, but to all who suffered under oppression - a vow to wield her future powers for liberation and healing.

Under the veil of a new dawn, the Munyazi homestead was a hive of somber activity. The family convened with the village elders in a meeting suffused with despair and unwavering resolve. Central to this solemn assembly was Me-Nzai, a mother entangled in the throes of inconsolable grief for her son, Kithi, spirited away by unknown hands. Her lament was a heart-wrenching aria, an echo of a mother's despair that reverberated through the very soul of the community. Each cry, each tear that fell, was a testament to the depth of her agony, her voice a ceaseless prayer woven with the threads of hope for her son's safe return. Desperation clung to her, a shadow that mirrored the tumult within her heart.

In this hour of profound sorrow, the women of the *Chifudu* organization, alongside other villagers, encircled Me-Nzai with a warmth that spoke of communal strength and empathy. Their presence was a beacon of solidarity, their shared grief a silent vow of support. Amidst this outpouring of communal heartache, the Menza family, bound by an unbreakable will, forged a plan born of desperation and a sliver of hope. They resolved to venture to the port of Malindi, a decision propelled by the possibility, however faint, that the Swahili people, with their intricate connections to the Arab traders, might hold the key to unraveling Kithi's fate.

Menza, the patriarch, along with a cadre of the village's most formidable warriors, led by Nzai, the eldest son, set forth on this daunting quest. Their journey was not merely a physical trek, but a pilgrimage fueled by fear, hope, and indomitable spirit. Each step taken towards Malindi was laden with the weight of anticipation, a shared determination to breach the shadows that had claimed Kithi from them. Yet, their quest did not halt at Malindi's shores; it stretched further to the bustling port of

Mombasa, infamous for its chilling role as a nexus in the nefarious web of the slave trade.

As they were navigating the labyrinthine alleys, the murmur-filled docks of these coastal towns. The group was driven by a singular, unyielding mission: to unearth the truth hidden beneath the veneer of commerce and conspiracy that cloaked the slave trade. Menza, a father besieged by a storm of anguish and hope, spearheaded this odyssey with a stoicism that belied the turmoil raging within him. Nzai, his presence a testament to the vigor and resilience of youth, stood as a pillar of strength beside his father, their spirits intertwined in their quest for justice and reunion.

This journey was more than a search; it was a testament to the power of familial bonds, a challenge thrown in the face of adversity. Each obstacle they encountered was a trial by fire, testing their resolve, courage, and the depths of their commitment to one another. In the face of uncertainty and danger, the ties that bound them were forged one more, more robust, and more enduring. Their path was fraught with peril, yet they pressed on, driven by the unquenchable flame of hope that Kithi, their son, their brother, would once again stand among them, a family reunited against the odds.

Days turned into an agonizing wait for the rest of the Menza family and their village, each moment stretching into an eternity of hope and despair. When Menza, Nzai, and the band of warriors finally emerged on the horizon, their silhouettes were those of men who had journeyed through the depths of hope and emerged into the shadow of defeat. They returned, not with the triumphant air of victors, but with the heavy, downtrodden steps of those who had confronted their limits and found them insurmountable. Their mission to uncover the fate of Kithi, to bring him back to the embrace of his family and community, had ended in heartbreak.

The warriors' once resolute faces were etched with the lines of exhaustion, their eyes reflecting the haunting emptiness of unfulfilled quests. The vibrancy that had fueled their departure, a myriad of determination and hope, now seemed a faded memory, replaced by the somber hues of reality. They had traversed the bustling ports of Malindi and Mombasa, navigated the intricate networks of Swahili and Arab traders, and faced the chilling silence of leads that went cold in their grasp. Yet, despite their valiant efforts, Kithi remained beyond their reach, a beloved son and brother still lost to the shadows.

Menza, a figure of stoic strength, now bore the weight of their collective sorrow, his shoulders sagging under the burden of a father's despair. His return was not the triumphant reunion he had envisioned but a silent testament to the cruel unpredictability of their world. Beside him, Nzai's youthful vigor was tempered by the harsh lessons of their journey, his resolve tested by the fires of adversity and the icy grip of defeat.

As they stepped into the heart of their village, their return was met not with celebrations but with a somber gathering of souls, a community united in their shared sorrow. The sight of these weary travelers, their mission unfulfilled, was a piercing reminder of the fragility of hope in the face of the vast, uncaring machinations of fate.

Yet, even in this moment of despair, the Menza family and their village stood together, a testament to the unbreakable community bonds and the human spirit's enduring strength. Their journey had not yielded the outcome they had so desperately sought, but it had reaffirmed the depth of their love for Kithi and one another. In the face of defeat, they found not the end of their story but the courage to continue writing it, each day a new chapter in their unyielding quest for reunion and healing.

The entire village, bound by ties of kinship and shared history, mourned alongside the Menza family. Their collective grief, each thread a testament to the love and esteem in which Kithi was held. The communal fires, once centers of joy and laughter, now flickered mournfully, their light dimmed by the shadow of loss.

Menza bore his sorrow silently, a stoic veneer masking the tempest within. Yet, the façade crumbled with each passing day, his grief finding solace in the bittersweetness of palm wine. His once-measured sips became deep, sorrowful draughts, a futile attempt to drown the anguish that gnawed at his being. Though fraught with good intentions, his path to oblivion only served to fracture the family further, leaving them unanchored in a sea of despair.

In this crucible of suffering, the Menza family stood as a poignant emblem of resilience. Though tested by the flames of adversity, their unity became their beacon of hope. Amidst the upheaval of their despair, they found strength in each other, their bonds fortified by the trials they faced. The journey ahead was fraught with uncertainty, but their resolve to reclaim their lost son from the clutches of fate was unwavering. And so, they embarked on a quest that would test the limits of their courage, a journey that would lead them into the heart of darkness and back, in the hope of reuniting their shattered family.

CHAPTER 5

Karisa's destination

Karisa's captors deemed his weakened body incapable of surviving the ocean's crossing and callously abandoned him in Bwagamoyo (Tanzania), considering him already lost to death. His physique bore the brutal testimony of wounds and fractures, a vivid map of suffering endured. Beneath the unforgiving Tanzanian sun, Karisa's spirit, though battered, emitted a faint but resilient glow.

In the mangrove shores of Bwagamoyo, Karisa's life threaded through the loom of destiny, weaving a tale not of despair but of resilience and hope reborn. His years had grown alongside his trials, marking him as a man who had seen the depths of human cruelty. Here, at the edge of despair, Chiku, a local fisherman, became the unexpected harbinger of hope. Discovering Karisa on the ocean's shores, Chiku extended the kindness that would become the salve to Karisa's battered existence. With water from his flask and the simple offering of bread, Chiku asked for his name in Kiswahili. Karisa nodded in response. Chiku was not sure of Karisa's identity. His face, now obscured by a dense thicket of facial hair, left only a portion of his sun-beaten and wrinkled forehead and eyes visible, telling tales of the trials and time passed.

He tried again, using hand gestures, facial expressions, and movements." Me," he said, pointing to himself on the chest. "Me, Chiku, you?" he asked, pointing at Karisa.

Karisa, his understanding dulled by pain, language barrier, and fatigue, managed to comprehend. With a voice as fragile as the dawn, he whispered, "Karisa."

Born to a Mijikenda mother - a woman deeply rooted in her people's traditions and spiritual life - Karisa's very essence was interwoven with the rich roots of African heritage. His mother's lineage grants him a profound connection to the land, its rhythms, and its ancient stories. Yet, his appearance whispers tales of distant shores; his complexion, a shade of fine caramel, is a delicate blend of his mother's rich, earthy tones and the lighter shades suggestive of an Arab lineage. This suspected heritage ties him to the Arab invaders of the time, a tumultuous period marked by conflict and cultural exchange along the coast.

Karisa's gaze, rich with the profound hues of enigmatic brown, captures the essence of a lineage woven from diverse threads. His eyes, alight with the resilience of his African heritage and the intricacy of his broader genealogy, serve as portals to a soul deeply rooted in the convergence of distinct worlds. These worlds, though occasionally at odds, are indelibly intertwined within his being, painting a picture of unity amidst disparity. In the warmth of his village, his unique visage sparked no discourse; to them, Karisa was simply one of their own - embraced, nurtured, and valued without reservation. His presence, marked by his distinctive hair - curly, abundant, yet subtly different in texture, tells a story of African lineage mingled with the gentle whispers of Arab ancestry.

Karisa stands with dignified grace, his physical stature mirroring the fortitude and adaptability that life demands at the juncture of contrasting heritages. The mystery that shrouds his paternity only adds depth to his persona, casting his path as one of exploration and coming to terms with a heritage that spans the spectrum of human experience. Karisa's story is a testament to the vibrant mosaic of identities that dot the African coastline, emblematic of a history that, while unique, is not wholly singular in its narrative.

Chiku, a man with hair that looked bleached by the sun, his skin evidence of his long hours in the coastal sun, glowed in a rich dark mahogany. He seemed much older than Karisa, an age of what could have been his father. He walked with a limp.

However, that did not disadvantage him. In his compassionate wisdom, Chiku guided Karisa away from the port of Bwagamoyo. A name given to the port that mainly exported enslaved people. A place where souls wept for their freedom. A Kiswahili word meaning drop or leave your heart/soul: when enslaved people were brought there, there was no point of return. A name that echoed the resignation of countless souls ensnared in the trade of lives. They left their hearts and souls before they boarded the sea vessels into the unknown.

Under the sheltering arms of a dense cashew nut tree, Chiku and Karisa found a sanctuary where words were unnecessary, and healing could begin. Each day, Chiku brought sustenance and, in the evenings, shared the fruits of his labor from the sea.

The air here was pure, filled with the salty tang of the sea, mingling harmoniously with the earthy fragrance of wet soil and plant life. The sound of waves lapping softly against the shore provided a constant, soothing background, occasionally punctuated by the distant calls of seabirds. Light filtered through the canopy, casting dappled shadows on the ground, creating a play of light and dark that added to the place's mystique.

"You have to swim in the ocean for the wounds to heal," advised Chiku. The advice to bathe his wounds in the salt of the ocean marked the turning of the tide for Karisa. The healing waters, coupled with the nourishment of cashew fruits and the bond forming between him and Chiku, stitched the fragments of his spirit back together. Karisa, once captive, now found himself captivated by the ocean's vastness, its waves whispering promises of strength regained and freedoms yet to be reclaimed.

Under Chiku's tutelage, Karisa learned the art of the fisherman. The boat became his new realm, the sea his teacher. In his generosity, Chiku not only shared trade secrets but also introduced Karisa to the words of Kiswahili and the principles of Islam. Their friendship, rooted in the kindness found in the most unexpected places, grew into a bond as enduring as the tides. Together, they constructed a humble abode beneath the cashew tree, a testament to Karisa's newfound resolve. The tools and weapons he crafted bore the mark of his heritage, a silent vow never to forget where he came from. Yet, the call of home, the longing to return to his people, never waned. Karisa, with every fish caught, every word learned, every prayer whispered under the vast African sky, nurtured the hope of reunion. Once a symbol of his salvation, the boat became the vessel of his dreams, carrying the promise of a journey back to the lands of the Mijikenda.

In the blends of Karisa's life, every thread pulled by hardship was countered by the weft of resilience, every night brightened by the dawn of new beginnings. His story, interwoven with that of Chiku, stood as a beacon of human kindness, a reminder that even amid despair, were souls willing to extend their hands, hearts open to those in need.

And so, as the seasons continued their eternal dance, Karisa's strength returned, his gaze fixed on the horizon, where the boundary between sea and sky blurred into the infinite possibilities of tomorrow. With a heart fortified by adversity and a spirit buoyed by friendship, Karisa prepared for the day when he would set his course back to the shores of his ancestry, to the embrace of his people, and to the land that held the echoes of his past and the whispers of his future.

Under the tutelage of Chiku, Karisa found solace in the rhythm of the sea, learning the art of fishing and the nuances of navigation that seemed so integral to his friend's existence. The language of the waves became as familiar to him as the contours of his heartache, a bittersweet symphony that spoke of both loss and discovery. Chiku, ever patient, introduced Karisa to the intricacies of Kiswahili and the tenets of Islam, each lesson weaving into the fabric of Karisa's new life, offering him a diversity of knowledge and belief that was both foreign and comforting.

Their days were filled with the silent camaraderie of shared solitude and the earnest efforts of bridging worlds through language and faith. Chiku's insistence on these teachings was not born of mere whim. Still, of a deep-seated belief, that understanding, integration were keys to a harmonious existence in this new realm, Karisa found himself. And so, amidst the ocean's vast expanse and the sky's embrace, Karisa learned to find his place in a world that once seemed impossibly alien.

Their success at sea one day brought them ashore laden with a bounty of fish, the setting sun casting long shadows as they made their way to fulfill the day's commerce. Chiku, ever the mentor, suggested Karisa assist in delivering their catch to his buyers, a proposition that carried the weight of trust and partnership.

The residence they approached stood as a testament to Omani architectural grandeur, nestled within the heart of East Africa. Its stone walls rose with an austere elegance, imposing yet inviting, crowned with large wooden doors that bore the intricate engravings of a culture rich in artistry and tradition. The patterns etched into the wood told stories of distant lands, of seas navigated and deserts crossed, a silent homage to the roots of its occupants. This residence, a microcosm of Omani influence in East Africa, was a bridge between worlds, it is very stones whispering tales of trade, conquest, and coexistence.

However, the awe that such grandeur inspired was quickly eclipsed by a turn of events that neither Karisa nor Chiku could have anticipated. As they made to leave, the guards, with sudden and inexplicable intent, barred Karisa's way, their actions casting a shadow of fear over the moment. Chiku, caught on the threshold of freedom and captivity, found himself thrust outside, "Let him go, let him free; he is not a slave!" his protests and pleas were silenced by the closing of the grand doors.

Karisa, captured once more by the specter of captivity, was led to a chamber where authority and expectation hung heavy in the air. At the room's far end sat a tall Arab, his presence commanding silence and submission with an air that spoke of undisputed leadership. His voice, when it broke the silence, was a thunder, its power sending tremors of dread through Karisa's weary soul.

As Karisa stood trembling, the guards embarked upon a dehumanizing inspection; they inspected Karisa's ears, teeth, tongue, eyes, and limps. And further, with another deafening command of their leader, the guards gripped at his groins, sizing them, then exposing his groin under his cloth, inspecting. The guards answered back to their leader and nodded in approval.

Finally, the guards' final nod of approval to their leader marked the end of the invasive inspection, a moment fraught with uncertainty for Karisa. Whether their judgment spelled further bondage or an unexpected reprieve, the implications of their judgment remained shrouded in the ambiguity of power and possession.

Karisa found himself cuffed once more, not by chains but by circumstances far beyond the comprehension of any soul seeking freedom. The chamber to which he was confined was a study in isolation, its existence a testament to the residence's darker facets. A single window, placed so high near the ceiling that the sky seemed a distant memory, allowed only the most stubborn rays of light to penetrate the gloom. The room was stark, the stone walls cold and unyielding, whispering secrets of despair to any who dared listen. Time became a fluid concept, marked only by the transition from light to darkness, as the sun's journey across the sky went unnoticed by all but the most attentive captive.

The arrival of food, unceremonious and devoid of empathy, was the only interruption to the monotonous dread that filled the chamber. Karisa, driven by a hunger that dulled his senses to all but the most basic needs, consumed what was given without thought or care for its origin. The subsequent washing, a forced cleansing, was yet another ritual in the dehumanizing process he was subjected to, each step stripping away layers of his identity, leaving him bare and exposed to the whims of his captors.

Guided into a room where the light danced a slow waltz with shadows, courtesy of a lone, flickering oil lamp, Karisa stepped into what seemed a scene conjured from the darkest corners of a nightmare. The room hosted a solitary bed, an oasis amidst an ocean of murk, cradling a figure wrapped in veils and mystery - a woman, an enigma. The guards' command to draw near, laced with a stark reminder of his status, cast Karisa into a bewildering role he had neither sought nor comprehended. As the lamp's flame was snuffed out, darkness enveloped the space, transforming it into a realm where scent and touch reigned supreme, the sole mediums through which existence asserted itself. Navigating through the blackness, Karisa's fingers grazed the bed's boundary, his hesitation palpable. It was then that a questing hand found his, startling him in the silent dark. This same hand, gentle yet firm, seized his, leading it in a tender exploration from the curve of her breast down to the secrets veiled by the night. Amidst this darkness, a delicate fragrance mingled with the scent of oil painted the backdrop for a grim tableau - an intimacy unbidden, a trespass against will and spirit, directed by invisible hands.

Karisa becomes Sahel

In the days that followed, Karisa, now given the name Sahel, was relegated to the margins of the residence, a ghost haunting the periphery of life within its walls. His existence was reduced to servitude, his identity supplanted by a name that was not his own. The room at the far end of the residence became his sanctuary, a place of solitude where the weight of his circumstances pressed heavily upon him.

As seasons melted into one another, the realization that the woman bore a child ignited a tumult of emotions within Karisa. The knowledge of his unwitting complicity in the perpetuation of his captivity, of a life brought into existence under such harrowing conditions, was a burden that threatened to unravel the very fabric of his being.

The night the cries of labor shattered the silence, followed by the first breaths of a new life, marked a turning point for Karisa. The reality of his situation, the complexity of the emotions that surged within him, and the understanding that his actions, however coerced, had consequences that extended beyond his suffering forged a resolve within him.

One night, as the residence lay enveloped in the stillness that preceded dawn, Karisa found himself at a crossroads of destiny. He realized that he could no longer remain a passive participant in his own life, that the existence of this child, innocent and yet so deeply intertwined with his own fate, demanded action and clarity of purpose.

In the quiet of the night, Karisa continued crafting his escape plan, a liberation not only from the tangible barriers of his dwelling but also from the constraints that imprisoned his soul. His planning was thorough, fueled by a desperation that honed his intellect to the keenness of a blade. Every movement and breath were a deliberate strategy in his quest for freedom.

The journey to reclaim his name, identity, and destiny was fraught with peril, a path that demanded every ounce of cunning, strength, and resilience he possessed. Yet, within Karisa, a fire had been kindled, a light that no darkness could extinguish. The resolve to face whatever challenges lay ahead, to forge a future where he could stand not as Sahel, the shadow, but as Karisa, the man, was the beacon that guided him through the darkest of nights.

In the shadowed confines of that darkened room, where secrets whispered and destinies intertwined, Karisa was caught in the web of a life he scarcely recognized as his own. Though uncertain, the night encounters had become the only semblance of connection in his isolated existence. The knowledge that he had fathered three children, seeds sown in the darkness, was both a source of deep, aching sorrow and a flicker of warmth in the cold expanse of his servitude. Their laughter, a sound he could only imagine, echoed like a distant dream in the corridors of the residence, a reminder of lives unfolding beyond his reach.

Violating sacred vows

After a brief hiatus, the routine of these nocturnal visits resumed with an unsettling familiarity. Yet, nothing could have prepared Karisa for the shock that awaited him one fateful night. As he navigated the darkness towards the bed, his hands reached out, seeking the outline of the figure that lay in wait. The revelation that the limbs his fingers encountered were unmistakably male sent a jolt of horror through his very core. A mixture of fear and disgust let his bile rush up his throat, giving him a strong surge of nausea. The familiar, yet wholly unexpected grip that seized him belonged to the voice that had haunted his arrival in this place - the commanding presence that all within the residence obeyed.

This encounter, a grotesque mirage of intimacy, was an affront to everything Karisa held sacred. The teachings of his youth, the rites of passage that had ushered him into manhood alongside his peers, Nzai and Harre, resonated with a clarity that cut through the darkness. The commandments they had vowed with an oath to uphold, the prohibition against such contact between men, was etched deep within his soul. To transgress was to face exile, to sever ties with the sacred lands of the sacred *Kaya* forests and the community that had nurtured him.

The realization that he stood on the precipice of an abomination, ensnared in a situation that defied the very essence of his beliefs and values, ignited a fire of defiance within Karisa.

"Do it!" The voice of the man on the bed, laden with authority and demand, now represented the ultimate betrayal, a violation of the sacred vows that had once bound him to his people and their traditions.

In that moment of profound turmoil, Karisa understood that his captivity had taken yet another dark turn, plunging him into depths of degradation that threatened to erase the remnants of his identity. The boundaries of his existence, already blurred by the trials he had endured, now seemed to dissolve entirely, leaving him adrift in a sea of moral ambiguity and despair.

Yet, Karisa's resolve hardened within this crucible of violation and conflict. The teachings of his youth, the values instilled by his community, and the rites that had marked his passage into manhood became the beacon that guided him through the darkness. The imperative to reclaim his autonomy, to resist the forces that sought to diminish him, became the driving force behind his every thought and action.

As the days melted into nights and the cycle of encounters continued, Karisa's spirit, though battered, refused to break. Each visit to the darkened room, each forced interaction, became a testament to his enduring strength and the determination to defy the circumstances that sought to define him. In the silent hours of contemplation, Karisa began to plan his escape, not just from the physical confines of the residence, but also from the chains that bound his spirit. The longing for freedom, for a return to the lands of his ancestors, and the sacred *Kaya* forests that held the essence of his identity grew with each passing day.

The journey ahead was fraught with uncertainty and peril, a path shrouded in the shadows of fear and the echoes of betrayal. Yet, Karisa knew that to surrender to despair was to forsake the vows of his youth, to abandon the hope of redemption and reunion with the land and people that had shaped the very core of his being. In the crucible of his trials, Karisa forged a resolve as unyielding as the ancient trees that stood sentinel over the sacred *Kayas*. Armed with the strength of his convictions and the indomitable will to reclaim his destiny, Karisa prepared to confront the darkness, navigate the treacherous waters of captivity, and emerge into the light of freedom.

CHAPTER 6

The union of Munyanzi and Mulewa

As the seasons turned and the sands of time whispered through the ancient lands of the Mijikenda, Munyazi's path, woven with the rituals and rites of passage that marked the life of a Giriama woman, was a testament to the enduring strength and cultural richness of her people.

Her passage through the rites of womanhood was a time of celebration and reverence as she was initiated into the mysteries and responsibilities that her role in society entailed. The young women were taken to a secluded camp called Jandoni. They were given different forms of knowledge, especially about managing, and caring for a household. They also learned about herbs and spices, diagnosing, and treating illnesses. Likewise farming skills, and nutritious foods. They were informed about marital intimacy, hygiene, living in harmony with neighbors, and being spiritually rooted. Unlike many other African cultures in those times, the Giriama subtribe did not practice genital mutilation. Only their men would be circumcised. The rites, a series of ceremonies steeped in ancient tradition, were a testament to her physical and spiritual maturity and a reaffirmation of her connection to the land and her ancestors. Each step, from the intricate dances to the sacred songs sung under the moonlit sky, was a narrative that would shape the legend she was to become. After completing the rites of passage, the young women were ready for marriage.

Munyazi was now a fully grown young woman, a figure of elegance and strength. She stood tall, her slim silhouette casting a graceful shadow on the sun-drenched earth. Her skin is a rich chocolate brown, smooth and radiant, glowing with the warmth of the sun and the depth of her heritage. It tells a story of resilience and beauty, a testament to the enduring spirit of the Mijikenda people.

Her hair, twisted into locks, cascades down her shoulders like waterfalls of dark silk, each twist a symbol of cultural pride and personal identity. These locks are not merely a hairstyle, but a declaration of her connection to her roots, to the traditions passed down through generations. They move with her, dancing to the rhythm of her steps and the gentle breeze, embodying her free spirit and the natural beauty of her surroundings.

Her smile, enchanting and radiant, illuminates her features, transforming her visage into a bastion of joy and warmth. This smile, a blend of grace and allure, serves as a beacon, inviting and comforting, embodying the very essence of hospitality and kindness. It is a smile that speaks volumes, inviting stories, sharing laughter, and expressing a deep-seated kindness intrinsic to her being. Her eyes sparkle with intelligence and compassion, reflecting the beauty of the world around her and the depth of her soul.

In her attire, she embodied the richness of Mijikenda culture. She wore a *kisuthu*; a wide rectangular cloth, with a particular pattern, colored in red, black and white. Her youthful feminine body wrapped around, accentuating her slender figure while honoring her cultural heritage. The vibrant colors and intricate patterns of her clothing tell stories of her community, of celebrations, of everyday life, and of the natural world that is so integral to Mijikenda's identity. Jewelry, made from beads, shells, or metal, adorns her neck and wrists, each piece meaningful, connecting her to her ancestry and the timeless beauty of African craftsmanship.

Her charm lies not only in her physical appearance but also in her presence, in the way she carries herself with dignity and grace. She moves with quiet confidence, aware of her heritage and her role as a custodian of her culture. Her beauty is magnified by her strength, resilience, and ability to bridge the past and the present. In her, one sees not just a beautiful

Mijikenda woman but the embodiment of a rich cultural legacy that continues to thrive through the ages.

In the fullness of time, Munyazi's path converged with that of Mulewa wa Duka, a man of substance and honor within the Giriama community. Mulewa, coming from the clan of Mwamkare of the Akadzini, lived in a nearby village, Bungale, and had heard impressive traits about Munyazi. Many praised her as an industrious, charming lady with good morals.

The prelude to the marriage

The dawn barely broke when Duka, a respected elder of his village, and his wife began their journey to Bamba. The air was crisp, filled with the promise of the day ahead. Their mission was of the utmost importance - to seek the hand of Munyazi, a young woman famed for her virtues, in marriage for their son, Mulewa wa Duka.

The anticipation grew as they traversed the paths well-trodden by the feet of those who came before them. Munyazi was not just any bride-to-be; her reputation for kindness, wisdom, and strength of character had reached the far corners of the neighboring villages, making her a sought-after companion in the sacred bond of marriage.

Upon reaching Menza's homestead, Duka-Mulewa's father traditionally announced their arrival, calling out, "*Enyeee, mbari hano Menza*!" His voice, seasoned with age and experience, carried across the compound.

Menza, a man of stature and warmth, responded with open arms, "Welcome, welcome, our friends and neighbors!" His voice echoed the hospitality the Mijikenda community held dear, a testament to the bonds that tied them together.

The proposal

"We have come to impress you with our goodness," Duka stated, his voice steady and sincere. By his side, his wife nodded. Her face was a mirror of the sentiment he expressed. "Accept our visit," he continued, laying the foundation for the purpose of their journey. Duka and his wife carried a gift of the finest palm wine, a token of their intentions, and a proposal gift for Munyazi's family. The palm wine, brewed with care and precision, was more than just a drink; it was a symbol of their desire to unite their families, a testament to their respect and the value they placed on Munyazi's virtue.

Menza and his wife, recognizing the significance of the moment, called upon the village elders. Together, they would witness the proposal, a momentous occasion that would determine their children's future.

The palm wine, *uchi wa mnazi*, was presented, its rich aroma filling the air. The parents poured the palm wine from the large guard into a newly branded woody cup with a bamboo straw. An array of buttery coconut milk, sweet-sour, earthy, popcorn-like smelling aroma filled the air. The wine was not just any brew; it was the best of what Mulewa's parents had to offer, a symbol of their commitment and the wealth of their affection.

The elders gathered, their faces etched with the wisdom of years. They took their seats on *chigoda* stools, symbolizing stability and respect for tradition. The first sip of the palm wine was taken, a moment of silence enveloping the gathering as they savored its richness.

"Ah, this brew," one elder exclaimed, "is the essence of the earth itself; its sweetness mingled with the strength of the tree from which it came. It carries the warmth of the sun and the whispers of our ancestors."

Another elder poured a generous libation on the ground, a gesture of offering, respect, and a petition for the ancestors' blessings. "Ancestors of our land," he intoned, "we seek your guidance and blessing. May this union be fruitful. May it bring joy and prosperity to both families." He continued, mentioning names of prominent forebearers as the palm wine sipped into the soil. After a slight silence "Our ancestors are pleased with us.", He finally declared. The small crowd exploded in sounds of jubilations.

The remainder of the wine was shared, a communal act that sealed their approval. The rich taste of the palm wine, embodying the essence of their land and traditions, was a sign of good things to come.

Pleased with the outcome, Munyazi's family set forth their request - a herd of 12 cattle, 8 goats, jewelry, teapots, cups, silk, and umbrellas. These items were not just material goods; they were symbols of wealth, stability, and provision for future needs. After thoughtful deliberation, an agreement was reached. The families embraced, a physical manifestation of their newly formed bond, their gratitude for this auspicious match palpable in the air. With hearts full of joy and anticipation for the future, Duka and his wife returned to their village in Bungale. Their steps were light, their voices lifted in song, a traditional expression of happiness and celebration. The high-pitched, jubilant sounds that accompanied their journey were a testament to the success of their mission.

Upon their return, they shared the news with Mulewa, their son, who listened with a heart swelling with pride and excitement. "You have found me a bride from a reputable clan," he said, his voice laced with gratitude. The promise of a future with Munyazi, a woman of good virtues, filled him with a sense of purpose and joy. Tradition, family, and the binding ties of marriage unfolded. It was a time when the bonds between families were strengthened not just by words but through the sacred rituals and the exchange of bride price, a tradition deeply ingrained in the fabric of the community.

Aaroni: The first meeting of the bridal couple

Munyazi's grandmother, Hawe Kache, was the bearer of significant news, a role steeped in tradition and weighted with the gravity of guiding Munyazi into the next chapter of her life. As the sun began its slow descent, painting the sky in hues of orange and pink, Hawe Kache called Munyazi to her side. The air around them was filled with the gentle hum of village life winding down, a fitting backdrop for the momentous conversation that was about to take place.

"Munyazi," Hawe Kache began, her voice carrying the wisdom of years, "the time has come for you to step into a new chapter. The Mwamkare clan of the Akadzini have proposed for your hand, an offer that speaks volumes of your virtues."

Munyazi's heart fluttered with a mixture of curiosity and anxiety. "What can you tell me about them?" she asked, her voice barely above a whisper, revealing the tumult of emotions within her.

Hawe Kache smiled, a warm, reassuring expression that seemed to ease Munyazi's nerves. "They are a clan of good repute, strong and kind-hearted. We would not have accepted their proposal if it were otherwise," she explained, her words a balm to Munyazi's anxious heart.

A formal arrangement was set for Munyazi to meet Mulewa at *aaroni*. It was a traditional place where future brides and grooms could see each other, talk, and begin to weave the threads of their future together without physical intimacy. The *aaroni* near Bamba nestled at the top of a small hill, away from the prying eyes of the village.

Draped in the most exquisite traditional attire, with beads glistening under the sun, Munyazi epitomized grace and beauty. Her grandmother, Hawe Kache, stood by her side as a beacon of comfort and laughter, their steps in sync as they ventured toward aaroni. Their journey was more than a mere walk; it was a celebration of their bond, filled with teasing and laughter that echoed through the fields and mango groves.

As they passed by verdant farmlands, greeting the toiling workers with warm smiles, they came upon a path lined with wild mango trees, heavy with ripe fruit. The air was thick with the scent of mangoes, a fragrance so intoxicating, it seemed to pause their worries and hasten their joys.

Hawe Kache, with a youthful gleam in her eye, stooped to pick up a mango, cradling it as if it were a precious jewel. "Mmmh, this is my best type, which is rare nowadays. It's called the sweet ear," she murmured, her voice a mix of reverence and delight as she inhaled the scent of the ripened fruit.

Munyazi, ever mindful of their purpose, gently chided, "Hawe, we have to hurry, or we'll be late."

Hawe Kache, undeterred and with a mischievous lilt to her voice, teased, "Oohoo, someone's eager to meet this man, eh?" She chuckled, continuing, "Remember, I'm returning with you today."

Munyazi's tone was a mix of impatience and affection. She barely managed a "Hawee..." before her grandmother added, "*aaroni* is merely for a greeting, at best from a respectful distance."

"At a distance?" Munyazi echoed, confusion coloring her voice. She helped pack more mangoes into the sling bag her grandmother had fashioned from her wrapper, her actions speaking of deep-seated care and respect.

Hawe Kache's laughter filled the air as she teased, "Ah, now I see. My stories have made you too curious. But remember, Munyazi, patience is a virtue." Their shared laughter was a testament to their bond, lightening their journey.

The conversation took a more intimate turn as Hawe Kache, with a twinkle in her eye, inquired, "But tell me the truth,

Munyazi, has anyone touched it?" Her question, though direct, was softened by the affection in her gaze.

Munyazi, exasperated yet amused, shook her head. "Hawee, why are you like this!"

"Because, my dear granddaughter, it's important," Hawe Kache replied, her tone a blend of seriousness and care. "We've told them you are untouched and innocent." She thought for a moment and added, "Remember Kasichana? Her grandmother took her for the first intimate night on her marriage day. What happened? They found out she was very much used to sexual intercourse!" Hawe Kache, sounding appalled, said, "Kasichana's grandmother was extremely embarrassed the next morning; they had to leave Kahenda's compound early the next morning. The Kahenda and his family did not want her anymore!"

"Where did she go? I don't hear of her anymore," inquired Munyazi.

"The family moved to the outskirts of Malindi; they were too embarrassed to stay. And the silly boy who used to wait for her behind their farm was punished," Hawe Kache explained. "You see how terrible it impacted all of them?"

"If that's so, it looks like we will all be sticking around here for a very long time," Munyazi chimed, almost giggling.

"I hope so child, ... I am too old to start over somewhere strange! I want to be buried where my ancestors were." Hawe Kache pointed.

Reassuring her grandmother, Munyazi affirmed, "I am untouched, Hawe. Don't worry." Her playful retort, "But how would you know?" was met with Hawe Kache's humorous demonstration, spreading her legs like a frog, a visual so comical they both erupted in laughter, their joy a vivid reminder of their unbreakable connection.

As they continued their journey, the laughter and teasing between Munyazi and Hawe Kache painted a picture of a journey rich with more than just tradition - it was filled with life, love, and the vibrant infinity of their bond. Each step towards *aaroni* was laden with anticipation, not just for the meeting but for the shared moments that defined their relationship, making the journey a celebration of their heritage and the love that bound them together.

Arriving at *aaroni,* they found themselves under the expansive shade of a cotton tree near a neatly constructed hut. The anticipation hung heavy in the air as they waited, seated on the wooden benches outside. A middle-aged woman emerged from the hut, her presence momentarily startling Munyazi, who had been lost in her thoughts of meeting Mulewa. Hawe gave her most of the mangoes they had picked. "Oh, these! The sweet ear! The best," she chimed. The woman's hospitality, offering coconut water and nuts, was a welcome distraction, easing the tension of the wait.

Then, as if summoned by Munyazi's beating heart, Mulewa appeared. His presence was commanding, his tall, muscular frame wrapped in rich chocolate skin. His hair, a perfectly combed afro with a wooden comb resting atop, framed his striking features.

Their eyes met, and smiles broke free, illuminating their faces with the glow of mutual admiration. Hawe Kache, sensing the importance of privacy for this pivotal moment, excused herself into the hut. Munyazi, overwhelmed by the intensity of the moment, found herself shyly gazing down, her foot drawing aimless patterns in the sand.

"Goodness, Munyazi, I knew you were beautiful, but I could have never imagined you to be this beautiful," Mulewa said, his voice a blend of awe and sincerity.

Flattered beyond words, Munyazi felt a blush warm her cheeks, a silent testimony to the effect of his words. "I am humbled, sir," she replied, her voice a soft whisper laced with the anxious fluttering of her heart.

"Don't be shy; look at me," Mulewa teased, his voice gentle, encouraging her to meet his gaze.

Raising her head, Munyazi allowed her eyes to lock with Mulewa's. At that moment, a sense of comfort and warmth enveloped her, a silent promise of shared tomorrows and a bond that felt ancient. They knew, without a word spoken, that their hearts had found a home in each other.

As days turned into nights and the sunrises painted the sky anew, the promise made at *aaroni* began to manifest. The family of Mulewa, true to their word, brought the full bride wealth. It was testament not to a transaction but to the forging of a bond, a mutual agreement between two families destined to unite. A confirmation to the esteem in which he held her. This bride wealth, a collection of goods and promises, was not a price but a symbol of alliance, respect, and the intertwining of lives and destinies; gesture that spoke volumes of the value placed on Munyazi, not as property, but as a cherished partner in the journey of life that lay ahead.

At this moment, traditions were honored, futures were forged, and the story of Munyazi and Mulewa wa Duka took its first breath, ready to unfold in the narrative of their community's rich history; of love, respect, and the unyielding bonds of marriage that would stand the test of time.

The day chosen for the union of Munyazi and Mulewa was one bathed in the golden light of early dawn as the village in Bamba awoke to a day of jubilation and celebration. Munyazi's parents, their hearts brimming with joy from the glowing report provided by Hawe Kache, had extended an invitation to Mulewa, his family, and their closest kin, marking the beginning of a new chapter in the lives of two families soon to become one.

The marriage celebration

As the sun rose higher, casting its warmth over Menza's homestead, the air filled with the vibrant rhythms and melodic tunes of Mijikenda dances. The "*mwanzele*" and "*sengenya*" and others were part of the *Mwaribe*, the wedding dances. The dances were vibrant, rich in colors, cultural heritage, and expression. Their bodies moving in unison to the beat of drums that echoed the heartbeat of their land brought the community together. Men, women, and children, adorned in their traditional attire, danced with abandon, their movements telling stories of joy, unity, and the sacredness of marriage.

During this celebration, the scent of food being prepared wafted through the air, mingling with the earthy aroma of freshly brewed palm wine. This feast, laid out with care and generosity, was a testament to the hospitality of Munyazi's family, eager to welcome their in-laws with open arms and full hearts.

Munyazi, the bride-to-be, was a vision of beauty and grace. She was adorned in a new *kisuthu* that hugged her figure, and a *hando* skirt that appreciated her hips. Her skin glowed under the gentle kiss of the sun, a natural radiance that needed no embellishment. Her hair, intricately styled and adorned with beads that caught the light with every turn of her head, cascaded down her shoulders like a waterfall of dark, shimmering silk.

Mulewa, her soon-to-be husband, complemented her perfectly. He wore a new linen wrapped around his waist and another slung across his chest, symbolizing his strength and readiness to embrace his new role as a husband. His presence, commanding yet tender, promised protection and love.

The highlight of the day's festivities was the couple's ritual blessing. Munyazi and Mulewa, seated on *chigoda* stools symbolizing stability and support, faced their parents in a moment steeped in tradition. With solemn grace, their parents performed the ritual, drawing water into their mouths from a coconut shell and gently spraying it onto the chests of the bride and groom. This act, a blessing for a fruitful and harmonious union, was a poignant reminder of the sacredness of marriage. Following the ritual, the celebration reached its zenith. The air was alive with music, laughter, and the joyous voices of people singing and dancing. The feast that ensued was a lavish spread, a testament to the abundance and generosity of the community.

As the sun began to descend, painting the sky in hues of saffron and lilac, Munyazi's family and relatives presented her with gifts: oils that gleamed like liquid gold, clothes woven with the dreams of her ancestors, beads that sparkled with the promise of happiness, and ornaments that whispered tales of love and endurance. Each gift was a blessing, a symbol of the journey she was about to embark on.

With nightfall casting its velvet cloak over the land, Hawe Kache, Munyazi's grandmother, prepared to escort her granddaughter to Bungale, the village that would soon be her new home. Their journey, taken under the watchful gaze of the stars, was one of quiet reflection and anticipation. Hawe Kache's presence was a comforting reminder of the strength and wisdom that Munyazi carried with her.

As they neared Bungale, the sounds of customary marriage songs greeted them, a melodious welcome that bridged the distance between the past and the future. Mulewa's family members emerged from the shadows, their voices raised in song, their arms open in welcome. Though the journey from Bamba to Bungale was taken in the quiet of the night, it was vibrant with the sights, sounds, and aroma of the earth that cradled their footsteps. The air was cool and fresh, carrying with it the scent of night-blooming flowers and the earthy musk of the forest. The soft fizzle of leaves and the distant calls of nocturnal creatures were the soundtrack to their journey, a reminder of the natural world that bore witness to their union.

As Munyazi and Hawe Kache paused at the edge of Bungale, the warmth of the welcome that awaited them filled their hearts with joy. This moment, a threshold between two worlds was a testament to the enduring bonds of family, community, and love. Munyazi's arrival at Mulewa's homestead marked the beginning of a new chapter in their lives. The air was thick with anticipation as they were ushered into Mulewa's freshly constructed dwelling, a testament to traditional craftsmanship. The house, built of palm leaves and sturdy wooden poles, stood proudly, its rustic charm inviting and warm. A handmade curtain dyed with the rich ochres of the earth divided the space into two intimate sections, each harboring a bed woven from the resilient fibers of sisal, promising comfort, and privacy.

As the moon illuminated the velvet blue sky, casting a soft silver glow that dipped below the horizon, sketching the sky in hues of deep blue, the world hushed. Munyazi and Mulewa were left to the sanctity of their new home. The air inside was cool, scented with the freshness of the palm leaves that made up the walls. The night outside was alive with the sounds of the Mijikenda night – a distant call of a night bird, the soft rustle of leaves in the gentle breeze, and the distant beat of drums celebrating the union.

Hawe Kache, Munyazi's grandmother, settled onto the adjacent bed, her presence a comforting shadow in the dim light. Tradition dictated her role tonight – a guardian of customs, listening for the tender whispers of new beginnings and the affirmation of Munyazi's virtue. As the night deepened, the silence between Munyazi and Mulewa was filled with whispered words of love and hopeful dreams. When the moment of their union arrived, it was marked by a soft sigh, a testament to the purity and innocence that Munyazi brought to this marriage. The air was charged with the significance of the moment, a sacred bond forged in the quiet of the night.

With the break of dawn, Hawe Kache emerged from the house, her face alight with pride. The news she bore was a cause for celebration – Munyazi had honored her family, her virtue intact. Mulewa's family gathered, their faces breaking into smiles as Hawe Kache shared the joyous news. The air was filled with the sounds of ululation, a vibrant expression of happiness and approval. Mulewa's grandfather, a venerable figure adorned in the traditional garb of the Mijikenda elders, stepped forward with a goat in tow. An offer that was no ordinary gift; it was a symbol of gratitude, a thank you to Menza's family for raising Munyazi with such care and honor. The goat, a prized possession, was presented with ceremony, and its significance was understood by all present.

In the days that followed, Mulewa's family busied themselves with preparations for the wedding ceremony. The village was a hive of activity, with neighbors and relatives contributing to the festivities. The air was filled with the scent of cooking food, the sweet aroma of palm wine, and the constant melody of Mijikenda music, setting the stage for a celebration that would be remembered for generations.

The main wedding day

The wedding day it dawned bright and clear, a perfect reflection of the joy and happiness that filled the air. Munyazi, adorned in a *kisuthu* of vibrant colors, her skin glowing under the gentle touch of the morning sun, her hair styled in intricate braids that shone like polished ebony, was a vision of bridal beauty. Mulewa, equally resplendent in his attire, a new cloth wrapped around his waist and another slung across his chest, stood proudly beside her, his heart full of love and promise.

Munyazi stepped into her new life with Mulewa, her heart full of hope and love. The journey they had begun was not just their own but a continuation of the traditions and customs that had shaped their people for generations. Together, they would build a future, their lives a testament to the enduring power of love, tradition, and community.

The day of Munyazi and Mulewa's wedding unfolded under a clear, bright sky, a perfect canvas for celebrating their union. The air was filled with the scents of tropical blooming flowers, mingling with the rich aromas of cooking food and the sweet fragrance of palm wine, creating an atmosphere of joy and festivity that enveloped the village of Bamba.

Munyazi, adorned in the *hando*, a thick white traditional skirt meticulously crafted by her grandmother, was the epitome of bridal beauty. The skirt gathered at the waist, cascaded down in soft folds, its purity symbolizing her transition into married life. Her skin, glowing under the gentle sun, was accentuated with colorful beads that adorned her crown, neck, upper arms, waist, and ankles, each bead a testament to the love and blessings of her family and ancestors. Her perfume, a delicate infusion of potpourri in coconut and castor oil, enveloped her in a scent as captivating as the aura of happiness surrounding her.

As the celebrations commenced, Munyazi received a heartfelt introduction to her extended in-laws, who welcomed her with open arms and warm smiles. Their acceptance was a comforting embrace that spoke of new beginnings and shared futures. Mulewa, standing tall and proud, wore a vibrant piece of cloth wrapped around his waist, its colors a vivid declaration of joy. A bow and arrow, adorned with feathers, hung gracefully on his back, a symbol of his strength and readiness to protect and provide for his new family. A headband with feathers crowned his head, completing his regal appearance and marking him as a handsome figure ready to embark on the journey of marriage.

The village came alive with the sound of festival songs and dances, a symphony of joy that resonated through the hearts of all present. Relatives, friends, and neighbors, each dressed in their finest, gathered to celebrate the union, their laughter and voices adding to the bounty of the day. Children played merrily, their innocent laughter mingling with the music, while women danced with grace and energy, their movements a beautiful expression of the culture and traditions that bound the community together. Others busied themselves with the preparation and serving of food, ensuring that the feast would be a memorable one.

The men, those not engaged in the dance, sat in semi-circles, their conversations a blend of wisdom and camaraderie. They shared palm wine, the traditional drink, passed from hand to hand, a symbol of unity and shared joy. Bright with happiness, their eyes watched over the celebrations, a testament to the community's spirit of togetherness and celebration.

As the day wore on, the air filled with the sounds of merriment, the village of Bungale a beacon of light and joy. The wedding of Munyazi and Mulewa was not just a union of two hearts but a celebration of community, tradition, and the enduring bonds of love and family.

The birth of Katilili

The birth of Katilili ushered in a new dawn for Munyazi and Mulewa, enveloping their lives with unparalleled joy and a deep sense of pride that only the arrival of a firstborn can bring. Katilili, a name that resonated with strength and promise, became not just a continuation of their lineage but a symbol of their love and unity, a tangible manifestation of their bond.

A profound transformation occurred from the moment Munyazi held Katilili in her arms.

"You are now Me-Katilili," Mulewa fondly affirmed to her.

A title that embodied her new identity as a mother, a role that she embraced with all the love and devotion in her heart. Her days and nights were now filled with the soft coos and gentle stirrings of her baby boy, each moment a precious memory etched into the fabric of her being. Katilili, the newborn son of Munyazi and Mulewa, was a radiant beacon of joy and pride for his parents. In him, they saw the perfect amalgamation of their features - his mother's striking deep brown eyes that sparkled with a curious light and his father's warm, rich chocolate skin that seemed to glow even in the dimmest light. Katilili's hair, soft and curly, lay like a crown atop his head, hinting at the strength and character he would grow into. His laughter, a melodic sound that filled their home, reminded him of the love and unity that created him. Every smile, every gaze, every touch from Katilili was a testament to the beauty of their union, making Munyazi and Mulewa feel an unparalleled sense of fulfillment and happiness. In Katilili, they saw not just their son, but a symbol of their love and a promise for the future.

Mulewa, too, found himself changed by Katilili's arrival. Watching over his son, he felt a surge of protectiveness and an overwhelming desire to provide for and nurture this new life he had helped bring into the world. Katilili was an excellent craft and a perfect work of art that merged. The sight of Munyazi cradling their son, the gentle way she whispered.

lullabies into the night, filled him with an indescribable warmth. Katilili's presence was a beacon of hope, symbolizing the future they would build together.

The joy Katilili brought to their lives was infectious, spreading throughout the household and beyond. His laughter, bright and clear, became the melody of their days, while his milestones - each smile, each step - were celebrated with jubilation that resonated through the hearts of all who had the privilege of witnessing them.

As Katilili grew, so did the bond between Munyazi and Mulewa. They watched in awe as their son took his first tentative steps, his eyes alight with curiosity and wonder. Each word he uttered was a testament to the love and care with which they raised him. Katilili was not just their son; he was a dream realized, a future unfolding before their eyes. The pride Munyazi and Mulewa felt for Katilili was immeasurable. They saw in him the best of themselves and their ancestors, a perfect blend of their virtues and strengths. He was their legacy, a living bridge to the future, carrying forward their people's traditions and values. In Katilili, they saw endless possibilities, a promise of continuity and renewal.

Their home, once filled with the anticipation of Katilili's arrival, now echoed with the sounds of his discoveries and adventures. Each day brought new joys, new challenges, and new reasons to be grateful. Munyazi and Mulewa now united not just as husband and wife but as parents, found a more profound sense of purpose in their shared journey through parenthood.

Katilili's presence in their lives was a constant reminder of the love that brought them together, a love that was now embodied in their son's life. He symbolized their union, a beacon of hope, and a source of endless pride. In him, they saw the future of their lineage, a continuation of their story, and the enduring legacy of their love.

Me-Katilili's firstborn, Katilili, was the embodiment of vitality and charm. With a sharp mind, a boundless curiosity, and a personality mirroring his mother's, his presence was a constant source of joy and amusement. In Mulewa's household, where Katilili's spirited antics were a daily occurrence, the air often vibrated with playful admonitions.

"Katilili, please don't climb the roof," his father would call out, only to find him moments later chasing the chickens with pebbles. "Katilili, stop that! You'll hurt them!" Not long after, a mischievous giggle would echo from the granary, prompting a gentle scolding: "Katilili, come out of there. It's not safe!" And in moments of cheekiness, even the neighbors would chuckle, "Katilili, you're such a handful!"

By the time he reached the age of seven, marking seven cycles of the seasons, Katilili's name was known to every villager, his charismatic nature weaving him into the fabric of the community. Though often mischievous, his antics were met with affectionate laughter, his ability to charm unmistakable.

On days Katilili chose solitude over play, the village felt his absence. "Where's Katilili today? It's too quiet without him," children would ask, their games lacking the spark he brought. Adults, too, would notice, "We missed you yesterday, Katilili. The village isn't the same without your laughter."

Despite his occasional troubles, Katilili always responded to reprimands with a grin and a nod of understanding. "I'll remember next time," he would say, his light-hearted acceptance a testament to his growing wisdom.

Raising a child was a collective endeavor in the Mijikenda community, as in many African cultures. "It takes a village to raise a child" they lived by, believing every child belonged to the community. "Katilili is just as much my son as yours," one mother would say, a sentiment echoed by fathers, "And he's every bit my responsibility too."

Katilili thrived under this communal care, showing early signs of leadership. "One day, you'll lead us, Katilili," an elder would say, watching him mediate a squabble among playmates. "You're everyone's child, and that's your strength."

Spiritual growth

Munyazi, who embraced the name Me-Katilili after the birth of her first son, found her life deeply intertwined with the spiritual essence of her surroundings. Her daily sojourns into the heart of nature - the dense forests for firewood, the flowing rivers for water, and the untamed bushes in search of edible herbs - became more than routine tasks. They were sacred pilgrimages that connected her soul to the earth and its creator, *Mulungu*, fostering a bond that transcended the physical realm.

Her relationship with the earth and its elements grew profound as she walked paths shadowed by towering trees and treaded by the rivers' ceaseless flow. In the solitude of nature, Me-Katilili found her spirit attuned to the whispers of the ancestors and the spirits that roamed the lands of her people. These entities, revered and omnipresent, began to impart to her ancient and profound wisdom, revealing secrets of the natural world that had been obscured from the eyes of the ordinary.

As her understanding deepened, Me-Katilili's connection to her religion and spirituality became a beacon that guided her through life. It was not long before she was recognized as a diviner, a conduit through which the divine communicated. Revelations were bestowed upon her in the quiet of the sacred *Kaya* Forest, by the riverbanks, and in the secrecy of the bushes - insights into the earth's healing powers. She learned of the unique properties hidden in tree roots, the healing barks, and the potent herbs that carpeted the forest floor.

Me-Katilili's newfound knowledge was not kept for her own enrichment but was shared with her community, offering solace and healing to those in need. She became a healer, revered, and sought after, not just for her remedies but for the spiritual guidance she provided. Her hands, once used for gathering firewood and water, now worked to mix concoctions that could soothe the ails of the body and the spirit. The sick came to her, those tormented by unseen forces sought her out, and even those burdened by the trials of life found a haven in her presence.

She bore more children, though this did not hinder her from actively practicing her healing powers. Her home, once a simple dwelling, transformed into a sanctuary where the boundary between the physical and spiritual worlds blurred. Here, under Me-Katilili's care, individuals were treated with herbs and offered prayers and rituals that invoked the protection and blessings of the ancestors and good spirits. Each treatment was a sacred act, a blend of physical and spiritual healing that reflected Me-Katilili's deep reverence for the interconnectedness of all life. Through her practices, Me-Katilili taught her community the value of maintaining a harmonious relationship with the earth and its divine creators. She reminded them that spirituality was not an abstract concept to be observed from afar but a lived experience, deeply rooted in the daily interactions with the world around them. Her life became a testament to the power of faith, the importance of respecting the natural world, and the profound impact of spiritual healing.

As word of her wisdom and healing spread, Me-Katilili's reputation grew, cementing her status as a respected and influential figure within her community. Yet, despite her prominence, she remained humble, always attributing her knowledge and power to *Mulungu*, the ancestors, and the spirits who guided her. In Me-Katilili, the people saw not just a healer but a bridge between the worlds, a guardian of tradition, and a living embodiment of their deepest spiritual values. Her legacy, enriched by her profound connection to the earth and its spiritual realms, continued to inspire and guide generations long after her time, immortalizing her as a symbol of wisdom, healing, and the unbreakable pledge between humanity and the divine.

By the time she was middle-aged, Me-Katilili was a figure of immense strength and wisdom. Her name echoed through the villages and into the very soul of the land. She was not just a healer but a beacon of hope, a guardian of tradition, and a fierce warrior in the spiritual and physical realms against the tides of oppression that sought to erode the very foundation of her people's identity.

Me-Katilili understood the Mijikenda's socio-religious structure, *Chikwehu*, profoundly. She saw it as a myriad of health, politics, development, and leadership, each thread a testament to the wisdom and resilience of her people. Her belief in *Chikwehu's* power was unshakeable, a conviction that it held the key to liberating the Mijikenda from the chains of foreign dominance that the Arabs and British had imposed upon their land.

Her healing hands were known everywhere, for she possessed an unparalleled knowledge of the natural world. People came from distant villages, their bodies and spirits battered by illness. They sought the solace of her remedies - herbs, roots, tree barks, leaves, all blessed by her prayers and offerings to the ancestors, and to God, *Mulungu*. Yet, Me-Katilili's gifts transcended the physical realm; she was a conduit for divine revelations, receiving guidance on confronting the invaders that threatened to extinguish the light of her culture. Me-Katilili's days were often spent in meditation, either within her home's comforting embrace or in the *Kaya* forests' sacred seclusion. These were places of power, where the veil between the seen and unseen worlds thinned, and wisdom flowed like the rivers that nurtured the land. Her communion with the stars and the psychic knowledge she garnered were tools that fortified her spirit, crafting her into a figure of awe within her tribe.

Her eloquence in public speaking was unmatched; each word she spoke was woven with the passion and conviction of her beliefs. Me-Katilili's courage knew no bounds; she was an upheaval of resolve, unafraid to stand against the storms of colonization that sought to ravage her homeland. Her journey from village to village was not just a movement through space but a rallying cry that awakened the hearts of her people. With every word, every meeting, she was knitting together a rebellion, a unified stand against the invaders that dared to claim dominion over their sacred land.

One day, under the ancient boughs of a sacred *Kaya* forest, Me-Katilili addressed a gathering of her people, her voice carrying the weight of their collective history and hope. "My brothers and sisters," she began, her gaze sweeping over the faces turned towards her, "the land beneath our feet whispers with the strength of our ancestors. It tells us not to falter or let our spirits be broken by those who do not understand the sacred bonds that tie us to this earth."

A young warrior, emboldened by Me-Katilili's words, stepped forward. "How can we, the children of this land, stand against the might of the invaders?" he asked, his voice a mixture of defiance and despair.

Me-Katilili's eyes met his, a spark of unyielding determination alight within them. "We stand as we have always stood - united by the strength of our beliefs, traditions, and love for this land. We will use the wisdom of *Chikwehu* and *Chimila*, the guidance of our ancestors, our mighty God, and the power of our spirits to reclaim what is rightfully ours. Our resistance is not just a fight for land; it is a battle for the soul of our people."

Her words ignited a fire within the hearts of those present, a flame that would grow into a fierce blaze of resistance. Me-Katilili's rebellion was more than a physical struggle; it was a testament to the enduring spirit of the Mijikenda, a declaration that though their bodies could be captured, their spirits would forever roam free, as untamed and majestic as the land they called home.

CHAPTER 7

From slave dhows to Frere town

In the cool embrace of dawn, the Indian Ocean murmured ancient secrets, its waves cradling *Tahmis Alriyah*. This dhow bore Baya, Katembe, Sidi, and many souls from Africa's verdant heart. Among them were Karisa, Kithi, and others, spirited away from diverse Mijikenda villages by Omani Arabs, their lives intertwined with the cargo that swelled with each caress of the southwest monsoon. Adrift upon the Indian Ocean's vast expanse, they sailed towards a destiny shrouded in dread, a path from which there was no retreat.

With the arrival of the northern monsoon came a caravan of Arab dhows, slicing through the waters to trade at ports like Mombasa, Malindi, Zanzibar, and Kilwa. They brought treasures from afar - silk, porcelain, and glass beads shimmering under the sun's gaze. This flotilla was a whisper in the chorus of hundreds that had braved the northern winds, trading silk and porcelain for a bounty of spices, coffee, tea, ivory, rhinoceros' horns, tortoiseshell, precious stones, and iron. Yet, as the southern monsoon loomed, they hurried to exchange other perishables and embarked on the grim pursuit of capturing humans for slavery.

Below deck, the air was thick with the scent of despair, salt, and sweat, a stifling abyss that had borne witness to nothing but the silent cries of the forsaken and the hushed resignations of the doomed. Baya, a youth not yet touched by time's full weight, pressed against the dhow's wooden belly, yearning for the warmth of his mother's embrace - a comfort fading into the shadows of his mind. Beside him, Katembe's gaze blazed with an undimmed fire of resistance, his spirit unbroken by the chains that bound him. Enveloped in silence, Sidi cast her eyes towards the distant horizon, conceivably in search of a sliver of mercy, an offering their captors had long abandoned. Each captive, enveloped in the solitude of their prayers, sought solace in whispered petitions to the heavens.

Katembe rose, his towering stature belying the frailty that clung to his bones. His gaze pierced the sailors with suspicion and wary hope. "Freedom?" His voice blended with disbelief and relief. He grappled with the concept as alien as the men who now spoke of liberation. This notion of freedom, so long elusive, felt as distant and foreign as the lands from which these sailors hailed.

Beside him, Sidi tentatively extended her hand, her fingertips grazing the deck as though to confirm its reality. Her eyes, wide with a blend of fear and fascination, mirrored the cautious awe that filled her heart. It was as if she needed to reassure herself that the ground beneath her was indeed solid, not another mirage conjured by her longing for liberation.

The air around them was imbued with the taste of salt mingled with the sweet, intoxicating essence of freedom - a flavor so exquisite, so unfathomable, that none among them had ever dared to dream it might one day caress their lips. As the sun ascended, its rays were no longer mere spectators to their plight but luminous heralds of dawn's promise; it cast a new light over everything. The bold and resplendent sun no longer bore witness to their suffering but seemed to proclaim the dawn of a new era. Under its benevolent gaze, the horizon stretched out in this moment, not as the boundary of their captivity, but as the vast canvas of possibility and hope.

 As they were led onto the deck of a British ship, the ocean around them sparkled with promise, a stark contrast to the dark hold they had known. Baya looked back at the dhow, now empty of its human cargo, and felt a surge of hope. Hopefully, in this vast world, there was a place for them where chains would no longer bind their fate. The deck of the British ship was flushed with the golden hue of morning light, casting long shadows over its newest occupants. Freed from the chains, the group huddled together, their eyes blinking against the brightness, their bodies unaccustomed to the freedom of movement.

Baya felt the deck sway beneath him, a gentle reminder of the sea's vastness. The British sailors moved among them, distributing bread and water - simple offerings that tasted of kindness in a world that had shown little. Baya watched as Katembe accepted the food with a nod; his wariness was evident, but his hunger was greater. Sidi, with a cautious smile, "Shurrkan" thanked the sailor in broken Arabic, a language she had picked up through overhearing on the Omani Arab captors. She naively thought all 'pale' people spoke the same language.

The sea air, once a marker of their captivity, now carried a different scent - a promise of beginnings. Baya could hear the murmur of his companions, their voices a mixture of languages and dialects, each telling stories of homes lost and futures uncertain. The voyage to Mombasa was marked by a transformation as visible as the changing hues of the sea. The former captives, each day a step further from their past horrors, began to forge a semblance of community aboard the ship.

Sidi found solace in the endless horizon, a visual metaphor for her burgeoning hope. Katembe, ever the protector, assumed leadership among the group, his strength and resolve to become a beacon for others. Baya, with an insatiable curiosity, spent hours with the crew, learning the ship's workings and the nuances of the sea. Once fragmented by despair, their stories began to patch together, creating a curtain of resilience. The ship's crew, initially distant, grew to respect the strength of those they had rescued, recognizing in their eyes a shared humanity.

As the African coast approached, a collective anticipation took hold. The sight of Mombasa, with its bustling docks and the promise of solid ground, ignited emotions long suppressed.

The group stood at the ship's edge, their gazes locked on the approaching land, each heart beating a rhythm of hope and apprehension.

Back on African soil

The landing in Mombasa was a cacophony of sights and sounds. The port teemed with life, a stark contrast to the isolation of the sea. As they disembarked, Baya, Katembe, and Sidi stepped onto the African soil, each step a declaration of their newfound freedom.

They were met by representatives from Frere Town, a settlement established for those like them. The welcoming faces of natives and the foreigners of the land, some bearing scars of past servitudes, offered a silent testament to the possibility of new beginnings. Frere Town was a patchwork of cultures and stories, its residents united by their shared experiences of liberation. The town, with its modest huts and communal gardens, represented a place of refuge and a promise of community and self-determination.

All felt a surge of relief as he walked the streets of Frere Town, the sounds of children playing and the smell of cooking fires sparking memories of his home. The sight of the locals dressed in unfamiliar clothes and speaking an alien language struck those who had newly disembarked from the rescue ships as surreal. Yet, in Frere Town, this oddity seemed to go unnoticed; most of its inhabitants were immersed in their daily routines, treating this cultural amalgamation as nothing out of the ordinary. Katembe, looking around at the budding settlement, saw the potential for growth and empowerment. Sidi, fascinated by the communal spirit, envisioned herself contributing through teaching, sharing the knowledge she had begun to acquire

The first weeks in Frere Town were a period of adjustment. The residents, each carrying the weight of their past, worked together to forge a collective future. They learned the value of labor, not as a means of survival under the whip, but as a path to rebuilding their lives and community. Baya found peace in the gardens, where he planted seeds that symbolized his hopes for the future. Katembe, with his innate leadership, became involved in organizing the town's defenses, ensuring that the horrors of their past would not find them again. Sidi, eager to give back to the community that welcomed him, started teaching the children, his classes a blend of academics and life lessons.

Evenings in Frere Town were a time of communal meals and storytelling. The formerly enslaved people shared tales of their homelands, their journeys, and dreams. Once filled with sorrow, these stories now carried a tone of hope. As the stars blanketed the sky, Baya, Katembe, and Sidi sat together with other newly rescued natives, reflecting on the journey that had brought them from the depths of despair to the shores of possibility. Frere Town's promise of a new day stood as a testament to their resilience and the enduring spirit of freedom. As Baya, Katembe, and Sidi began to settle into their new lives in Frere Town, the presence of British missionaries and local converts introduced them to a world far removed from the beliefs they were raised with. Their traditional religion, *Chikwehu* and *Chimila*, had always been a guiding force, offering comfort and community within the Mijikenda. Yet, in this new setting, Christianity promised spiritual solace and tangible benefits that were hard to ignore.

One Sunday morning, as the sun cast a soft glow over Frere Town, the trio stood at the threshold of a modest yet inviting structure. St. Mark's Church was a beacon of the missionaries' efforts to spread their faith among the new settlers.

"I never thought we'd stand before a house of their God," Baya whispered, his voice tinged with curiosity and skepticism.

Katembe, arms crossed, surveyed the gathering crowd. "Nor did I. But look," he gestured towards the congregation, "they dress in interesting clothing and speak confidently ... "

Ever the inquisitive soul, Sidi added, "And they offer to teach us to read and write. Knowledge is freedom, they say."

They were greeted with warm smiles and handshakes as they entered the church. The interior was simple, with wooden pews and a pulpit adorned with a cross. The air was filled with the sound of hymns, a stark contrast to the traditional chants of their homeland. Baya, Katembe, and Sidi attended the missionaries' classes in the following weeks. They were taught to read and write, a skill that opened new worlds to them. With each word they learned, the missionaries' promises seemed less like foreign concepts and more like opportunities.

"We were told that accepting their faith would bring us closer to their community," Sidi remarked one evening, her fingers tracing the letters in a book.

"Yes, but it's more than that," Baya responded, looking up from his own book. "It's about understanding. We learn their ways, and they begin to see us as equals."

Katembe, who had been listening, added slowly. "And yet, we must not forget where we come from. Our beliefs, our traditions - they are part of who we are." He looked up, trying to force back tears. "I want to go home," he sighed.

A few days later, the trio and other residents of Frere Town visited the bustling market in Kongowea. The market was a lively blend of colors, sounds, and smells. Merchants hawked their wares, from vibrant textiles to fresh produce, as people from all walks of life mingled and bartered.

Suddenly, a loud sound pierced the air, sending a wave of panic through the crowd. Memories of slave raids flashed in their minds, and the market descended into chaos. Women and children sought refuge, while men prepared to defend their families.

"It's the slave traders! They've come for us again!" a woman cried out in terror.

Baya, Katembe, and Sidi exchanged glances, their hearts racing. But as they braced themselves, a local merchant approached them, his expression calm.

"No, no, my friends," he said, "it's not what you think. That sound - it's the new bell at St. Mark's. It calls us for an announcement, nothing more."

Days later, the reaction was markedly different when the bell rang again. The residents of Frere Town, now informed of its purpose, gathered at St. Mark's with a sense of community rather than fear.

As they assembled, a missionary, Father Michael, stood before them. "We ring this bell as a call to gather, to share news, or to pray. It's a symbol of our unity, not a cause for alarm," he explained.

Baya turned to Katembe and Sidi, his face reflecting a newfound understanding. "Perhaps this is what belonging feels like," he mused.

Katembe nodded. "A new beginning," he agreed.

"And knowledge," added Sidi, holding up a book. "The power to decide our own fate."

New faith

In the months that followed, Baya, Katembe, and Sidi navigated their faith and identity within the diversity of Frere Town's community. They engaged in dialogues with the missionaries and the locals, blending the teachings of Christianity with the wisdom of *Chikwehu*.

Following a sermon one afternoon, in the presence of approximately twenty native attendees, "Your beliefs hold great value," Father Michael conveyed during their conversation, "and we embrace the depth and diversity of your traditions within our community. Yet, practices such as honoring the ancestors, summoning spirits, and venerating your gods, along with other aspects of your cultural heritage, are unfortunately not permissible."

"Father," Baya paused, the word 'Father' feeling foreign on his tongue when directed at a man viewed as an interloper by his tribe. Yet, in Frere Town, such titles were the norm. "In our belief, the Mijikenda recognize only one God, *Mulungu*. He is the architect of the earth, the air, and all celestial entities, both seen and unseen. He sculpted the first man, Muyeye, and blessed him with two wives, Mbodze and Matsezi..."

Before he could continue, Father Michael, barely concealing his vexation, interjected firmly, "There is but one God, Jehovah, who created Adam as the first human and Eve as his sole partner." With a swift motion, he opened the Bible he held, his fingers briskly leafing through the pages in search of the relevant scriptures.

A young man, seated thoughtfully beside Katembe, posed a question with a tone of genuine curiosity, "You mentioned your God had a son. How is it possible for Him to have a son if He is indeed God? I mean …"

At this, Father Michael could feel his patience fraying, a mounting frustration at the challenge of bridging the vast expanse between their worlds of belief.

During the conversation, Katembe's curiosity was piqued, leading him to pose a question that mirrored his bewilderment. "Is Jesus considered your ancestor?" he queried; his tone laced with confusion. "Your faith seems to revolve around a singular ancestor and just one spirit, or ghost, as you say. Our traditions are enriched by numerous ancestors and a multitude of spirits. This concept of your religion is quite foreign to me. I believe I would rather stay true to the teachings of *Chikwehu*." Katembe's candid expression of his spiritual preference aligned him with a group of natives who similarly resisted the allure of Christianity.

Due to their refusal, they found themselves subtly penalized by being denied food for several days under the guise of 'fasting'.

"Fasting serves to purify your mind, allowing the holy spirit to descend upon you," Sister Martha explained, offering this explanation to justify the deprivation and suggest a spiritual benefit. Nonetheless, for Katembe and his peers, this enforced fast was experienced less as religious enlightenment and more as a covert punishment.

As Frere Town grew, so did its inhabitants, weaving together a community as diverse in belief as it was united in its quest for a peaceful existence. The bell of St. Mark's no longer signaled fear but a call to gather, learn, and celebrate the many paths that had led them to this shared space of hope and renewal. Numerous locals embraced Christianity, yet some remained uncertain or refused to adopt the new culture and beliefs.

Sister Martha addressed the group resistant to converting to Christianity with a stern warning, "If our faith and way of life find no room in your hearts, I regret to say, the only path left is your return to the villages hidden within the wilderness. But be forewarned, in such places, the shadow of enslavement looms large, threatening to ensnare you once more." The mere mention of captivity sent shivers down their spines, reviving memories of past atrocities they desperately wished never to relive. The fear of facing those horrors again left them deeply unsettled.

Sidi, initially doubtful, felt a newfound appreciation for the missionary's candidness and raised her hand, declaring, "We will learn from you." Inwardly, she affirmed, "Yeah, we will not forsake our ancestors. We will carry both legacies forward."

CHAPTER 8

Dividing the continent without consent

The Berlin conference (also known as Congo conference) started on 15 November 1884. The conference hall, a grand chamber adorned with the emblems of empire and the heavy scent of anticipation, starkly contrasted with the bleak weather outside. The city was overcome by an unusually bitter fall, with iced rain that painted everything with a gloss of silver frost. The trees, stripped of their leaves, stood as silent sentinels to the changing seasons, their branches etched like dark veins against the heavy, gray sky.

Within this solemn setting, the air was electric with the undercurrents of imperial ambition. Excluding the rulers of the continent under discussion, every leader of the major European and American empires was either personally in attendance or represented by a close delegate. The Sultan of Zanzibar's attempts to secure an invitation were swiftly dismissed, met with derision by the British. Leaders from other African nations were entirely overlooked, and their inquiries, if any were made, met with indifference.

The conference culminated in an agreement with three key outcomes. Firstly, it acknowledged the region that King Leopold II had declared as his private estate. Secondly, it validated various territorial claims across Africa that were already in place. The most significant consequence of the conference, however, was the establishment of a framework that allowed European nations to lay claim to and annex African territories.

King Leopold II of Belgium stood. A figure of authority, his gaze fixed upon the vast map of Africa that dominated the room. "I will keep this part of the continent," he declared, his finger landing with finality on the heart of the Congo Basin. His voice, firm and unwavering, filled the room with the weight of his claim.

Otto von Bismarck, the orchestrator of this diplomatic ballet, acknowledged King Leopold's declaration with a nod, his eyes scanning the assembly. "Indeed, your Majesty," he began, his voice smooth and diplomatic. "But let us remember, not all Africa bears the same fruit. As you've rightly identified, the Congo Basin is a treasure trove - rich in resources like gold, diamonds, and rubber. Our division must be equitable."

King Leopold's response was immediate, his tone laced with a mix of pride and defensiveness. "Let me remind you, Chancellor, the Congo is already under my protection. I have bestowed upon its people the gifts of civilization, Christianity, and education. It is, by all rights, my land."

A murmur of unrest stirred among the representatives, the weight of Leopold's claim hanging heavily in the air. The brutality of his rule in the Congo was an open secret, tales of amputation, enslavement, and murder whispered but never openly acknowledged.

In a grail to Gather the room's focus, Bismarck's voice cut through the tension by clearing his throat before speaking. "Gentlemen, our goal here is a peaceful division of Africa. Those areas under occupation should naturally fall under the occupier's sovereignty."

Nods of agreement followed though the air remained thick with unspoken objections.

Sir Henry Morton Stanley, seated beside King Leopold, remained conspicuously silent, his earlier explorations having paved the way for Leopold's claims. His eyes, however, betrayed a knowledge of the Congo's suffering under Belgian rule.

Edward Baldwin Malet of the United Kingdom interjected, pointing to the map. "The British Empire shall retain parts of Eastern and Western Africa," he stated, his voice confident.

"And let us not overlook Southern Africa, where we've already established a foothold," added John A. Kasson of the United States, his American accent pronounced among the European timbres.

"To dismiss the North as barren is to overlook potential riches," countered Alphonse de Courcel of France, his remark adding another layer to the complex variety of claims.

Questions of clarity and borders arose, and Phillip van der Hoeven of the Netherlands voiced the collective uncertainty. "Which parts are we discussing, precisely?" he inquired, seeking clarity amidst the voracious partitioning.

Clemens Busch, tasked with detailing the proceedings, reassured him, "A division map is forthcoming, detailing every nation's share." Clemens, tasked with delineating their conquests, assured him, "The division map is in progress, a blueprint of our new world order."

At the same time, Henry Morton Stanley dipped his quill in ink, jotting points: his quill, a silent witness to history's making. As the meeting adjourned, a conclusion set for the following year. The very absence of African representatives in the room was a silent testament to the imperial disregard for the voices of the colonized. The decision to reconvene on 26th February left many questions unanswered, but the path forward was clear - a continent divided, its fate sealed by those who knew it not.

The decision was a testament to the era's imperialist zeal, a moment captured within the confines of a Berlin conference hall, now silent yet echoing with the whispers of a continent's fate being drawn without its consent.

The conference hall emptied, leaving behind the echoes of a future carved from ambition and greed. Outside, the chilly rain continued to fall, indifferent to the destinies altered within those walls. The representatives dispersed - the air still heavy with the gravity of their undertaking.

On The following year on February 26th the partition of Africa, decided without its voice.

Sitting on her throne Queen Victoria, alongside her esteemed British royal council, lent their undivided attention to the royal herald's proclamation the following day:

"The nations gathered at the conference have successfully divided Africa into fifty separate nations.

The major colonial territories were as follows:

The United Kingdom aimed to create a continuous stretch of colonies from Cape to Cairo, nearly achieving this through their dominion over Egypt, Sudan (known as Anglo-Egyptian Sudan), Uganda, Kenya (referred to as British East Africa), South Africa, and what are now Zambia, Zimbabwe, and Botswana (formerly Rhodesia). Additionally, the British Empire held sway over Nigeria and Ghana (formerly known as the Gold Coast).

France established its presence across a vast expanse of Western Africa, extending from Mauritania to Chad (collectively called French West Africa), as well as Gabon and the Republic of Congo (French Equatorial Africa).

Belgium, under King Leopold II, assumed control over what is now the Democratic Republic of Congo (then the Belgian Congo).

Portugal laid claim to Mozambique in the east and Angola in the west.

Italy managed to secure Somalia (Italian Somaliland) and a section of Ethiopia.

Germany acquired Namibia (German Southwest Africa) and Tanzania (German East Africa).

Spain secured the smallest parcel of land, Equatorial Guinea (Rio Muni), as its territory."

By the dawn of the 1890s, the British Protectorate made its presence known along the eastern shores of Africa, ostensibly to safeguard the indigenous peoples - a noble declaration, or so it was portrayed. As the British traversed this new terrain, they were struck with wonder at the vast stretches of fertile land unfolding before them. Enthralled by the lush tableau cradled in the generous warmth of the equatorial sun, they found themselves in a land where the climate composed a harmonious blend of soft breezes and nurturing sunlight. This idyllic setting formed the perfect canvas for the grand designs they harbored in their hearts.

Word went around that the British were driven by motives cloaked in the guise of trade, exploration, and the spread of civilization, they claimed. To the natives, however, their intentions were clear: to exploit the land's resources and people.

In the waning years of the 19th century, a shadow loomed over the vibrant landscapes and communities along the East African coast. The 1890s marked a pivotal moment in the region's history, as the Imperial British East Africa Company, under the auspices of a British Royal Charter, took a decisive step that would irrevocably alter the lives of the indigenous peoples. This entity, driven by the insatiable appetites of commerce and imperialism, claimed the Sultan of Zanzibar's mainland territories, stretching from north of Kipini to Vanga. This coastal strip was the lifeblood of countless communities, including the Giriama.

The British sought to establish control through treaties and force, imposing their rule and disrupting the indigenous way of life. They introduced new laws, taxes, and land appropriation measures that upended social and economic structures, leading to widespread displacement and discontent among the local populations.

With their eyes set on the untapped wealth of the land, the British envisioned vast plantations of sisal, cotton, and rubber flourishing along the banks of the Sabaki River. This river, a vital artery that nourished the land and its people, was now to be the backbone of their commercial enterprise. But this vision of agricultural exploitation came at a grave cost to the Giriama, whose lives were intertwined with the river and its surrounding lands.

For generations, the Giriama had cultivated the fertile arable lands along the Sabaki, their fields yielding bountiful harvests that sustained their communities through seasons of plenty and want. The river's banks were sacred, a testament to the harmony between the people and the earth that nurtured them. Moreover, the tapping of palm wine, a practice as old as the community itself, was not merely a source of income but a cultural ritual that bonded the people to their ancestors and the natural world. The decree from the British forbidding these age-old traditions was a strike at the very heart of Giriama society.

The proclamation of the Protectorate was more than a political maneuver; it was an assertion of control over a region that had, until then, resisted European imperialism's full grasp. The Giriama and other indigenous communities were caught in the crosshairs of a global struggle for territory, resources, and power. The fertile lands along the Sabaki, once the source of their sustenance and prosperity, were now coveted by foreign powers with designs that extended far beyond the immediate needs of the people who called them home.

As the British established their Protectorate, the landscape of East Africa began to change. The traditional ways of life honed over generations and deeply rooted in the land were challenged by the demands of colonial administration and economic exploitation. Yet, amid these upheavals, the spirit of the Giriama and their neighbors remained unbroken. Their resistance to the encroachments of colonial rule and their determination to protect their lands, traditions, and way of life would be a beacon of hope and defiance in the face of adversity.

Edward, the expedition leader, a man of robust stature with piercing blue eyes, stood tall and authoritative. His face, marked by the sun and sea, bore an expression of unwavering determination. Dressed in a rugged ensemble of khaki, he looked a little unkempt. Despite that, his presence was as commanding as his voice, which carried the crisp, unmistakable timbre of British resolve. He inhaled the scent deeply when he approached a wild mint bush, its leaves vibrant against the soil's rich hue. The scent, a potent mix of earth and freshness, invigorated him. "Oh yes! This is what I am talking about!" he exclaimed, echoing through the clearing. With a swift motion and the reminiscent of a seasoned swordsman, he drew his blade and etched a cross into the earth. "This is a treasure, very fertile! We are going to build our station here," he declared, his eyes alight with visions of empire.

William, another expedition member, leaned in his attire a slightly more refined version of Edward's, yet bearing the dust of travel. His hair, a sandy blonde, was swept back, revealing a skeptical brow. His accent, thick with British slang, carried a note of caution. "That will be quite some work; this place is quite bushy," he observed, his gaze sweeping over the dense foliage that threatened to reclaim the land.

Edward's response was swift, a smirk playing on his lips, revealing a hint of arrogance. "Ach, not an issue. We will get a few natives and force them to work if they want to live," he stated, his voice a chilling blend of casual imperialism and determination.

Charles, the youngest of the trio, shifted uncomfortably at Edward's words. His features were softer, less hardened by the elements, and his eyes held a glimmer of reluctance. "I am not in the mood for another raid; the one near Mombasa almost got me killed!" he protested, his voice tinged with a mix of fear and defiance.

Edward, undeterred, laughed off Charles's concerns. "Oh, come on, we have our guns, granites, and canons; they have bows and arrows and their bush religion," he scoffed, his confidence unshaken.

Charles, attempting to bring reason into the conversation, mentioned the Giriama, a local tribe known for hunting prowess. "I heard the Giriama are good hunters, very accurate with their bow and arrow," he said, hoping to instill some caution.

Edward's response was dismissive, a teasing retort that underscored his underestimation of the local population. "Don't worry, Robin Hood is not here," he jested, his laughter mingling with the rustle of leaves.

The conversation took a turn as Edward, unable to resist the allure of the land's bounty, plucked a guava from a nearby tree. As he bit into the fruit, his eyes closed in bliss, a momentary escape into the sweetness that enveloped his senses. "Mmmh, the best ever," he murmured, the taste of the fruit a testament to the land's richness.

However, the shadow of competition loomed wide as Charles mentioned Sultan Majid of Zanzibar's interest in the area. Edward's reply was dismissive, a reflection of his single-minded pursuit of glory. "Oh well, we will deal with that later," he stated, brushing aside the concern with a wave.

Charles, ever the strategist, suggested manipulating local fears to their advantage. "I have an idea: We can simply convince the natives we have come to protect them against the Arabs. They fear the Arabs," he proposed with a glint of cunning in his eyes.

Edward, seizing upon the suggestion, ordered action. "William, get the rest of the crew. We have work to do," his voice resolute, echoing the onset of a campaign that would alter the course of history.

At this moment, amidst the whispering winds and the rustle of leaves, Malindi's fate hung in the balance. It was a land caught between empires' ambitions and its people's resilience.

CHAPTER 9

The disappearance of Katilili

Katilili, now a youth, had witnessed the passing of fifteen full seasons. The sun had barely peeped above the horizon when Katilili and his band of brothers Kalama, Karema, and Dyeka, and four friends, set out towards the Sabaki River. The air was filled with the promise of adventure, the morning dew glistening on the tall grasses that lined their path, whispering secrets of the day to come. Their laughter and chatter echoed through the air, a melody of youth and camaraderie.

As they navigated the familiar trails, a sudden realization pierced his excitement - he had forgotten an essential tool, a gift from his father Mulewa, a symbol of his transition into manhood and a vital aid for their fishing expedition. Stopping in his tracks, he faced his friends, the weight of disappointment heavy in his voice. "I must go back. I've left behind father's gift. Wait for me at the river; I'll return swiftly and join you soon."

Understanding the tool's importance, his brothers and friends nodded in agreement. "Hurry, Katilili. We'll await your return," Kalama said, clapping him on the back. And with that, Katilili turned, his pace quickening as he retraced their steps, leaving a trail of dust swirling in his wake.

But as the sun climbed higher, casting its golden warmth across the land, Katilili did not return. Unbeknownst to his brothers and friends, who were now fully engrossed in the day's catch, laughing, and shouting each time they snagged a fish from the rushing waters of Sabaki, their friend's absence stretched into hours. When the shadows began to lengthen, and the river no longer sparkled with sunlight, they gathered their catch, their thoughts turning homeward. "Katilili must have decided to stay home," Karema mused, a hint of disappointment tinging his words. The others agreed, albeit with a growing sense of unease.

Upon their return, the village was awash in the soft glow of the evening. Their homes, a collection of warmth and welcoming light should have been a comforting sight. Yet Katilili's absence cast a shadow over the village. Me-Katilili, seeing her other sons return without Katilili, was immediately engulfed in panic.

"Where is Katilili? He did not return with you?" Me-Katilili's voice, laced with fear, cut through the evening's calm. The boys exchanged worried glances, their joy from the day's adventure evaporating like morning dew under the sun.

"We thought he stayed behind," Kalama explained, the unease evident in his voice.

Me-Katilili's heart sank. "No, he left with you. He hasn't come back since you all left at dawn," she gulped, her voice barely audible, a testament to her growing dread. Her eyes welled up.

The village's tranquility was shattered as the news of Katilili's disappearance spread. Neighbors gathered, their faces etched with concern, expressing words of comfort and prayers for his safe return. Yet, no one had seen him since he parted ways with his friends and brothers that morning. As darkness enveloped the village, a sense of foreboding took hold. Me-Katilili, her spirit deeply intertwined with the ancestors and the divine, felt a chill of premonition. "Something is terribly wrong," she murmured, her eyes reflecting the fear that gripped her heart.

Mulewa, upon hearing of his son's disappearance, organized a search party. Despite the dangers that lurked beyond their village of raiders and slave traders prowling the night -they could not wait for daylight. "We must find him," Mulewa declared, his voice a mix of determination and fear, rallying the men to action.

Armed with torches and weapons, the search team set out into the darkness, calling out for Katilili, their voices carrying across the fields and forests. In each village they passed, they asked and pleaded for any sign of their missing son, but each inquiry was met with shaking heads and expressions of sympathy.

As the night deepened, the search team ventured further, driven by a mix of hope and desperation. The dangers they faced -wild beasts and lurking invaders -paled compared to the thought of losing Katilili to an unknown fate. As the moon climbed high, casting its silver glow over the searching party, the men moved urgently, their torches flickering like fireflies against the vast darkness. Mulewa led them, his resolve unbroken, though his heart was heavy with dread. The night was alive with the sounds of the wilderness, a reminder of the perils they faced.

In the depths of the night, the search party encountered other villages, waking their inhabitants with their urgent pleas. "Have you seen Katilili?" became a refrain that echoed through the darkness, met too often with confusion or concern, but no answers. The terrain grew more treacherous as they ventured into the dense forest, a place whispered about in the village as the domain of spirits and unseen dangers. The trees stood like silent sentinels, their branches stirring in the wind as if whispering secrets to one another.

Mulewa paused, lifting his torch high, casting light upon the shadowed path. "We must not falter," he declared, his voice steady despite the fear gnawed at his insides. "Our son, our brother, is out there, and we must bring him home."

Back in Bungale village, Me-Katilili, surrounded by her fellow women and the *Chifudu* women organization, had gathered the children, their voices rising and falling in a haunting melody of prayers and songs of protection. They created a circle of unity; their joined hands symbolized their collective hope and strength, their eyes reflecting the flames of the fire that burned at the center of their gathering. The scent of smoked wild *chan* plant and the soft murmur of prayers filled the night air, a concur to the discernible tension and fear that gripped everyone's hearts.

The mysterious disappearance of Katilili, the eldest son and a gleaming beacon of hope and pride among his parents and siblings -Karema, Kalama, Kavumbi, Kanazi, Mwathethe, Dyeka, Mwakidhiru, and Mwedya -set aflame a relentless quest. This quest united Me-Katilili, her husband Mulewa, and the vibrant ensemble of *Chifudu* dancers in a season-long odyssey across their ancestral domains, fueled by a fervent hope to embrace once again the spirit that once made their family whole.

Their journey crossed through villages, communities, and sub-tribes - their hearts heavy but spirits undeterred.

"Have you seen our son, Katilili?" Me-Katilili's voice, laced with desperation and hope, would echo through each new settlement, Mulewa by her side, his gaze piercing each respondent, searching for a flicker of recognition.

One villager suggested with a tone of warning, "Try the notorious ports of Malindi or Mombasa. The Arabs maintain hidden slave camps there." Their words were a grim reminder of the dangers lurking in their quest.

Another, older and worn by the sun, advised with a hint of bitterness, "The British posts might hold your answer. They claim to shield us from the shackles of slavery, yet whispers abound that they, too, capture our people, forcing them to toil on distant plantations."

And from a somber group, the revelation came, "We also lost a couple of young men a few days ago..." Their voices trailed off, a shared understanding of loss uniting them momentarily with Me-Katilili and Mulewa.

As Me-Katilili and Mulewa traversed the landscapes of their ancestors, the absence of Katilili felt ever more profound. Yet, their resolve to find him grew, fueled by the stories and warnings of those they met. Each piece of advice, each shared tale of loss, added layers to their search, painting a complex picture of hope, despair, and the unyielding strength of their family.

As the next season unfolded, Katilili's parents continued their relentless search for their son.

"My people, we are searching for our child, Katilili, my firstborn. He is a strong boy, stands about this high," she made a gesture indicating shoulder high. "He is slim, his muscles still young, his dark brown eyes are large like mine, has thick eyebrows, and his skin color exactly like his father," she glanced at Mulewa, "And when he smiles, he has a dimple on his left cheek," painting a vivid picture of Katilili, a Mijikenda boy of fifteen full seasons, whose laughter once filled their home with endless joy.

The response they met was a blend of shared sorrow and empathy. In every village, amidst the whispers of the wind and the rustle of the trees, the same refrain of unspoken understanding passed from one family to another. The disappearance phenomenon of children had touched many, yet the void left by Katilili's absence seemed to pierce the essence of the community's spirit.

Me-Katilili, embodying the resilience and deep reverence for the *Chimila* and *Chikwehu* traditions and religion, led the search for her missing son with a heart burdened by sorrow but driven by an unyielding spirit. Her voice, rich with the depth of a mother's boundless love, resonated across the villages as they pursued their vanished kin. Alongside Mulewa, select family members, and the steadfast companions from the *Chifudu* women's association, their presence drew significant crowds, capturing the attention of the communities they visited.

Amidst the unplanned gatherings sparked by their journey, Me-Katilili recognized an extraordinary chance that fate had woven into their path. It was not merely a quest for Katilili anymore; it was a beacon calling her to a grander destiny. The air, charged with the collective breath of the assembled, awaited her words like dry soil thirsts for rain. She stood before them, not merely as a seeker of assistance but also as a visionary ready to share a profound insight. With every soul present hanging onto her words, Me-Katilili seized the moment to transcend her initial pursuit. She became a mentor and a guide, weaving a narrative that served a dual purpose: seeking aid and, more importantly, enlightening the hearts and minds before her. She leveraged this unexpected platform to shed light on the looming shadows cast by foreign invaders, their sinister motives creeping silently into their midst.

Her words were not mere warnings but a clarion call to awareness and empowerment. Me-Katilili enlightened the community about the subtle dangers posed by the invaders, urging them to peer beyond the veil of deceit. Through her compelling oratory, she stirred a sense of unity and resilience, inspiring her people to safeguard their heritage against the insidious encroachments. In her mission, Me-Katilili did not just seek to find Katilili; she aimed to fortify the very soul of her community, turning every listening ear into a vigilant eye against the threats that sought to undermine their existence.

She stood before them, not merely as a warning voice but as a powerful summon to solidarity and defiance. Her words were more than cautionary tales; they were a vibrant battle cry for unity and resistance, echoing the profound strength woven through the fabric of their collective spirit and ancestral sagacity. Me-Katilili's speech transcended a simple plea for her family's reunion; it was a deliberate act to steel her community against the creeping darkness that threatened their way of life. She aimed to anchor their heritage in unyielding resilience, ensuring it would remain unshaken in the wake of foreign dangers.

In these moments of personal trial, her leadership blossomed into a luminary of hope, illuminating the path forward. It stood as a resounding declaration of the unbreakable spirit that courses through the veins of the Mijikenda people. Her resolve, fueled by the fires of passion and the depths of her love for her people, transformed her anguish into a bastion of strength. Me-Katilili's rallying call did not just seek to safeguard the physical bounds of her community; it sought to immortalize their spirit, ensuring that the legacy of the Mijikenda would forever echo, resilient and undimmed, in the annals of history.

Mulewa, flanked by a cadre of the village's most stalwart and brave men, set forth on a demanding odyssey. This was not merely a journey but a test of endurance and courage that spanned several grueling days, during which they trod the thin line between survival and peril. Their path led them to the vibrant, teeming docks of Malindi and Mombasa, where the air was thick with the scent of sea salt and the murmur of countless languages. In these bustling epicenters of trade and turmoil, uncertainty was as palpable as the humid air, casting a shadow that harbored both the glimmer of hope and the specter of despair.

Their quest stretched further to Frere town, a haven of solace for souls emancipated from the cruel shackles of slavery. Here, amidst the whispers of trees and the gentle breeze, the air was heavy with tales of sorrow and songs of freedom, a poignant mosaic of human endurance and the thirst for liberation. It was a place where each breeze carried the weight of tragic and triumphant narratives of life reborn from the ashes of captivity.

The expedition ventured to Kengeleni, where the Missionary church stood as a luminous symbol of faith and rebirth. Against a backdrop of verdant greenery and the tranquil chorus of nature, the church's spire reached towards the heavens, a beacon for those seeking solace and a new path in the light of their newfound faith. Here, among the hallowed grounds where faith and fate intertwined, the group encountered stories of transformation and redemption, of lives redirected towards hope and communal harmony under the watchful gaze of the divine.

Through each step of their journey, Mulewa and his companions navigated the intricate web of human experience, encountering the dual faces of despair and hope, bondage and freedom, all while the specter of their mortality loomed ever close. Their voyage was a testament to the resilience of the human spirit, a vivid chapter in the ongoing saga of their people's struggle, endurance, and ceaseless quest for a brighter tomorrow.

These men, driven by a fuse of determination and desperation, combed through every nook, cranny, and potential hideaway they suspected might conceal their beloved Katilili. Their search was exhaustive, spanning regions known and hidden. They were all hoping to find a clue, a sign, anything that would lead them to Katilili. Yet, despite their relentless efforts and the breadth of ground covered, their search yielded nothing but heartache. Katilili remained lost, his presence missing from every corner they turned, every shadow they investigated. The harsh reality set in - despite their courage and resolve, Katilili was nowhere to be found. The silence following their inquiries was a heavy burden, a testament to the vastness of their loss, leaving Mulewa and his companions to return empty-handed, their spirits weighed down by the emptiness of their quest. Refusing to let despair tether her hope, Me-Katilili turned to the ancient pearls of wisdom, delving into the spiritual realms with a fervor born of desperation. She sought counsel from the guardians of the unseen, the diviners and religious specialists, whose connections to the world beyond promised a glimmer of hope. Her journey through the spiritual landscape was as tumultuous as the physical one, with revelations that twisted the knife of sorrow more profound into her heart. While some whispered of realms unreachable by the living, others spoke a truth more harrowing - that Katilili had crossed the threshold into the realm of ancestors, leaving behind the world he once danced upon.

In the wake of such devastating revelations, the customs of their ancestors provided a semblance of solace. The family, cloaked in the garb of mourning, undertook the somber ritual of the customary burial. In place of their son, they could not find or lay to rest; they were required to bury a stem of a banana tree, embodying the spirit of Katilili, as the community gathered to perform the funeral rites. The act of shaving their heads served as a poignant testament to their grief, a physical manifestation of the void that now lay within their hearts.

Though steeped in tradition, this ceremonial farewell was but a fragile balm to the searing pain of loss. Yet, in this act of communal mourning, the bonds that tethered them to their ancestors, to each other, and to the land they called home. A place that offered a whisper of comfort, a promise that Katilili, though absent in body, would forever dance among them in spirit, a reminder of the love, the loss, and the enduring strength of a family united in sorrow and hope. This sorrow was not just a brief shadow but a deep, pervasive ache emanating from the disappearance of Katilili, Me-Katilili's son. For Me-Katilili, a mother whose heart was as expansive as the lands she walked upon, this loss transcended personal anguish; it was a rip in the very fabric of her being, mirroring an age-old pain - a mother's mourning for a child who stood at the precarious threshold between youth and manhood.

This was not merely Me-Katilili's story but a communal wound that bled through the heart of the Mijikenda community, reviving the collective grief and solidarity among the Agiriama. The echoes of mourning for Kithi, another soul lost to the insatiable maw of fate, intertwined with the current despair, deepening the sense of loss as ancient as it was immediate. Yet, amidst this abyss of sorrow, a flicker of purpose emerged, kindled by the traditions and rituals that had long defined their people. In this landscape of mourning and memory, Me-Katilili's sorrow became a reflection of a profoundly personal and expansively communal grief. This sorrow was about to catalyze a movement of resistance and unity, grounded in the rich soil of their traditions and beliefs.

The hidden power of the *Chifudu* dance

As the sun rose, painting the sky with strokes of gold and crimson, Me-Katilili and her entourage embarked on a journey that would pave the way for legends. Adorned with the vibrant expressions of the *Chifudu* dance, their movements were of grace and grief, each step a testament to their unyielding spirit. With its rhythmic beats and spirited gyrations, this dance transcended its origins as a mourning medium. Instead, it evolved into a potent symbol of resistance, a rallying cry that echoed through the hills and valleys of the Giriama lands.

Within Me-Katilili's strategic grasp, the *Chifudu* dance - traditionally a profound expression of grief and a means to honor the spirits of those who had passed - was ingeniously repurposed as a cloak for a more clandestine agenda. This dance, deeply rooted in the rituals of remembrance, subtly transformed into an instrument of stealthy defiance. It offered a guise of mourning, a clever facade that allowed the fragmented individuals of her community to converge in unity while their true purpose remained shrouded from prying eyes.

These solemn assemblies sprouted into resilient outposts of resistance. Like seeds quietly sown in the rich soil of shared history and identity, they germinated into a silent rebuke of the British dominion's attempts to suppress their cultural practices and collective expressions. This veiled defiance, embedded within the mournful steps of the *Chifudu* dance, stood as a silent testament to their refusal to let the winds of foreign control extinguish their cultural flame. Through this ingenious use of tradition, Me-Katilili not only preserved the essence of her people's identity but also stoked the embers of resistance hidden beneath the surface of mourning.

As Me-Katilili led her people in these dances, the air vibrated with the energy of unity and defiance. The vibrant colors of their attire, the determined tilt of their heads, and the unyielding glint in their eyes spoke of a people not broken by sorrow but fortified by it. The *Chifudu* dance became more than a ritual; it was a declaration that though they mourned, they would not be cowed. In the shared rhythm of their dance, the Agiriama found a voice that whispered of resilience, undiminished hope, and a steadfast commitment to preserving their culture and beliefs.

Rallies catching British attention

Me-Katilili's gatherings began to stir the embers of resistance and unity. These assemblies, born from the rhythmic steps of the *Chifudu* dance, became crucibles of solidarity, defiantly brimming with the collective strength of a people united under the shadow of grief. As Me-Katilili moved from village to village, the dances served not only as expressions of mourning but as powerful magnets, drawing the scattered sons and daughters of the Giriama back to their roots, culture, and shared resolve against the oppressive yoke of British rule.

Within these gatherings, the air pulsed with more than just the shared rhythm of dance; it vibrated with the words of Me-Katilili, who, with the authority of a spiritual leader and the passion of a bereaved mother, breathed new life into the ancient wisdom of the Chikwehu. Her voice, rich with the timbre of conviction and the warmth of maternal love, resonated through the crowds, weaving tales of past glories, present struggles, and future hopes. She spoke of the importance of economic independence, the virtues of governance by the people, and the sacredness of their land and traditions. Her words urged her people to renew their faith in themselves and stand firm against the encroachments that threatened to erode their identity.

Under Me-Katilili's guidance, the gatherings became more than mere congregations; they transformed into forums of enlightenment and empowerment. Through her, the Agiriama found a voice to articulate their grievances, a platform to share their aspirations, and a beacon to guide them through the darkness of colonial subjugation. Me-Katilili's message was clear: their traditions were not relics of the past but the foundation of their identity and resistance. Her call to action reverberated through the community, igniting a sense of pride and a determination to preserve their heritage against all odds. In these moments of collective defiance and solidarity, the Agiriama rediscovered the strength of their bonds. Each gathering, each dance, each shared story, and each echoed chant became threads in a beacon of resistance, lightening a narrative of resilience and hope. Me-Katilili, through her leadership, became the embodiment of this resistance - a symbol of the unbreakable spirit of the Agiriama.

Her efforts did not go unnoticed. The British authorities saw these gatherings as a threat to their control, a challenge to their authority. Yet, the Giriama, inspired by Me-Katilili's fervor, remained undeterred, their resolve hardened by the collective will to protect their way of life. Amidst the oppressive shadows of colonial rule, the Giriama found in Me-Katilili a guiding light, leading them in a dance of defiance that resonated with the power of their ancestors and the unyielding hope for their future.

She and her followers ingeniously masked their gatherings from the British authorities by cloaking them in the guise of funeral processions. Utilizing the *Chifudu* funeral dance as their cover, they moved stealthily from one village to another. Amidst the melancholy rhythms and mourning dances miming bereavement, they whispered messages of resistance, sewing seeds of defiance against British imperialism among the natives. This clandestine dance of rebellion allowed them to spread their message under the watchful eyes of colonial rule, turning grief into a powerful tool of unity and resistance.

Faced with the escalating turmoil that enveloped her community, Me-Katilili's resolve only strengthened. Her religion became her sanctuary, a beacon of hope and resilience amidst the chaos. In seeking solace for her "multiple mains," or deep-seated pains, she found refuge in meditation and prayer, her spirit communing with the divine in the serene embrace of the sacred *Kaya* forests. Here, amidst the whispers of ancient trees and the soft caress of the wind, her spirituality deepened, intertwining her essence with the soul of the earth and the fabric of human society.

Me-Katilili sought solace and strength in the sacred solitude of the *Kaya* forests, where the air hums with the wisdom of the ancients thrived. These ancient groves, veiled in mist and mystery, were the living heart of the Mijikenda lands, a sanctuary where the spirits of the ancestors whispered through the rustle of leaves and the wind's caress. Here, amidst the towering sentinels of trees that had stood watch over generations, Me-Katilili found solace from the storm of her grief and purpose. The sacred *Kaya* forests were not merely a retreat but a place of profound spiritual communion, where the veil between the worlds thinned, allowing for the exchange of divine wisdom and earthly woes.

Guided by the whispers of the ancestors and the subtle language of nature, Me-Katilili deepened her connection to the spiritual realm. She walked the forest paths as both a student and a vessel, learning the secrets the land held close - the healing virtues of herbs, roots, and leaves; the sacred geometry of stones; and the invocations that called forth the blessings of rain and bounty. These secrets, passed down through the murmur of the forest, became the threads with which Me-Katilili wove her rituals of appeasement and protection, seeking the favor of both God and the ancestors.

Her practices, rooted in the ancient wisdom of the *Chikwehu*, were acts of faith and defiance, reaffirming her people's bond with the land and their resistance to the forces that sought to sever it.

Divination

In the profound stillness of *Kaya* Jilore, a place where the spirits danced in the dappled sunlight, Me-Katilili experienced a transformation that transcended the boundaries of the physical world. It was as if the very essence of the divine permeated her being, bestowing upon her a gift of divination - a bridge between the seen and the unseen, the known and the mysterious. This gift was not merely a personal enlightenment but a call to action, a mandate to use her newfound abilities to guide her people through the encroaching darkness.

Armed with the wisdom of the ancestors and the strength of her convictions, Me-Katilili emerged from the sacred *Kaya* forests not simply as a bereaved mother but as a beacon of hope and resistance. Her communion with the spirits in the sacred groves had endowed her with a deep understanding of the interconnectedness of all life, a knowledge that she would wield like a torch against the shadows of colonial dominion. In the embrace of the *Kaya* forests, Me-Katilili had found more than solace; she had discovered her purpose, power, and the path that lay before her, illuminated by the ancient light of her people's wisdom. Within the hallowed tranquility of *Kaya* Jilore, a profound transformation unfolded for Me-Katilili, a moment of divine intervention that would forever alter the path of her destiny and that of the Mijikenda people. As she knelt upon the earth, her heart open to the heavens, the boundary between the temporal and the eternal seemed to dissolve, enveloping her in a light that was neither of the sun nor the moon but of something far more ancient and profound. In this sacred communion, where the ancestors' whispers mingled with the breath of God, Me-Katilili was bestowed with the gift of divination, marking her as a chosen conduit between the worlds of the living and the spirits.

This divine endowment was far more than a personal honor; it was a responsibility, a calling that imbued her with a sense of purpose as deep as the roots of the *Kaya* forests themselves. With this gift, Me-Katilili could see beyond the veil of the present into the realms of possibility and warning. Her visions, though cryptic, offered guidance and insight, shedding light on the path her people must tread to preserve their identity and resist the encroaching shadows of colonial rule.

Equipped with her newfound abilities, Me-Katilili emerged from the *Kaya* forests not just as a bereaved mother but as a beacon of hope and resistance for the Agiriama. Her divination powers became a symbol of divine favor, affirming the righteousness of their struggle and the sanctity of their traditions. In the eyes of her community, Me-Katilili's gift was a testament to their ancestors' enduring presence and protection, a sacred bond that no external force could sever.

The divine intervention reinvigorated the Giriama resistance, infusing it with a spiritual fervor that transcended the physical realm. Me-Katilili's visions guided her leadership, offering strategies that were as much about spiritual alignment as tactical resistance. Through her, the Agiriama saw the embodiment of their faith and the tangible presence of their ancestral guardians, inspiring a collective resilience that would echo through the annals of their history. In receiving the gift of divination, Me-Katilili became not only a guardian of her people's past but a visionary leader for their future, navigating the tumultuous waters of colonial resistance with the steady hand of one guided by the divine.

From the depths of personal despair and communal sorrow, Me-Katilili rose, transformed by divine intervention and profound communion with the ancestors in the sacred *Kaya* forests. Her emergence marked a pivotal moment in the history of the

Agiriama, symbolizing the birth of a leader whose spirit was alighted with purpose and whose heart was fortified by the wisdom of the ages. This was not merely a personal triumph but a beacon of hope for her community, a testament to the resilience of the human spirit and the unyielding power of faith.

Me-Katilili's path was marked by profound personal grief, enduring the loss of both a mother and a sister. Yet, from these depths of sorrow, she rose to become a beacon of spiritual and cultural leadership. Her journey embodies the unyielding spirit of the Agiriama. Her divine gift of divination and the authority with which she spoke of the revelations bestowed upon her in the *Kaya* forests resonated deeply with her people. They saw in her not just a leader but a manifestation of their ancestors' protection and guidance, a living symbol of their struggle against the forces that sought to diminish their identity and sovereignty.

With every village gathering, every ritual performed, and every word of wisdom she shared, Me-Katilili inspired a revolution of the heart and soul among the Giriama. Her leadership was not enforced by might but nurtured through her people's collective memory and shared aspirations. She rallied them not to arms but to unity, to a steadfast commitment to preserve their culture, land, and traditions against colonial encroachment. Under Me-Katilili's guidance, the Giriama found a renewed sense of purpose and direction. Her visions offered both foresight and insight, enabling her people to navigate the challenges of their time with a blend of ancient wisdom and newfound resilience. The accretions of resistance she instilled were imbued with the pillars of solidarity, defiance, and hope, crafting a legacy that would endure beyond her years.

Me-Katilili's profound connection to the natural and spiritual realms bestowed upon her remarkable gifts made her exceptional. She became a healer of unparalleled skill, diagnosing diseases with uncanny precision and liberating those afflicted by evil spirits or burdened by life's tribulations. Her gaze, attuned to the celestial dance of the stars, the moon, and the sun, granted her insights into the cosmic order. With this celestial knowledge, she could foretell impending calamities, offering warnings to her people and guiding them through the storms foreseen in her visions.

Healing powers

Reacting to the catastrophes the community was experiencing, Me-Katilili took her religion even more seriously. To soothe her multiple mains, She spent a lot of time meditating and praying. Her spirituality deepened; she spent much time in the sacred *Kaya* forests. Her knowledge linked her with the earth and human society. She could correctly diagnose diseases and accurately heal people of ailments, evil-spirit-possessed, and those with life problems. She observed the skies, the heavenly bodies, the stars, the moon, and the sun and understood the universe. She possessed the remarkable ability to predict future disasters accurately, offer people warnings, and provide insightful and prudent advice and guidance.

As the Giriama rallied around Me-Katilili, her fervor ignited their spirits, and the echoes of resistance reverberated through the hills and valleys of their homeland. It was a call to arms, a declaration that they would rather breathe their last as free souls than live under the yoke of oppressors. Me-Katilili wa Menza, the mother of resistance, had awakened the lion within her people, and together, they stood ready to defend their land, identity, and future. Each thread woven in Me-Katilili's life was a testament to her resilience, spirituality, and unwavering commitment to the well-being of her kin and the wider community. With the poise and wisdom of a leader, she united the fragmented spirits of those battered by the storms of colonial invasion - most profoundly, the women who had suffered immensely. These were mothers and wives plunged into despair by the loss or capture of their husbands and sons to the merciless hands of foreign oppressors.

Me-Katilili's profound understanding of women's essential role in the fabric of society fueled her mission. She became a beacon of hope and strength, guiding them to rise above their circumstances.

In gatherings that blossomed into forums of enlightenment, Me-Katilili imparted invaluable knowledge spanning from agricultural best practices to cultivating personal fortitude of their spirits. Her rallying cry, "Mudzi be ni Muche!" (The active presence of woman completes community/village), echoed through the hearts of her listeners, a potent reminder of their indispensable value in weaving the community's collective tapestry. "Empowering women is our path to liberation," she proclaimed, her voice imbued with a conviction as unwavering as the ground beneath. "In uplifting the women placed in adverse social and political contexts, we ignite the beacon of hope and inspiration. My resolve is unshakable in mobilizing women towards this cause."

Her teachings transcended ordinary lessons; they were profound revelations that uncovered the immense power lying dormant within each woman. Me-Katilili's voice, rich with passion and resolve, ignited a spark within these women, awakening them to their innate abilities and the crucial role they played in the socio-economic fabric of their community.

She envisioned a future where gender equality was not merely an ideal but a reality, where women stood alongside men as equals and pioneers of transformative change. Me-Katilili ardently fought for women's empowerment, challenging them to cast aside passivity and assert their influence as a formidable force against the dual oppressions of colonialism and patriarchal British laws.

Among the folds of her profound maternal foresight was the pivotal decision to safeguard her youngest child, Mwedya, which underscored her protective vigilance. Me-Katilili, a matriarch sculpted by the harsh contours of loss and struggle, was acutely aware of the perils that shadowed the boundaries of their home. Her advice to her children, steeped in the wisdom of her years, emphasized the necessity of adult supervision to ward off the veiled threats of an evolving world.

The thought of her absence - whether in pursuit of spiritual enlightenment or rallying her community against colonial onslaughts - cast a heavy shadow over her heart. Conscious of how her pursuits might alter the fabric of her family life, Me-Katilili broached a subject laden with selfless foresight. She proposed taking a second wife to Mulewa, her rock, amidst the storm of life. This suggestion did not come from a place of whimsy but from a profound understanding of her family's need for continuity and stability.

Request for a co-wife

One evening, after a day spent traversing from one community to another, weaving stronger bonds of unity and resistance, Me-Katilili decided to share her thoughts with her husband.

"My husband, the ancestors have entrusted me with burdens that weigh heavily upon my shoulders..." Me-Katilili began, her voice a blend of determination and solemnity.

"My wife, I understand. This is the path you are meant to walk," Mulewa responded, his voice laced with unwavering support.

"I have been thinking of Kavunje. Her life took a tragic turn when her husband was unjustly taken from her soon after their marriage. She is hardworking, virtuous, and a pillar of strength," Me-Katilili continued, her words painting a picture of the woman she deemed fit to join their family.

Mulewa, caught in a whirlpool of emotions, hesitated for a moment before voicing his deepest fear, "Don't you want me anymore, my wife?"

"Why would you think that my husband?" Me-Katilili chuckled, the warmth in her laughter softening the tension. "It's precisely because I want you and cherish our family that I suggest this. Kavunje is a woman of substance, and by welcoming her into our home, we're not just strengthening our family but also honoring our community's duty to support young widows."

Me-Katilili spoke with conviction, her argument for Kavunje interwoven with broader concerns for their people's survival amidst the threats of abduction and violence. "The rate at which our people are captured is alarming. We must ensure the Mijikenda thrive, and part of that is making sure procreation continues unabated."

"I will think about it," Mulewa said, his mind tumultuous thoughts touched by the depth of Me-Katilili's foresight. Mulewa's contemplative acceptance and trust in his wife's judgment guided him, so they approached the council of elders. They arranged a meeting, and after several sunrises, Me-Katilili and Mulewa stood before Kavunje's family, humbly requesting her hand in marriage.

Mulewa's marriage to Kavunje, from which came Dama, Kitsao, and Kahonzi -children Me-Katilili embraced as if they were her own flesh and blood - served as a vibrant testament to their united commitment to their family's lineage. This development strengthened the ties within their family and reverberated with the values of resilience, nurturing, and dedication to the community that Me-Katilili epitomized. Through this union, the core of their heritage and the vigor of their communal spirit were set to flourish for generations to come

CHAPTER 10

Wanje wa Mwadorikola and other prominent elders

As Me-Katilili wa Menza journeyed through the heartlands of Mijikenda villages and communities, her fervent calls to arms against the oppressive forces of colonialism kindled a fire of resistance in the hearts of many. Her crusade for freedom meticulously crafted a close-knit network of loyalty, drawing together a league of dedicated souls whose fates became intrinsically woven with the struggle for autonomy. Central to this alliance were Bembe wa Bembere, an esteemed elder, Bogosho wa Menza, a celebrated elder and spiritual authority, and the dynamic Wanje wa Mwadorikola, a revered medicine man whose very essence burned with the resolve to confront the British encroachment. His bond with Me-Katilili transcended mere collaboration, evolving into a profound fusion of mutual destinies and steadfast determination.

Wanje wa Mwadorikola epitomized the quintessential Giriama warrior spirit despite his unassuming stature and economical use of words. His appearance, marked by the beginnings of baldness in his mid-years and the modest presence of hair, narrated a story of wisdom and extensive life experience. Despite his lesser height, Wanje's demeanor was imposing. His physique, etched with the vigor and suppleness indicative of a life harmoniously entwined with nature, testified to his pivotal role as healer and custodian of his people's ancient wisdom. His skin, rich with the tones of the earth, narrated the tale of generations deeply rooted in their land. A distinctive nose and the enigmatic scar adorning his lips added dimensions of intrigue and endurance to his character - a silent testimony to past adversities bravely confronted.

The depth of insight and wisdom harbored in his gaze was profound, offering a glimpse into a soul steeped in understanding far beyond the ordinary. Wanje's speech, when he chose to vocalize his thoughts, was measured and compelling, each word resonant with the gravity of his beliefs and the careful consideration of his strategies. This methodical approach to communication was strategic, ensuring his contributions to the cause were both meaningful and considered.

The partnership between Wanje and Me-Katilili stood as a pillar of the resistance, symbolizing the unity and collective resolve that powered their fight. Their alliance was more than a strategic collaboration; it was a powerful amalgamation of spiritual strength and tactical insight. Together, they became the embodiment of defiance against colonial domination, their concerted efforts rallying their community towards a common goal far more significant than any individual ambition. This collaboration was not just cooperation; it was a potent synergy that galvanized a whole community to unite against colonial intrusion, epitomizing the relentless spirit and resilience of a people steadfast in their quest to preserve their heritage, land, and future.

Charles Hobley, the District commissioner and Arthur M. Champion, his Assistant

Charles William Hobley was a key British Colonial administrator in Kenya, starting his service in 1894. He arrived in Kilifi in 1912. As the district commissioner, Hobley, alongside Arthur Champion his assistant, were instrumental in managing British colonial efforts from their base in Mwangea, Kilifi. Hobley, a man in his middle years, was distinguished by dark hair and skin bronzed from the African coastal sun. He was tall and slim, his facial features marked by a long, slender nose and a perpetually thoughtful and stern expression, reflective of the weight of his responsibilities. A pipe was often a fixture between his lips, symbolizing his contemplative nature. His attire epitomized a British colonial administrator, complete with the uniform that marked his status and role.

January 1913. On a remarkably serene afternoon in Kilifi, Charles and his wife Alice enjoyed the comfort of their home's exterior. They were seated in chairs, embraced by the gentle breeze that whispered through the surroundings. The scene was set for a quiet afternoon tea, with a teapot nestled between them on a table, releasing the warm scent of tea into the air alongside two cups awaiting their use. Alice was engaged in knitting, her hands moving with precision and grace. At the same time, Charles was absorbed in reading an old newspaper, possibly drawing connections between past events and the current state of affairs under his administration. One of the soldiers guarding the well fenced residence came forth to Hobley and announced they had a guest from Britain.

At Hobley's base that afternoon arrived a figure both imposing and out of step with the world he stepped into. Arthur M. Champion, a young British officer of twenty-nine years, carried the air of the empire on his shoulders, his presence starkly contrasting the vibrant and untamed spirit of the land. Tall and slim, his stature was as much a part of his authority as the official British uniform he wore with a meticulous sense of pride. His hair, a light blonde, caught the sun in ways foreign to this part of the world, and his blue eyes, piercing and cold, mirrored the distant skies of his homeland rather than the warm, earthy tones of the Giriama lands he was sent to dominate.

Arthur's chin was broad, a foundation for a face that was all angles and dominance, with a long nose that seemed to sniff out dissent and subversion even where it did not lie. Hobley perceived Arthur as someone who viewed the world not through the lens of reality, but rather through the prism of his own convictions about how it ought to be. Despite this, Hobley could not help but admire Arthur for his unwavering dedication.

Arthur's mission was unambiguous: to conduct a census, levy taxes, and assert the empire's mandates with a fervor that spoke of his deep-seated belief in the legitimacy of his actions, as decreed by the British Empire.

By May 1913, Champion's mark on the region was indelible. He had, with unyielding zeal, appointed headmen who were met with open hostility by the native council of elders. These actions, emblematic of his ignorance and dismissive nature, did not consider the intricacies of Giriama societal structures, nor did they respect the traditions that had sustained these people for generations. His decisions, driven by an ego that saw the native people as primitive and incapable, led to a systematic undermining of their way of life.

On the orders of the district commissioner, Hobley, Champion aimed to dismantle the longstanding and vital ivory trade that connected the Giriama with the Sanye hunting people and, through them, to the broader world via the Baluchi traders. This trade, a lifeline for many, was deemed illegal under the pretext that its proceeds were used for purchasing *tembo/uchi wa mnazi*, a local brew. This justification, however, thinly veiled, was part of a broader strategy to subjugate and control, to replace a thriving economy with one dependent on the whims of the empire.

But Arthur M. Champion's ambitions continued beyond economic disruption. In a move that symbolized the erasure of Giriama heritage, he planned the relocation of *Kaya* Giriama, the heart of tribal ritual life, dismissing it as nothing more than a "dilapidated refuse heap." This was not merely an act of physical displacement but a profound disrespect to the spiritual and cultural foundations of the Agiriama. His actions, fueled by arrogance and a profound misunderstanding of the land and its people, rendered him deeply unpopular among the natives. They saw him not as a bearer of civilization but an invader, a force of disruption and disrespect. His very name symbolized his disconnect from the community he sought to govern.

They called him "Chembe," (which means a crumb or a tiny grain in the Mijikenda language). This seemingly insignificant moniker was laden with meaning. It spoke of how the Giriama perceived Champion as minor, easily overlooked, and inconsequential in their culture's vast and enduring legacy.

Arthur M. Champion, in his hubris, failed to see the true strength of the people he deemed primitive. In their resilience and unwavering commitment to their heritage, the Giriama stood as a testament to the enduring power of culture and community in the face of colonial arrogance.

CHAPTER 11

The revolts begin

4th August 1913, within the hallowed confines of the sacred *Kaya* Fungo forest, a sanctuary that had stood the test of time, safeguarded by the whispers of ancestors and the solemn vows of its protectors, an assembly of unparalleled significance was convened. The air, heavy with the scent of earth after rain, was charged with an urgency that pulsed through the roots of the towering trees. Underneath the canopy that filtered the sun into a dichroic of light and shadow, all ranks of the Mijikenda government and the religious specialist, along with priests and diviners, formed a circle, an embodiment of unity and resistance. Me-Katilili, Wanje wa Mwadorikola, Pembe was Bembere, and Bogosho wa Menza sat next to one another quietly exchanging insights.

Their voices, low and imbued with the gravity of the moment, spoke of the British invaders, of the disrespect and the disenfranchisement that had befallen their land. Me-Katilili, her eyes alight with the fire of determination, her voice a blend of wisdom and wariness, addressed the gathering. "The land of our ancestors, the sacred soil that nourishes our people, faces a threat unlike any before. The British, led by Champion, see not the spirit of our people but only the shadows of their greed."

Wanje wa Mwadorikola, his gaze steady, added, "Their ignorance blinds them to the sanctity of our traditions, our *Kaya*. We must stand united, for the roots of our resistance are deep, watered by the blood of those who came before us."

As the gathering focused on devising plans to reclaim their freedom, they barely crossed the sacred *Kaya* Fungo Forest boundary when devastation struck. A Dynamite, unleashed with ruthless precision, tore through the heart of the sacred *Kaya*. In an instant, chaos reigned supreme. The air, once a vessel for solemn vows and determined spirits, became heavy with the dark plumes of smoke. The sharp scent of charred timber cut through the peace of *Kaya* Fungo was an assault on the senses. The sacred grove, long-standing as a symbol of spiritual unity and community resilience, fell victim to a ferocious onslaught. Directed by Hobley's command and executed by the infamously despised Arthur Champion, the police force set the forest ablaze. Flames, sinister as specters from forbidden tales, blazed through the trees and underbrush, their destructive dance fueled by tangible, scorching wrath. Panic ensued as the dynamites exploded into the sacred space and its surroundings. The elders and their congregation, faces illuminated by the fire's glow, raised voices in a cacophony of distress and scrambled to flee.

Me-Katilili's voice rose above the turmoil: "To the river, quickly! Our ancestors guide us; this fire will not be the end of our story."

Amidst the chaos, Pembe was Bembere, ever the beacon of calm, chanted prayers to the ancestors, seeking their protection as the community navigated through the inferno. "O ancestors, shield us with your wisdom, guide our steps through these flames," he intoned, his voice a steady drumbeat against the crackling of fire.

The community, bound by a resolve forged in the heat of adversity, moved as one. The act of setting fire to the sacred *Kaya* Fungo was perceived as a profound and heretical affront by the British administration, a violation that resonated with piercing clarity among the natives. This blasphemy was not merely an insult; it was an act that sliced deeply into the very sinews of Mijikenda history, a sacrilege that bled into the collective memory of the people, staining their ancestral legacy with the ash of desecration. The attendants with their clads singed, faces soot-streaked, emerged from the forest's embrace, their spirits unbroken despite the assault on their sanctuary. As they reached the safety of the river, the flames continued to devour the forest behind them, a stark testament to the violence inflicted upon their sacred lands. The sacred *Kaya* Fungo was completely burnt down. There were a few casualties with minor to moderate injuries.

Back in the villages, the natives were overwhelmed and stricken. The attack on *Kaya* Fungo, a sacrilege against their heritage, ignited a fervor that transcended the immediate threat. It was a call to arms, a rallying cry for the preservation of their identity, their culture, and their right to self-determination. A state of emergency was declared in the aftermath, not just by the colonial administration but within the people's hearts.

The elders, their faces illuminated by the nascent dawn, looked upon their people with a renewed sense of purpose. "This fire has not consumed us; it has ignited a flame within us that no force can extinguish," Me-Katilili proclaimed, her voice echoing across the waters, a beacon of resilience and defiance.

The events of that day, marked by loss and betrayal, also sowed the seeds of resistance, of a collective resolve to reclaim the sanctity of their land and the dignity of their people. In the face of adversity, the elders of sacred *Kaya* Fungo, united by the flames that sought to destroy them, emerged stronger, their spirits like the phoenix reborn from the ashes of despair.

Granary hideout

In the shadowed underbelly of colonial intrigue, where loyalties were as shifting as the sands beneath the relentless African sun, there emerged a figure whose name would be etched in infamy. Mtawa, a son of the soil, had turned his back on his people. He was lured by the cold clink of coins and the hollow promises of favor from an occupying force. He slithered through the underbrush, a serpent in human guise, to deliver whispers of betrayal to Arthur Champion, the man whose very presence was a blight upon the land.

Clocked with an arrogance like a second skin, Champion met Mtawa's revelations with a dismissive snort. "They plan to poison me, you say? And my interpreter?" His laughter, a sound devoid of mirth, echoed off the walls of his makeshift office, a tent that stood as a testament to his transient conquest. Yet, beneath this veneer of indifference, the seeds of fear took root. With a sleight of hand, he passed a handful of coins to Mtawa, his gaze cold. "Keep the information coming," he commanded, the bribe a silent testament to his reliance on treachery for survival.

In the days that followed, the local population tactically cut off the vital supply of food to the British camp, executing this action with a precision that took Champion by surprise. Additionally, they obstructed access to water sources and contaminated the camp's water reserves with Euphorbia leaves, a move that further destabilized Champion's position. In response, Champion issued a stern warning, decreeing harsh penalties for anyone found responsible for these disruptions.

Amidst escalating tension and disorder, a figure emerged from the depths of duplicity: Ngoyo wa Mwavuo, a wealthy man (rumors had it, that he got his wealth through slave trade and bribes from colonialists). With motives veiled in the dense fog of betrayal, he extended a clandestine offer of assistance to Champion, revealing the natives' plan to set the British camp ablaze under the veil of night. He stealthily escorted the imperiled officer to a sanctuary unbeknownst to others - a granary situated within Ngoyo's own compound. This granary, a repository for the season's yield, was to become Champion's unlikely refuge.

Enclosed within the granary's walls, Champion was enveloped by the land's plenty. He found himself amidst towering stacks of maize, coconut husks, surrounded by the dense, hearty blocks of cassava, and the distinctive aroma of dried fish. For that night, this emblem of sustenance and prosperity morphed into a haven for Champion. Outside, the darkness was pierced by the flames consuming his camp, the fire a vivid symbol of the natives' determination and their unrelenting quest for autonomy. Meanwhile, Champion, the focal point of their wrath, remained hidden within the granary, amidst the maize, coconuts, cassava, and dried fish.

The aftermath of this fiery onslaught and the revelation of Champion's survival, aided by betrayal, spread swiftly among the communities. This act of defiance, sparked by the news of the granary's role as a sanctuary, stoked the flames of resistance among the natives. The granary, once just a storehouse for the harvest, had now played a pivotal role in a night of survival, echoing the enduring spirit of freedom among those who stood against subjugation.

But peace was a stranger in these tumultuous times. The villagers, their suspicions aroused by whispers and wary glances, turned their eyes towards Ngoyo's abode. Accusations flew like arrows, sharp and unerring, piercing the veil of secrecy that Ngoyo had hoped to maintain.

"He harbors the enemy!" they cried, their voices a chorus of anger and betrayal. Ngoyo, cornered and desperate, refused them entry, a futile attempt to stem the tide of inevitable discovery.

As the men departed to summon the elders, the arbiters of justice and tradition, Ngoyo faced a choice that would define his legacy. With urgency borne of fear and a flicker of remorse, he ushered Champion out of the granary into the night alive with the sounds of a community betrayed. And so, under cover of darkness, Champion fled, leaving behind a village that had been a crucible of resistance, loyalty, and betrayal, of battles fought not just with weapons but with the soul of a people.

Once a symbol of revelation, the granary stood void of Champion as the elders returned, a testament to the flight of a man whose name would be whispered in cautionary tales for generations to come.

Me-Katilili confronts Champion

On 13th August 1913, Chakama in Kilifi, Kenya, beneath a sky marred by the ominous shadows of colonial oppression, the air was heavy with a tension palpable enough to choke on, laden with the acrid scent of an impending storm brewed from confrontation and strife. A couple of days ago, the British police, emissaries of a distant, indifferent crown, had descended upon the unsuspecting village in Vitengeni like a plague, leaving behind a trail of devastation - lives claimed in cold blood, innocence desecrated, and souls shackled to the yoke of forced labor. The egregious act against two young women and the abduction of ten men, bound for toil under the scorching sun for roads and a water project in Mombasa, was not just an attack on individuals but an affront to the spirit of the Mijikenda people. Rage simmered within their hearts like a tempest waiting to burst forth.

In the heart of this brewing maelstrom stood Me-Katilili wa Menza, a matriarch whose spirit was as indomitable as the ancient baobabs that fused their land. She was more than a leader; she was the embodiment of the Mijikenda's unyielding will to fight against the shackles of subjugation. Her presence at the forefront of a fervent protest was a beacon of hope, rallying the Mijikenda to voice their dissent against the manifold injustices inflicted by the British colonialists - their fertile lands stolen, families torn asunder, and the future of their youth imprisoned by chains of greed.

As dawn broke over Chakama, near Malindi, the British colonial administrator's station stood stark against the horizon - a monolith of oppression. Champion and his police force were present in the marketplace. Yet, before this edifice of domination, a sea of protestors gathered, their spirits undeterred. Amid this crowd stood Me-Katilili, her gaze steel, her resolve unbreakable, bearing a basket that cradled a mother hen and her chicks - a poignant symbol of the natural bond of care and protection, a bond the colonialists sought to obliterate.

The air was charged with anticipation as a meeting convened, attended by Me-Katilili, Wanje wa Mwadorikola, and other venerable community elders, outraged parents, and the British-appointed headsmen. Words were exchanged, but the dialogue turned barren and yielded no fruit. Frustrated yet undaunted, Me-Katilili went forth, her basket in hand. Her act was not just a protest but a declaration, embodying the philosophy that "The parent is the one who knows the pain of bearing a child."

Releasing the mother hen and her chicks from the basket onto the ground, she challenged Arthur Champion, the embodiment of colonial disdain, to grasp the essence of protection by taking away the chicks.

Me-Katilili, with a defiant tone, proclaimed, "Chembe, Chembe! I challenge you, go ahead and snatch a chick. You will see the consequences of taking our sons."

With a sneer that spoke volumes of his contempt, Champion underestimated the gesture's gravity. "Is this your rebellion, Me-Katilili? A hen and her chicks?" he mocked. Yet, the moment he laid hands on one of the chicks, the mother hen's fierce instinct to protect her brood was unleashed - an upheaval of pecks and flaps on Champion's arm that served as a stark lesson in the innate power of maternal protection.

The crowd seethed with a tumultuous mix of emotions - horror, awe, and defiance - their collective breath held in taut anticipation. In a bold and reckless instant, Champion drew his weapon and executed the mother hen with a gunshot that shattered the tense silence. Without missing a beat, Me-Katilili retaliated with a slap of such ferocity it hurled Champion sprawling to the ground, her movements swift, her resolve unbreakable. Her action, a vivid flash of defiance. "Don't you ever touch our children!" she forbade, her voice not just a warning but a solemn vow, a luminescent flare of courage against the dark skies of oppression.

"Madwoman! Witch!" The words burst from him, tainted with contempt, as a spray of blood flecked his lips. Laboriously, he attempted to regain his footing, his frame trembling with effort. Heavy with defiance, each movement underscored the intensity of the battle he waged within himself to stand tall once more.

The aftermath was prompt and brutal. The police officers unleashed a flurry of gunfire that claimed the lives of the young men, a tragic symphony that marked the culmination of an execution most foul. Yet, in the chaos, Me-Katilili vanished, a phantom in turmoil, her spirit unbroken, her legacy a testament to a people's undying will to fight, hope, and endure. In her wake, she left not just the echoes of gunshots but a call to arms, a reminder of the lessons of resistance and the undying spirit of the Mijikenda. As Me-Katilili escaped, she, alongside Wanje wa Mwadorikola and their companions, hastened to notify other men to sound the emergency horn. The British administration's brutal shootings were a declaration of war against the Mijikenda.

The following morning, the sun rose over Malindi, painting the sky with hues of fire and blood, a warning of the day's turmoil. The air, heavy with the scent of the ocean and the earthy aroma of the surrounding forests, carried within it the murmurs of a community on the brink of rebellion. At the heart of this brewing storm stood Me-Katilili wa Menza and Wanje wa Mwadorikola, figures of unwavering defiance against the colonial yoke that sought to bend their people to its will.

Arthur Champion, the assistant district commissioner, set into motion a manhunt that would ripple through the very core of the community. With a cold, unwavering resolve, he dispatched the British police force across the sprawling expanse of Giriama territory. Their mission was singular and clear: to hunt down Me-Katilili, Wanje wa Mwadorikola, and all the elders who dared stand against the might of the British Empire. The landscape of Giriama, once a sanctuary of tranquility and vibrant life, transformed into a stage for relentless pursuit. The rustle of leaves and the whisper of the wind carried the heavy boots and stern commands of the British police, a foreboding presence that sent ripples of tension through the villages.

As days turned into nights and the search proved fruitless, frustration gnawed at Champion and his administration. The elusive spirits of Me-Katilili and Wanje, along with the steadfast elders, seemed to merge with the land itself, evading capture with a defiance that echoed the resilience of the Agiriama.

In a desperate bid to break the resistance, Champion resorted to the age-old tactics of coercion and betrayal. He summoned a select group of headsmen whose loyalty could be swayed by the glint of silver and the weight of gold. He sought to corrupt the fabric of Giriama society with heavy bribes, turning brother against brother and leader against follower. These headsmen, swayed by greed or coerced by pressure, were tasked with a grim directive: to lead the colonial forces to their prey.

The betrayal bore fruit in quiet, unsuspecting moments. Me-Katilili, the lioness of Giriama, was captured in Garashi, betrayed by a small fraction of the people she sought to protect. Wanje, too, found his sanctuary breached, taken from his home at a dawn that promised despair rather than hope.

The convoy attack

16th August 1913. The air was charged with a palpable sense of anticipation as dawn broke over Giriama lands. Wanje's clan, alongside the revered members of Mekatilili's lineage, gathered in a clearing surrounded by the ancient whispering trees of their homeland. The elders, their faces etched with the wisdom of ages, stood with solemn dignity, their presence a testament to the gravity of the moment. Sons, daughters, and extended family members of these storied clans stood united, a living cuneiform rock of shared history and collective resolve. They were joined by a mob of those who, moved by a deep alignment with Me-Katilili and Wanje's principles, had come to lend their strength to the cause. Together, they formed a congregation bound by a singular purpose: to confront the injustices that had long shadowed the Giriama community and the Mijikenda tribe at large.

Under the canopy of the sky, now a vault of endless azure, the assembly embarked on a series of clandestine meetings. The very air seemed to thrum with the weight of their deliberations. They spoke of forming potent armies, each a spearhead of their burgeoning resistance, stationed strategically across the breadth of their lands. These discussions were not merely tactical; they were imbued with a sense of destiny, a collective understanding that their actions would carve a path toward freedom for their people. Secretly, they gathered intelligence, piecing together a mosaic of information that would undermine the British colonial grip.

Their plan was audacious, a bold stroke aimed at the heart of oppression. It centered on a daring rescue, a mission to liberate their brethren languishing in the feasible grim confines of the Kisii detention camp. Time was their adversary, urging them forward, and they embraced the urgency with a fierce determination.

The night became their cloak as they launched their first forays against the British forces. A convoy laden with soldiers, officials, and police officers - all symbols of the colonial yoke - fell to their coordinated assault. Flames, bright as the stars above, consumed British stations in Vitengeni and across the Giriama lands, each blaze a declaration of their unyielding resolve.

For days, the land was alive with the sounds of conflict, with clashes that were verses in the epic of their struggle. Men and women, fueled by a deep-seated desire for retribution, fought with a ferocity that belied their numbers. They fought for freedom, justice, and the right to live on their land without the shadow of subjugation. They fought for the memory of those taken from them, for the innocence stolen, and for the dignity eroded by forced labor and dehumanizing acts. Amidst the turmoil, their voices rose, a chorus of defiance that pierced the heavens.

"Let our people free! Freedom, freedom!" echoed across the valleys, a rallying cry that bound them together.

"Release Me-Katilili, release Wanje," they demanded, invoking the names of their revered leaders as beacons of hope.

"Go back to your land; this is our land!" they declared, staunchly affirming their sovereignty. Their words were a typhoon, hurling defiance at their oppressors with each breath.

"Chembe, you are nothing but a tiny grain," they taunted, a rebuke that diminished the might of their enemies.

"Give us back our people!" they demanded, their voices a torrent of anger against the theft of their kin.

"All invaders are thieves! All invaders are murderers! Criminals, get out!" The air was thick with their accusations, each slogan a testament to their resolve, a refusal to be silenced or subdued. As they rioted and fought, their cries became the anthem of their resistance, a symphony of spirit and determination that resonated far beyond the battlefield. In their defiance and courage, the Agiriama carved a legacy of resistance, a testament to the enduring power of unity and the unquenchable thirst for freedom.

With fervent intensity, they hurled curses laden with venom at every interloper of their sacred lands, targeting Champion and his British overseers among them. Their declarations, potent and dynamic, were sent skyward, seeking the ears of their ancestors, invoking their strength and guidance in this moment of defiance.

Meeting and resisting

On 6th November 1913, a day etched in the collective memory of the people with a clarity that belied the passage of time, the air in Biria, the domain of the resilient Bogosho, held a charge. Under the vast expanse of the African sky, it was here that the forces of the British Empire, led by Hobley and his assistant, Arthur Champion, alongside twenty-five police officers, converged to dictate the terms of a peace that bore the weight of oppression. With them, as symbols of their supposed triumph, were two figures of defiance: Me-Katilili and Wanje wa Mwadorikola, their spirits unbroken despite their chains.

The meeting ground, a clearing that had borne witness to countless gatherings of unity and resistance, was now a stage for enacting colonial authority. The natives, a sea of determined faces, stood firm and unwavering, their resolve a testament to the deep roots of their rebellion. Despite the imposing presence of the colonial force, their spirits remained indomitable, and their stance was a silent defiance against the erosion of their way of life.

As the proceedings began, the elders, guardians of the community's conscience, took a step that was both a concession and a strategy. The anti-government oath, a symbol of their resistance, was revoked. This act, however, laden with the bitterness of the moment, was a necessary sacrifice in the eyes of those who sought to protect their people from further harm. The immediate consequence of this decision was heart-wrenching; Me-Katilili and Wanje, embodiments of the fight against subjugation, were to be exiled to Kisii the following day, their absence a void in the hearts of their community.

In the wake of this, the police patrols, emboldened by the veneer of victory, began to exact fines from each location, a sum of 1500 rupees, a demand that bled the community of its resources. This act of levying fines was not merely a financial burden but a deliberate attempt to weaken the people's resolve, to break their spirit under the guise of enforcing peace.

In his reports, Hobley dismissed the uprising as a "trifling conspiracy of vague import," a statement that belied the fear and respect that the rebellion had instilled in the colonial administration. Yet, in this dismissal lay an acknowledgment of the actual outcome of their actions. The events had provided a pretext, however unjust, to entrench their control further. The concentration of the people around the new station at Mwangea, the closure of the old *Kaya*, and the clearing of the area north of the Sabaki River were strategic moves designed to dismantle the social and spiritual fabric of the community, to relegate their traditions into the shadows of forgotten history.

This moment, though framed as a formalization of peace, was, in reality, a stark illustration of the colonial strategy of divide and conquer, of the imposition of authority through the erasure of identity. Yet, even in the face of such adversity, the spirit of the people remained unquenched. The exile of their leaders to the Kisii detention camp, the fines imposed upon them, and the strategic reconfigurations of their lands were but chapters in the more extended narrative of their resistance. The legacy of Me-Katilili, Wanje, and the countless unnamed warriors of the Giriama uprising was a beacon of resilience and defiance against the forces that sought to silence them.

Bound for prison

7th November 1913. The square erupted into chaos, screams mingling with the cries of despair as Me-Katilili and Wanje wa Mwadorikola were swiftly apprehended, their wrists and ankles bound as the police force led them away. Yet, even in this moment of arrest, they held their heads high, their spirits unbroken.

As the British forces descended upon them, the air was split by the cries of the Agiriama, a chorus of anguish and defiance that rose from every corner of Mijikenda land. Me-Katilili, her eyes alight with the fire of resistance, stood resolute as the soldiers approached, her voice cutting through the chaos. "You may chain us, but you cannot chain the spirit of our people," she declared, her gaze locked on the approaching authority figures.

Wanje, standing by her side, nodded in silent agreement. His presence a steadfast support to Me-Katilili's fiery leadership. The community rallied around them, their voices a unified cry against the injustice that sought to tear them from their land, their families, and heritage.

Yet, as the British forces closed in, the reality of their situation settled like a heavy cloak upon the gathered crowd. Me-Katilili and Wanje were swiftly apprehended, their hands bound as they were led away. The community's cries of protest followed them like a haunting lament.

Within the confines of the colonial building, Me-Katilili and Wanje faced the cruelty of their captors with a dignity that belied their circumstances. Stripped of their clothing and subjected to the lash, they endured each blow with a stoicism that spoke volumes of their inner strength. "Is this the strength of your rule? The whip and the chain?" Me-Katilili taunted, her voice a beacon of defiance even in the face of torment.

Wanje, his body bearing the marks of their captors' brutality, remained silent, his resolve a silent testament to the cause for which they fought. Amidst the pain and humiliation, a spark of hope remained within them, fueled by the knowledge that their struggle was not in vain. Together, they embodied the unbreakable will of their people, a beacon of resistance in the face of colonial tyranny.

As Arthur dispatched his telegraph to England, his words were a cold calculation of colonial policy. The fate of Me-Katilili and Wanje hung in the balance. England's directive was shrouded in bureaucratic coldness, yet it sealed their immediate future, a relocation meant to silence their voices and erase their influence.

Outside, the community's vigil continued, a constant presence that defied colonial authority with every chant and cry. The people's voices, a blend of sorrow and resistance, carried the stories of their ancestors, a reminder of the land and the freedoms that had been theirs long before the colonizers arrived.

"Do you not possess any shame? Where is your dignity?" a protester bellowed, his voice rising above the tumult as Me-Katilili and Wanje were forcefully led by the police force toward the vehicle.

Under the oppressive glare of the midday sun, Me-Katilili and Wanje were marched toward the vehicle, a Land Rover, which awaited them. Amidst this grave procession, the air became thick with tension, a palpable force that seemed to suffocate the breeze. It was then that the voices of the Agiriama rose a tumultuous wave of defiance and sorrow that crashed against the indifferent façade of their oppressors.

"Let our people go!" they thundered, echoing through the oppressive atmosphere. Their plea was a clarion call for freedom that refused to be silenced.

"Release our people!" the cry followed. A demand laced with the raw edge of desperation as if each word carried the weight of countless unspoken stories of suffering and resilience.

"Stop killing our people!" This shout was a stark accusation, a reminder of the blood that stained the hands of those who dared claim authority over life and death, a rebuke so powerful it seemed to shake the very foundations of injustice.

"Go back to where you came from!" This was a defiant command, thrown like a spear through the heart of colonial arrogance, a declaration that this land and its people would no longer tolerate the presence of those who sought to strip them of their dignity.

"Heartless animals!" The final insult was hurled with all the venom of a wounded soul, painting their oppressors not as humans but as beasts devoid of compassion, empathy, or any semblance of humanity. The British guards responded with a chilling silence, their guns a stark reminder of their power.

Each outcry was a testament to the Agiriama's indomitable spirit. A collective expression of anguish, anger, and an unyielding desire for freedom resonated through the air, a vivid cry of resistance braced with hope and the unbreakable will of a people united in their struggle.

In a moment frozen in time amidst the chaos that enveloped them, Me-Katilili's gaze pierced through the crowd of faces, finding solace in the wise, weathered eyes of an elder from the council. She imparted an earnest plea, her voice a fragile thread of sound, strained and hoarse from the tumult of emotions that choked her words. "Go to the sacred *Kaya* forest, call upon the spirits, tell the ancestors and God to bring us back to our ancestral land," she implored, her voice directive barely escaping her parched lips as the forceful hands of the British officers urged her towards the Land Rover that stood ready to tear her from the land she held dear.

The elder's nod was a beacon of hope, a silent vow that her message would be carried on the winds to the very heart of the sacred forest. As he melded back into the sea of faces, a symbol of unspoken solidarity and resilience, the crowd surged forward in a desperate attempt to thwart the departure, their bodies a testament to the collective will to protect their own. Yet, their efforts were swallowed by the relentless advance of the vehicle, which roared to life and tore away, leaving nothing but a billowing shroud of dust and the heavy weight of despair. The protestors, undeterred, continued their chants, a chorus of solidarity and defiance that followed the Land Rover as it disappeared into the distance.

As the vehicle cleaved through the landscape, carrying Me-Katilili and Wanje into the maw of uncertainty, a solemn pact was forged within its confines. Me-Katilili, with resolve as steadfast as the ancient forests, assured Wanje, "We will return to our homeland soon. I will do everything within my power to bring us back home."

Together, they intertwined in prayer. Their voices rose to *Mulungu*, the supreme God, invoking protection and favor. With incantations that carried the weight of centuries, they summoned their ancestors, beseeching them to pave the way for their return. As the landscape blurred past, their spirits remained anchored in the land of their birth, calling out to the unseen forces that govern the balance of all things. In this sacred communion, they laid bare their souls, entrusting their journey to the hands of those who had walked the paths of the earth long before. They draw strength from the unbreakable bond that ties the present to the past and the living to the spirits that watch over them from the realms beyond.

The journey embarked upon them, Me-Katilili and Wanje unfurled along the rugged contours of a less traveled road, a path that carved its way from Malindi to Kisii. This was not merely a route marked by the dust of the earth but a testament to an era of transformation, where the dreams of progress clashed with the harsh realities of colonial ambition. The road itself was a vein of turmoil and toil, flanked on either side by legions of workers who bent their backs under the searing kiss of the sun, each one a cog in the colossal endeavor to lay the tracks of what would be known as the iron snake.

Surrounded by the vigilant gaze of British soldiers, these laborers were silent witnesses to imperialism's relentless march. Their sweat mingled with the dust that rose in clouds around their feet. Commands barked in foreign tongues, slicing through the air, urging them to push beyond the limits of human endurance. The natives dictated by the British to pave the railway path that would forever alter the face of their land.

Within the confines of the Land Rover, its canvas hood marred by the wear of time and journey, Me-Katilili and Wanje found themselves peering out through a tear that offered them a window to the world outside. Then, with a rumble that grows into a cacophony, a monstrous creation of metal and steam appears, moving with a life of its own. Me-Katilili and Wanje watched the astonishing beast slithering along the iron path with a series of interconnected carriages following obediently behind. Smoke billows from its top, and its sound - a constant, rhythmic chugging - echoed through the air, unlike anything heard before. This mechanical serpent, which could devour distances that once took days to traverse in mere hours, was a spectacle of awe and wonder, signifying the dawn of a new era of exploration and connection.

"Ooh, this is the iron snake that Mepoho prophesied..." Me-Katilili whispered, her words heavy with realization. The prophecy, once a distant echo of caution, now unfolded before their eyes, a tangible manifestation of change that none could have foreseen.

As the vehicle trudged along, the scenery outside morphed with each passing mile, a visual symphony of change that painted the story of a land in transition. The lush, verdant embrace of the coastal region gradually gave way to the rugged majesty of the uplands. This journey was more than a mere relocation; it was a passage through the very heart of a nation's soul, a voyage that bore witness to the shifting sands of identity, culture, and destiny.

Through the tear in the Land Rover's canvas, Me-Katilili and Wanje watched, their eyes tracing the contours of a landscape caught between the past and an uncertain future.

As the journey progressed, the embrace of the climate shifted, casting aside the familiar warmth of the coastal regions for a cooler, drier atmosphere that heralded their approach to higher altitudes. The evening air, crisp and unforgiving, bit into their skin with a chill they had never known. Me-Katilili and Wanje, clad only in garments suited for the warm embrace of their homeland, found themselves shivering, unprepared for the sudden descent into a chill that enveloped them as the sun dipped below the horizon.

The journey's relentless pace came to an abrupt halt, and the vehicle's engine stopped its steady rumble, cutting through the evening's silence. With a swift motion, the two British officers exited the Land Rover, their forms momentarily silhouetted against the fading light. They had arrived in a small town, a modest constellation of shops dotted the landscape, starkly contrasting the vast, open spaces they had traversed.

Curiosity stirred within the local populace as the vehicle's back canvas was slightly drawn back, revealing its human cargo to the fleeting glances of those nearby. A shop owner, drawn by the unusual sight, ventured closer, his inquiry hanging in the air. "What do you have there?" The driver's response was curt and devoid of any semblance of empathy. "Prisoners," he declared, as if the word were a shield against further questioning.

The British officers took turns disappearing into the bush, seeking momentary respite, while Me-Katilili and Wanje watched, their presence reduced to mere spectacles in their captors' eyes. Upon their return, the men indulged in a brief reprieve, consuming food and drink with a casual disregard for the hunger and thirst that gnawed at their prisoners.

With the vehicle refueled, the journey resumed with a jolt, the Land Rover lurching forward into the night, leaving behind the small town and any fleeting hope for compassion or mercy. Me-Katilili and Wanje denied even the most basic human kindnesses and were left to endure the cold, their bodies and spirits tested by the ordeal, yet unbroken. In the silence that followed, their resolve hardened, a silent vow shared between them that this journey, no matter how arduous, would not define their spirit nor diminish the fire of hope that burned within.

The sun set and rose again. The emotional toll of their captivity weighed heavily on Me-Katilili and Wanje. Each moment of silence was filled with reflections on their journey, the memories of their people, and the uncertain future ahead. Yet, even in their darkest moments, their bond remained unbroken, their shared resolve a source of comfort and strength. The journey to their unknown destination was a trial of endurance. The rugged terrain and their cuffs constantly reminded them of their plight. Yet, amidst the adversity, moments of defiance shone through, each act of resistance a testament to their unbreakable will.

The vehicle came to its final halt. The uncertainty of their new circumstances loomed large, yet Me-Katilili and Wanje faced it with an unwavering resolve. "We may be far from our land, but our spirit remains with our people," Me-Katilili whispered, her voice steady despite the weariness that clung to her.

Wanje, his gaze fixed on the horizon, nodded in agreement. "Our struggle does not end here. It lives on in the hearts of our people," he replied, his voice resolute.

As the soldiers led away from the vehicle, the weight of their journey was evident in their every step, but Me-Katilili and Wanje remained undaunted. Though fatigued, their eyes burned with an undimmed light - the light of resistance that no force could extinguish.

In the face of adversity, their spirits remained unyielding, their resolve unshaken. The journey ahead was fraught with uncertainty, yet they stepped forward with the knowledge that their fight was part of a larger struggle - a struggle for freedom, dignity, and the right to live on their terms. In their hearts, the voices of their people continued to sing, a chorus of hope and defiance that would carry them through the darkest of times, a reminder that even in captivity, they were never truly alone.

The grueling journey from Malindi to Kisii, a stretch spanning over 900 kilometers, was nothing short of a test of endurance and spirit for Me-Katilili and Wanje. They were confined to the merciless bare floor of a dilapidated vehicle; their bodies jostled and jarred by the relentless bumpy, dusty roads that seemed to stretch into infinity. The wear and tear of this arduous journey were visibly etched on their attire, a mere shadow of what it once was. Wanje was cloaked in remnants of a once vibrant blue cloth, now torn and soiled, paired with what used to be a pristine white cloth wrapped around his waist, now tainted by the harshness of their travels. Me-Katilili, on the other hand, adorned herself with a traditional *kisuthu*, draped gracefully above her breast, and her *hando* skirt, now reduced to tatters. The chilly embrace of the evening air was an unwelcome companion, its cold fingers piercing through their light, worn clothing.

Kisii (Getembe), Gusii land, Nyanza Province

In the heart of Gusii land, where the whispers of their ancestors lingered through the lush highlands, and the skies weep with rain that nourishes the earth, Kisii town - once known as Getembe - holds stories of resilience and transformation. The presence of *'Abasongo'* or the British, marked a new era for the indigenous Gusii people. This era saw the merging of worlds and the challenging of ancient traditions.

In their strategic retreat from the battles at Lake Victoria, the British found refuge in these lands, planting the seeds of colonial dominance amidst the green embrace of Kisii. They brought faces unfamiliar to the Gusii - Nubians, Maragoli, Baganda, and Suba - each group playing a role in the new societal fabric woven under colonial rule. While some of these newcomers found a way to blend their stories with those of the Gusii, others, like the Nubi, remained distinct, a reminder of the diverse identities that Kisii town would become.

The British viewed the warrior spirit of the Abagusii as a threat to their control, responding with punitive measures that sought to break the will of a people born on the earth they fought to protect. Despite the adversity, the heart of Kisii remained untamed, its climate a mirror of the resilience of its people. Nestled within the hills, the town thrived under a tropical highland climate, a sanctuary from floods, its atmosphere charged with the frequent rumblings of thunderstorms, a testament to the vibrant life force of the region.

Using similar tactics as on Mijikenda, the British quest to quell any form of resistance and solidify their dominion, the British launched targeted raids against the Abagusii. These raids were not merely military maneuvers but calculated efforts to strike at the heart of the community's way of life. By seizing cattle, the British aimed to cripple the economy, diminish the warriors' status, and erode the social structure that had sustained the Abagusii for generations. The cattle, revered and central to the

Abagusii culture, were not just economic assets but symbols of wealth, power, and prestige. The loss of livestock to British raids was a blow to the community's morale, a theft of their heritage, and a clear message of dominance.

Despite their valiant efforts to defend their land and way of life, the Abagusii found themselves ensnared in the oppressive web of colonialism. The British, leveraging their military might and technological superiority, invaded Abagusii territory, expropriating land and imposing their will with relentless zeal. The sovereignty of the Abagusii was usurped, their lands annexed, and their autonomy eroded as the British colonial machinery ground forward, indifferent to the cultural devastation in its wake.

Compelled by circumstances beyond their control, the colonialists coerced some of the Abagusii into serving those who had usurped their lands and disrupted their ancestral way of life. The British, exploiting the very people they had subjugated, imposed labor and taxation systems designed to extract maximum economic value while ensuring submissiveness. For the Abagusii, this was a bitter pill to swallow; to work for the very architects of their suffering was a daily reminder of the loss of their freedom and dignity.

An undercurrent of resistance and resentment marked the relationship between the Abagusii and the British. Though forced to navigate the realities of colonial imposition, the Abagusii never fully consented to British rule. The flames of defiance and the yearning for self-determination continued to burn in the depths of their hearts. The British had invaded their land, plundered their resources, and sought to dismantle their cultural identity, but the spirit of the Abagusii, tempered in the forge of adversity, remained unbroken.

This tumultuous era, characterized by conflict and cultural upheaval, laid bare the stark disparities between colonial ambition and indigenous resilience.

The Abagusii, like many other communities subjected to the colonial yoke, faced immense challenges.

Sakawa the Abagusii Diviner

Sakawa, the visionary seer, was the architect of destiny for the Bantu Abagusii people. Esteemed for his deep communion with the invisible realms, Sakawa stood as a pillar of wisdom and peace. His foresight into the impending colonial invasion and the resultant tumult was far more than a simple caution; it was a clarion call to the essence of his people, urging them to brace for the looming challenges. Through his eyes, the future unfolded not just as a series of frightening events but as a battleground for resilience, a testament to the strength and spirit of the Abagusii.

Sakawa's influence grew, and his name became synonymous with foresight and preserving Gusii's heritage. His prophetic gift foresaw the arrival of two souls from afar, a female diviner and a medicine man, whose fates were entwined with the well-being of Getembe, later renamed Kisii. The spirits and ancestors were clear in their directive to Sakawa: these individuals must not be held in Getembe, for their detention would spell calamity for the land and its people.

In a move that would set the wheels of fate in motion, Sakawa summoned Morani, a young man whose loyalty to the British had placed him in a unique position. This meeting, shrouded in the secrecy of sacred duty, was a testament to Sakawa's strategy. He recognized the value in Morani, a bridge between two worlds whose actions could alter the course of history.

Morani, aware of the reverence accorded to Sakawa, approached the meeting with a mix of curiosity and apprehension. The seer, with the tranquility that had come to define him, laid bare the urgency of the message from the spirits. He spoke of the diviner and the medicine man, warriors of the spirit, whose presence in Getembe was a harbinger of change. Sakawa entrusted Morani with a mission of paramount importance, a task that would challenge his allegiances and test the very fabric of his being. As Morani left Sakawa's presence, the weight of his newfound responsibility bore down on him. The town of Getembe, the current Kisii, with its verdant hills and storied past, stood at the precipice of a new chapter - a chapter that would be shaped by the actions of a young man caught between loyalty and destiny. The seer's mandate was clear, and the path ahead, fraught with uncertainty, promised to redefine Getembe's legacy and the destiny of its people.

Upon arriving the Kisii detention camp, they were greeted by an atmosphere of despair and desolation. The camp, an isolated enclave, seemingly detached from the world, was alive with the sounds of barking dogs and the wailing of prisoners - each cry a haunting reminder of the camp's grim purpose. This place, initially carved out by British soldiers in retreat from the advancing German army's heavy gunfire during the Great War, bore the scars of its turbulent beginnings. Its L-shaped structure loomed ominously, a project of containment still under construction, its incomplete form a testament to the ongoing conflict and the British effort to suppress the burgeoning spirit of anti-colonial resistance, which would eventually later fuel the Mau-Mau uprising among other rebellions.

The atmosphere was charged with tension as the camp official, upon unfolding the letter handed to him by the driver, announced with a tone of caution, "A woman, and a man, notorious for their escapades along the coast." This proclamation stirred a whirlwind of curiosity within the ranks of the soldiers. A figure stood out among them, accompanied by a vigilant guard dog, who, with a head tilt, questioned, "A woman?" The driver nodded, "Indeed, she is the leader and mastermind behind their schemes."

The directive that followed was issued with cold efficiency, stripping the moment of any shred of compassion, "Escort them to cell 9." Ethel, the stern overseer of the detention facility, interjected.

"By the letter of our regulations, cohabitation is prohibited - firstly due to their differing genders, and secondly, because they're suspected to be in collusion, to be confined in the same cell," objected the soldier, the guard dog at his side sensing the growing intensity.

"Then segregate them!" Ethel's command cut through the air like a blade.

"Commander, our cells are at capacity. The troublemakers from the Mount Kenya region have overwhelmed our facilities! Moreover, we're grappling with a cholera outbreak in several cells," the prison clerk interjected, his presence near Ethel underscored by the urgency of the situation.

As guards forcibly ushered Me-Katilili and Wanje into their cell, Ethal's voice dripping with sarcasm remarked, "This is where notorious criminals like you end up. I'm sure you'll find it to your liking."

The local guards, natives of Abagusii, dressed in ill-fitting khaki shorts and oversized shirts, were complicit in their silence, their underpaid servitude a stark reminder of the colonial hierarchy. Questions about the duration of their imprisonment were met with a chilling response from a British official, "Nothing less than five years… if they survive. Or for life..." The implications hung heavily in the air as they were led, still shackled, through the dim corridors of the detention camp, past the agonized faces of other prisoners and the menacing snarls of the kennel dogs, to their designated cell.

Cell 9 was a void of despair, its dark, cold interior punctuated only by the stench of decay. The moist earth floor and a lone clay pot, meant to serve as a latrine, were the only "amenities" provided. The walls, adorned with dried blood markings, told tales of unspeakable horrors that had transpired within these confines. A British soldier slammed the iron barrier shut with a resounding thud and secured the lock, leaving an echo in the prisoner's mind. A momentary silence fell before a young native Abagusii guard hesitantly stepped forward to offer them a meager meal of bananas and water from a calabash.

"My son," Me-Katilili began, her voice a blend of maternal warmth and unwavering resolve, "where I come from, many men like you are murdered by the invaders." Her attempt to forge a connection was abruptly cut short by the young guard's command for silence, yet her words, "I am a mother fighting for you so that we don't all perish," spoken with tears in her eyes, resonated with a poignant urgency.

The young guard's hasty departure left Me-Katilili and Wanje enveloped in the pervasive cries and groans emanating from the other cells, a harrowing symphony of suffering. Yet, in the depths of their despair, they found solace in prayer. Their voices joined in a fervent appeal to *Mulungu* and the ancestors for divine intervention, and their spirits intertwined in a bond of shared hope and unyielding resilience.

As dawn unfurled its first light over the Kisii detention camp, a hazy veil of unease settled over the landscape, presaging a day that would etch itself into the annals of history with the sharpness of a double-edged sword. For Me-Katilili and Wanje, the relentless passage of time within their cell had blurred the line between hope and despair, making each day indistinguishable from the last, save for the subtle shifts in the air that hinted at the world beyond their imprisonment.

The British soldiers, embodiments of colonial dominion, commenced their customary morning rounds with mechanical precision, their boots thudding against the earth in a rhythm of authority and control. The sound reverberated through the camp, a constant reminder of the oppressive force that governed their lives. Following closely behind, the local guards received their training, instilling in them the techniques and discipline required to maintain order, an order imposed by foreign rulers upon a land that once thrived under the stewardship of its indigenous peoples.

As evening approached, cloaked in the cool embrace of twilight, a young guard, his features softened by the fading light, made his way to cell number 9. The lock clicked open, and he presented Me-Katilili and Wanje with their modest dinner: maize pulp and bananas. This simple offering belied the complexity of the moment that was about to unfold. Seizing the opportunity, Me-Katilili, with a resolve that expressed strength from the very earth beneath her feet, "I have a message for the great diviner of your people," her voice a whispered force. In a gesture that bridged worlds, she plucked a lock of her hair, and then, with a nod of silent understanding, Wanje did the same. These strands, imbued with their spirit and resolve, were placed in the palm of the young guard, a tangible symbol of their plea to the unseen forces that moved within their homeland.

Upon receiving this sacred charge, Sakawa, the revered diviner, acted with the urgency of one who understands the delicate balance between the seen and unseen worlds. In the seclusion of his dwelling, he brewed a potent concoction of herbs, the aroma filling the space with a sense of ancient wisdom and power. This elixir, encapsulated in a small fruit shell and sealed with leaves, was a testament to the enduring connection between the people and their ancestral land. Entrusting it to Morani with instructions that carried the weight of centuries, Sakawa set in motion events that would challenge the very foundations of the colonial apparatus.

"Handle with care. This is for those greedy Abasongo (white men in the Gusii language)," Sakawa instructed, his words a blend of caution and resolve. He entrusted Morani with further instructions. "Tell the two to run towards the sunrise and never to be seen here again. The ancestors have spoken. They should never speak a word of this; otherwise, it will cost us precious lives, which is not a fair treat after saving theirs."

The following days unfolded with the monotony that had characterized life in the camp. The hours stretched into an eternity, marked only by the sun's changing position in the sky. Yet, beneath this veneer of normalcy, currents of change were stirring, their potency yet to be unleashed.

As night descended again, a different guard delivered their dinner that evening, the silence between them heavy with unspoken words. The British soldiers, vigilant in their routine, conducted their rounds, the clinking of keys a reminder of the chains that bound the people's spirit to the will of their oppressors.

The morning that followed broke with an unusual quiet that enveloped the camp in a silence that spoke volumes. The sun, climbing higher in the sky, cast its light on a scene that deviated from the colonial masters' script of subjugation. The British soldiers and native guards awoke to a world that appeared to resist their awakening. The officials' minds were clouded, and their bodies were unwilling to move.

It was in this state of confusion and drowsiness, a battle against the fog that clouded their consciousness, that the absence was discovered. Cell 9, securely locked yet hauntingly empty, stood as a silent testament to the defiance of the human spirit, a defiance that had outwitted the colonial machinery. The alarm that ensued was not merely a signal of escape but a clarion call that resonated deep within the hearts of those who had been silenced. The other prisoners, initially unaware of the cause of the tumult, soon joined in a chorus of jubilation and slogans, their voices rising in unison: "Freedom to our people, freedom to our land!" The gunfire that sought to silence them only served to amplify their resolve; each shot a punctuation mark in the narrative of resistance they were authoring collectively.

Escape from Kisii detention camp

Embarking on their escape under the shroud of night, Me-Katilili and Wanje carried with them no more than the essentials for survival: gourds filled with life-sustaining water and sour milk alongside a modest supply of sorghum bread that was handed to them by an unfamiliar man. These humble provisions marked the totality of their worldly possessions as they ventured into the unknown, guided only by the faint light of the stars and the deep, instinctual desire for freedom. The terrain underfoot was treacherous, uneven, and unforgiving, their path illuminated only by the occasional glimmer of moonlight piercing through the dense canopy of trees overhead. Each step forward was a testament to their resolve, their feet bearing the brunt of the harsh landscape with bruises and wounds as silent witnesses to their plight.

Despite the physical agony, the threat of being pursued by the British soldiers injected their weary bodies with a surge of adrenaline, propelling them forward through the darkness. As the first tendrils of dawn stretched across the sky, painting the world in shades of gold and crimson, they adjusted their course, steering towards the nascent sun with a determination that seemed to transcend their human limitations.

Their journey was a relentless push against the natural elements, a passage through the heart of the wilderness that demanded every ounce of their strength and cunning. They navigated through dense forests, where the air was thick with the sounds of unseen creatures, and across vast plains that stretched out like an endless sea of grass while avoiding the lurking dangers of wild animals and the prying eyes of human settlements. It was a voyage through the very essence of nature's untamed beauty and ferocity. When the sun had ascended to its zenith, casting a blanket of heat upon the earth, Me-Katilili and Wanje allowed themselves a moment of respite. Sheltered beneath the boughs of a solitary tree, they partook of their meager rations. The water and sour milk provided a brief solace from their thirst, and the sorghum bread a fleeting relief from their hunger. Their bodies were a landscape of exhaustion and resilience, worn and battered yet unyielding in their quest for liberty.

In the sanctuary of their makeshift haven, Wanje took on the role of healer, his hands skilled in the ancient art of herbal medicine. He foraged the surrounding area, returning with plants known for their curative properties. With a practitioner's care, he prepared remedies to ease their physical sufferings, his actions a quiet ode to the enduring spirit of survival. "My sister," he whispered, his voice carrying the weight of their shared ordeal, "our journey is long, and our path is strewn with challenges yet unseen. But we are far from defeated."

Me-Katilili, with a resolve as steadfast as the rising sun, responded, "The diviner's wisdom has set us on this path, and it is by the grace of God and the guidance of our ancestors that we shall persevere." She stepped away, her silhouette framed against the sun's light, as she invoked the blessings of their forebears, her voice a soft murmur blending with the rustle of the leaves.

Fortified by their brief rest and Wanje's herbal concoctions' healing properties, they set forth once more, their eyes fixed on the horizon, where the sun heralded the promise of a new day. Their strategy was to shadow the path of the "iron snake," the railway, a symbol of the invaders' presence, and maintain a cautious distance to avoid detection.

As dusk enveloped the land, casting its cloak of shadows and cooling the scorched earth, Me-Katilili and Wanje sought refuge for the night. The darkness brought the threat of animal and human predators, compelling them to find a safe place. They discovered a small cave, a natural fortress at the base of a hill, where they crafted a barrier from branches, a primitive yet effective defense against the dangers that prowled in the night.

With the break of dawn as their signal, they resumed their odyssey, each step a stride towards freedom, each breath a testament to their unbreakable will. Vast and wild, the land around them was both adversary and ally, a constant reminder of the fragility of life and the indomitable strength of the human spirit. Under the relentless African sun, Me-Katilili and Wanje's journey morphed into a saga of survival, resilience, and the quest for freedom. With the vast landscape stretching before them, each step was a leap of faith, a move away from their past entrapments towards an uncertain future. They navigated through the wilderness with a wary eye, avoiding the telltale signs of human settlements and the potential wrath of British soldiers and colonial patrol police.

Their path paralleled the colonial railway's skeletal framework, an iron artery cutting through the heart of their homeland. They subsisted on nature's generosity, plucking wild fruits that burst with sweetness on their parched tongues and wrapping their lips around leaves that dripped with dew at dawn. Rivers and streams became sanctuaries where they could quench their thirst and wash away the grime of their toil. As they ventured further, the climate began its gradual transformation. The air thickened with warmth, and the lush greens gave way to expansive fields that stretched towards the horizon. From their hidden vantage points, they glimpsed the colonial agricultural enterprise in full swing - plantations of tea, coffee, sugar cane, and cotton painting the landscape in varied hues. The sight of native workers, bent and broken under the oppressive yoke of British supervision, ignited a fire of rage in Me-Katilili's heart. She muttered curses under her breath, each word a venomous dart aimed at their oppressors.

"Look at them, Wanje," she whispered fiercely, her eyes never leaving the toiling figures in the distance. "Stripped of their dignity, laboring on their own land as if they were strangers."

Wanje's gaze was downcast, and he nodded. "It's a sight that wounds the soul," he agreed, his voice laced with sorrow.

Amidst the sprawling fields, Me-Katilili's thoughts drifted to her son, Katilili, and her brother, Kithi. The possibility that they might be among those trapped in the colonial machinery haunted her. The thought of calling out to them, of potentially reuniting, however fleeting, spurred a storm of emotions within her.

"My heart aches, Wanje," she confided, her voice cracking with emotion. "Each face I see from afar, I wonder... could it be Katilili? ... Or Kithi, now aged and worn out by years we have not shared?"

Wanje placed a comforting hand on her shoulder. "We carry them in our hearts, Me-Katilili. And in our fight for freedom, we honor their spirits."

The Akamba's hospitality

Their journey led them across arid plains where the earth cracked under the sun's scrutiny, and water scarcity tested their limits. Faced with the dire need for sustenance, Me-Katilili decided to approach an Akamba village, her declaration of peace echoing with a blend of desperation and hope.

"I come in peace," she announced boldly at the village's edge, her arms raised in a universal gesture of surrender and goodwill. Wanje, perched in a nearby tree, arrow nocked to bow, watched over her with the intensity of a guardian spirit, prepared to defend at the first sign of hostility.

The villagers' initial wariness gave way to curiosity as they surrounded Me-Katilili. The air vibrated with the sound of the *kivoti* flute, summoning the council of elders to deliberate their response. Me-Katilili, drawing upon her repertoire of gestures, shared their harrowing tale. Though foreign to the Akamba tribe, her words were laced with a universal pain and hope that transcended language barriers.

"We seek only water... and a moment's rest," she pleaded, her eyes scanning the faces of the elders, searching for a sign of empathy.

Wanje, from his leafy concealment, remained vigilant, the bowstring taut between his fingers, a silent promise of protection.

After a hushed consultation, the council of elders, *Atumia ma Thome*, signaled their acceptance. "Let them be welcomed," the chief elder declared, his voice carrying the weight of authority and compassion. "We are all children of this land."

Relief washed over Me-Katilili as Wanje descended from his perch, his weapons laid aside as a gesture of trust. They were ushered into the heart of the village, where they were offered water that tasted of the earth and food that spoke of the villagers' simple generosity. The beans and vegetables, though humble, were a feast for their depleted bodies.

As night enveloped the village, Me-Katilili and Wanje were granted a place to rest, a respite from their endless journey. The distant roars of lions and the subtle rustle of elephant grass outside the village boundaries reminded them of the awaited wilderness. Yet, for a brief moment, they found solace in the kindness of strangers, a shared bond of humanity that offered a glimmer of hope in the darkest times.

Though their hearts were heavy with the burden of their quest, the simple acts of kindness they had encountered lightened them. In the Akamba village, under a sky punctuated by the timeless dance of stars, Me-Katilili and Wanje found not just shelter but a renewed sense of purpose. Their journey was far from over, but the path ahead seemed a little less daunting, buoyed by the knowledge that they were not alone, even in the vastness of their struggle.

The first light of dawn caressed the Ukambani landscape, Me-Katilili and Wanje found solace under the sprawling branches of a short acacia tree. In the serene embrace of the morning, they engaged in a quiet meditation, their hearts and spirits intertwined in prayer. This moment of reflection was their way of preparing to bid farewell to the Akamba villagers who had extended their kindness and hospitality, a rare solace in their tumultuous journey. The villagers intrigued, and somewhat in awe, observed them from a respectful distance - their curiosity piqued by these strangers who had suddenly become part of their community's narrative.

As they rose to express their gratitude and continue on their path, a middle-aged man in a sisal kilt approached them. His demeanor was one of respectful urgency as he gestured towards the left, beckoning them to follow. With cautious steps and silent understanding, Me-Katilili and Wanje complied, their curiosity mingling with a sense of anticipation. They were led to a secluded area that radiated authority and tradition. At its heart sat the chief of the Akamba tribe, his presence commanding yet welcoming. He sat ensconced on a sizeable woven chair that seemed to hold the stories of generations. Beside him, a gracefully poised woman, likely his consort, shared the dais, her gaze kind and observant. A circle of elders completed the assembly, each embodying the wisdom and experience of their people.

The chief's voice resonated with the weight of authority as he addressed the gathering. Confronted with the challenge of a language barrier, he quickly dispatched his aides to fetch a translator. Upon the translator's arrival, the dialogue resumed, yet Me-Katilili and Wanje found themselves navigating through a linguistic maze. The translator's speech was a complex of Kiswahili, Akamba, and sprinkles of Mijikenda dialect, all delivered with a distinct Akamba inflection. Despite the confusion, Me-Katilili and Wanje managed to grasp enough Bantu words, piecing together the fragmented sentences. This effort to understand marked a delicate bridge, connecting their divergent worlds across the expanse of cultural and linguistic divides.

"My chief says you can stay longer," the translator conveyed, his eyes flickering between the chief and the guests. Again, the chief's voice filled the air, and the translator relayed, "He says you are powerful people of great knowledge. It would please him if you exchange knowledge. Our great healers and diviners were captured during a raid, and our village now has little knowledge."

Me-Katilili and Wanje exchanged a glance, a silent conversation passing between them in the comfort of their native Giriama. After a moment of contemplation, Me-Katilili responded, her voice firm yet imbued with the warmth of gratitude. "We appreciate your hospitality, and to show our gratitude, we will share our knowledge. However, please note that our knowledge shall never be used to harm the natives. Neither should it be given to foreigners of this land."

The chief nodded in agreement, a gesture of respect and understanding sealing their pact. In the days that followed, Me-Katilili and Wanje became teachers and students, sharing the wealth of their knowledge with three men and a woman selected by the Akamba tribe. They delved into the secrets of medicinal plants, unraveling the mysteries of healing and disease, and imparted wisdom on communicating with the spiritual realm. This exchange was not just a transfer of knowledge but a fusion of cultures, a testament to the power of unity and shared human experience.

In gratitude for their generosity, the Akamba tribe offered gifts of sustenance and protection. Water, food, and antivenin became their provisions against the perils of the journey ahead. Items of clothing, including a heavy blanket, were given to shield them from the elements, while weapons ensured their safety. Wanje's bow and arrow, symbols of his strength and skill, were returned to him, a gesture of trust and respect. As the time came for Me-Katilili and Wanje to depart, two young men from the village escorted them beyond the boundaries of the Akamba lands. This farewell was marked not by sadness but by a profound sense of mutual respect and hope. The knowledge they exchanged had woven a bond of indelible strength, a bridge across the chasms of difference.

As they stepped back into the wilderness, Me-Katilili and Wanje carried with them not just the physical gifts of the Akamba people but the intangible wealth of shared wisdom and the promise of enduring connections. Their journey was far from over, but the legacy of their encounter with the Akamba tribe would remain a beacon of light, guiding them through the darkness of their quest and beyond.

Meanwhile, Mulewa is being captured

Mulewa wa Duka was engulfed in a sea of despair following the imprisonment of his wife, Me-Katilili; she was not only his life partner but also his closest ally and friend. He approached the council of elders earnestly, urging them to devise strategies to free Me-Katilili and Wanje from the cold, unforgiving cells of Kisii Prison. Mulewa, with a mind as fertile as the lands he cultivated, proposed a myriad of schemes and plans in his quest for their freedom. Yet, amidst this turmoil, he did not falter in his duties as the family's provider. Tasked with the well-being of his children and Kavunje, his second wife, he poured his energy into the land, farming with a diligence that served as a balm for his wounded heart, a distraction from the relentless ache of his loss.

When the delicate hues of dawn began to cast their light across the landscape of Mulewa wa Duka's ancestral home, the world seemed to pause in reverence. Mulewa, a man whose soul was as intertwined with the earth as the crops he nurtured, led a life deeply rooted in the essence of his heritage, his family, and the age-old traditions that had been the compass for his forebears. Renowned for his steadfast commitment to his eleven children,

Mulewa stood as a towering figure of strength and insight within his community, embodying the enduring resilience and vibrant spirit that defined his people.

Every day, upon returning from the fields or a hunt, Mulewa brought small tokens of nature's bounty to his children, whom he affectionately called "*Mbeyu mbidzo*" - his great seeds. He was not just their father; he was their mentor, imparting lessons on farming, hunting, and the wisdom of their forefathers. Mulewa's teachings were not confined to skills and traditions; they were imbued with stories of their ancestors, the importance of community, and warnings of the encroaching dangers posed by colonial invaders. Despite his outward strength, Mulewa carried a silent sorrow for Katilili, his first child lost to the cruelties of life, and his first wife, his life partner, and best friend, Me-Katilili, being arrested and sent to prison in a very distant place. Though often masked by the day's duties, his pain found solace in the palm wine company and the village elders' shared understanding at the end of the day.

On a day that began like any other, with the land bathed in the soft glow of morning, an ominous shadow loomed on the horizon. The British colonial forces, driven by the insatiable demands of the First World War, descended upon Mulewa's village with a cold, calculated intent. The morning's tranquility was shattered, replaced by chaos that threatened to upend the community's very foundation.

Mulewa and thirteen other men stood firm, their hands still stained with the soil of their labor as the colonial forces encircled them. The air was tense, a palpable force that seemed to choke the courage from the bravest of hearts. Yet, Mulewa's voice rose above the clamor, a beacon of defiance in adversity. "Our spirit cannot be caged," he declared, his eyes burning with a resolve that belied his calm demeanor.

The capture was swift, a blur of motion that saw Mulewa and his brethren bound and led away from their ancestral lands. As they were marched through fields once tended with love and care, the reality of their plight sank in. They were to be porters and laborers, tools of the force that sought to erase their identity and break their spirit.

Yet, in the darkest moments, Mulewa's resolve only strengthened. He became a pillar of hope among his fellow captives, reminding them of the strength in their bonds to each other and their land. "Remember who we are," he would say under the cloak of night. "We are the children of the Mijikenda land, and like the seeds we sow, we shall find a way to grow, no matter the soil we find ourselves in. We shall return!"

Taita Taveta, the neighbors on the hills

Traversing across diverse terrains, they journeyed through the highlands and the expansive plains, ventured into the depths of forests and across the vast savannahs. Their path took them over lands nurtured by the Agikuyu, Maasai, and Akamba peoples. Finally, their expedition led them to the verdant, undulating hills of Taita Taveta, a mosaic of natural beauty and cultural heritage. Through the verdant landscapes of the Taita Taveta Hills, Me-Katilili and Wanje pressed on, their journey marked by the resilience of the human spirit against the backdrop of colonial upheaval. The rich and fertile hills whispered of a time when the land was untouched by the iron grip of foreign dominion. From their hidden vantage points, they watched the "iron snake" carve its path through the earth, a constant reminder of the changes that had swept across their homeland.

As they journeyed forth, they crossed paths with the members of the Taita Taveta tribe, a people known for their humility and warmth. The Taita Taveta people initially met them with cautious reserve. However, the air soon filled with a burgeoning sense of mutual respect and understanding. Under the canopy of night, they were offered shelter and sustenance alongside other hospitalities. Gathered around the fires, which danced like hopeful flames against the dark, they shared tales, beliefs, and wisdom that bridged the gaps between their distinct cultures. The Taita Taveta folk bestowed Me-Katilili and Wanje guidance toward the Mijikenda lands. They also advised them to forge eastward but to steer clear of the railway lest they find themselves at the bustling port of Mombasa.

Amidst these instances of profound connection, an undercurrent of disquiet lingered in Me-Katilili's soul. She repeatedly confided in Wanje, her words heavy with an ominous foreboding - an unshakeable and persistent shadow of dread that clung to her spirit.

"I am afraid I have a terrible feeling that my family is not well," she confessed, the weight of her anxiety palpable in the silence that followed her words.

Wanje, ever the steadfast companion, sought to offer reassurance. "Don't overthink," he advised gently. "Let us arrive safely first." His words were to comfort, yet the shadow of worry remained a silent specter that accompanied them on their journey.

"Wanje, you are a man of virtue, a very good man." Me-Katilili declared with sincere enthusiasm. "Taking my daughter's hand in marriage would fill me with immense honor, Me-Katilili her words imbued with profound gratitude."

Despite the Taita Taveta elders' fascination with Me-Katilili and Wanje and their invitation to extend their stay, the duo felt the urgent pull of their journey home. The time spent within the Taita Taveta village was brief, their departure hastened by Me-Katilili's growing apprehension for her family's well-being.

As they ventured closer to their homeland, the familiarity of the Mijikenda language wrapped around them like a warm embrace, a sign that they were nearing the end of their long journey. The ease with which they communicated with the Taitas Taveta in Giriama was a comforting reminder of their shared heritage, a beacon guiding them home.

Finally, after days and nights of relentless trekking, they arrived at Taru, a territory deeply rooted in Mijikenda culture. Overwhelmed with relief and gratitude, they sought the sacred *Kaya* forests, where they would share news of their return with the council of elders in secrecy, far from the prying eyes of the British.

Together with the diviners and special religious priests, they held a ceremony to thank *Mulungu*, the supreme God, and appease the spirits and ancestors for their protection throughout the journey. This moment of profound spiritual significance was a reconnection with their roots and the divine forces that had guided their steps. Yet, amidst the rituals of gratitude and renewal, Me-Katilili's heart was heavy with concern for her community, especially her children. The council's revelations shattered the fragile peace she had found upon her return. Her husband, Mulewa, along with thirteen other men, had been captured by the colonial forces, condemned to labor under the oppressive yoke of the British.

The news struck Me-Katilili like a physical blow, her worst fears realized in the stark reality of her people's suffering. The Mijikenda, once free to roam their lands and uphold their traditions, were now shackled by forced labor, foreign religions, and an alien culture that sought to erase their identity. Villages lay abandoned, homes stood incomplete, and the people were displaced to barren lands, all while British churches and offices rose from the ruins of their desecrated heritage.

The disaster that had befallen the Mijikenda during her absence was a wound that cut deep, a stark reminder of the price of resistance and freedom. Devastated by her people's plight, Me-Katilili found herself at a crossroads. Her journey had brought her back to a homeland forever altered, a community fractured by colonial ambition. Yet, within her burned the flame of defiance, a determination to reclaim the dignity and autonomy of the Mijikenda. Her return was not just a homecoming but a call to arms, a rallying cry for those who yearned to break the chains of oppression and restore the spirit of their people. The road ahead would be fraught with challenges. Still, Me-Katilili and Wanje were fortified by their experiences and the knowledge shared with allies along their journey back. They were ready to face whatever trials lay in store, united in their quest for justice and liberation.

CHAPTER 12

A Taste Of Peace

In the early days of 1914, a fleeting moment of tranquility unfolded, coinciding with the departure of the widely reviled Arthur Champion for a two-month respite. During his absence, J.M. Pearson assumed command, his attention fragmented by the looming responsibilities and preparations for a global conflict on the horizon. Pearson's lack of engagement with the local populace meant that the simmering tensions remained unprovoked, a stark contrast to the usual atmosphere of unrest.

However, this lull was abruptly disrupted upon Champion's return, invigorated from his hiatus. He orchestrated a meeting with Giriama elders, joined by Pearson and two other British officers, Logan and Taylor, at a colonial outpost in Vitengeni on 11th March 1913. With calculated guile, they sought to coerce the elders into swearing allegiance to the British crown through the highly revered *Fisi* (Hyena) oath during a ceremony scheduled in the hallowed grounds of *Kaya* Fungo the following day. Yet, the British were met with staunch resistance instead of submission. The Giriama elders, unyielding in their defiance, unleashed a barrage of insults towards Champion and Pearson, branding them as thieves and killers. This public affront left the British officers stunned.

In the aftermath, Taylor and Logan left posthaste, unable to shoulder the weight of their public disgrace. A fragile quietude settled over the region, a tense interlude that hung like a thin veil over the ensuing weeks, a testament to the unbroken spirit of the Agiriama and their relentless pursuit of sovereignty.

Arriving at Kilifi, from Kisii

Late April 1914, in Bungale village, the void left by Mulewa's absence carved deep into the fabric of the community, transforming Me-Katilili's once vibrant home into a silent testament of loss. The walls that had resonated with laughter and love now stood in stark silence, a reminder of the warmth and protection that once filled their spaces. Despite this, the community, bound by the strength and unity Mulewa had instilled, encircled Me-Katilili and her children with a solidarity that defied the bleakness of their reality. This circle of support was a beacon of hope, illuminating the resilience of a people who, even under the oppressive shadow of colonization, clung fervently to the roots of their traditions and the bonds that tethered them to one another.

In her most profound moments of despair, Me-Katilili found solace not only in the cherished memories of her husband's wisdom and unwavering affection but also in the indomitable spirit of her community. Their resolve to withstand the trials imposed upon them served as a wellspring of strength for Me-Katilili, inspiring her to confront the pain of her loss head-on. In her quest for closure and the sincere hope of reunion, Me-Katilili delved into the ancient practices of her ancestors, engaging in soul-search rituals that transcended the physical realm.

Secluded from the world's prying eyes, she called out to the essence of her husband, her voice a soft, haunting echo in the stillness, "My soulmate, my beloved, hear my plea. Return to me, for I am adrift without you. Your children yearn for your guidance; your people crave your wisdom. In the name of our undying love, I beckon you - come back to us."

Through the veil of the spiritual world, Me-Katilili sought communion with Mulewa, her incantations and offerings, a bridge between the living and the ethereal. The revelation that Mulewa's spirit lingered within the realm of the living ignited a flicker of hope, a promise of his presence still tethered to their world.

This ritual of seeking and communing with the spirits became a recurring solace for Me-Katilili, a way to touch the intangible and to keep the memory of her loved ones alive. The fate of Kithi, whose spirit also roamed the earthly plane, and Katilili, now among the ancestors, wove a complex narrative of loss and connection, of souls caught between worlds.

As the seasons ebbed and flowed, the village of Bungale bore the weight of absence, a collective yearning for the return of Mulewa and the other men who had vanished into the maw of uncertainty. Yet, amidst this landscape of longing, the enduring spirit of the community flourished with hope, steadfastness, and unyielding belief in the reunion of souls. This belief rich in the colors of perseverance and unity, stood as a testament to the power of love and tradition to transcend the barriers of time and circumstance, binding the hearts of the people to each other and to the essence of those they yearned for.

Devoted, back to more rallies

Fueled by a renewed sense of purpose and the deep-seated pain of their community's suffering, Me-Katilili and Wanje embarked on a vigorous campaign for liberation. They refused to succumb to the exhaustion that tugged at their limbs, choosing instead to harness the raw energy of their anguish and transform it into a catalyst for action. Alongside the *Chifudu* dancers and the *Mikushekushe* women's association, whose vibrant performances had long been a medium for storytelling and cultural expression within the Mijikenda community, they traversed the breadth of their homeland. Their journey took them from village to village: Marafa, Ulaya, Chakama, Mwange, Langobaya and many others, where they stood at the heart of each community, their voices ringing out with a message of resistance and unity.

Me-Katilili, with her commanding presence, captivated her audiences. She narrated tales of their ancestral strength with the harsh realities of their present circumstances. She spoke of the need to stand united against the British, reclaiming the autonomy they had wrestled from them through deceit and coercion. Her words, imbued with the passion of her convictions, stirred the hearts of those who listened, reigniting a flame of resistance that colonial oppression had sought to extinguish.

Yet, as they rallied their people, a chilling revelation came to light - traitors were among them. These betrayers had whispered the secrets of their resistance to the enemy, divulging the guerilla tactics that had once given them the element of surprise. The British, forewarned, had adapted their strategies, now shooting at the slightest hint of movement in the grasslands and bushes where the Mijikenda warriors lay in wait. The tactics that had once allowed them to strike with the stealth and precision of the hunter were now compromised, leaving them vulnerable to the firepower of their adversaries.

Before an expansive sea of attentive faces, she stood with an air of defiance, her voice echoing through the assembly. "It is a sorrow beyond measure," Me-Katilili proclaimed, her tone imbued with palpable grief, "that among us, there are those willing to trade our very essence - our blood, our land, our souls!"

Her eyes, piercing and resolute, swept across the crowd, settling with intention on Mtawa, Wanje wa Mugaya, and Ngonyo wa Mwavuo. At that moment, her gaze was an unspoken challenge, a mirror reflecting the weight of their choices. "What depth of despair must one plum to betray their kin?" she asked, letting the question hang in the air, a poignant pause that resonated in the collective conscience of those gathered. Raising her voice, she declared, "I, along with the elders, demand the return of the stipends you've received from Chembe." Her statement was a call to action, a plea for redemption. "And should fear grip your heart at the thought of returning these tokens of betrayal, know that I will bear that burden. I will return them myself."

In her assertion lay an unshakeable courage, "I fear neither weapon nor man, least of all Chembe! Who is he?" With a dismissive flick of her finger, she reduced the formidable Chembe to nothing more than a speck, an insignificant crumb to be brushed aside. "Merely a *Chembe* (meaning a crumb/a grain in Mijikenda language)," she stated, her gesture trivializing his presence as if he were no more than a grain, an imaginary crumb of inconsequence. At that moment, Me-Katilili stood as a beacon of resilience, her words a clarion call to reclaim dignity and defy subjugation.

This treachery cut deeper than any physical wound, for it was a betrayal of trust, shared heritage, and the collective struggle for freedom. Me-Katilili and Wanje realized these revelations' grave impact on their people's spirit. Fear had taken root, a pervasive dread that stifled the once fierce devotion to their cause. The *Kaya* forests, sacred groves that had served as bastions of their culture and spirituality, now lay deserted, a testament to the erosion of their way of life under the shadow of colonial rule.

Amidst these trials, Me-Katilili's resolve only hardened. She recognized that the path to liberation was fraught with obstacles, both from without and within. The challenge was not only to combat the physical might of the British but also to restore the unity and resolve of her people, to mend the fractures that fear and betrayal had wrought. With Wanje at her side, Me-Katilili embarked on a mission to rebuild the Mijikenda's bonds of trust and solidarity. They sought to weave together their community's frayed threads and inspire a renewed commitment to the struggle for freedom.

Through their words and actions, they aimed to demonstrate that their people's strength lay not in the secrecy of their tactics but in their unity and the righteousness of their cause.

Mulewa returns home

As the sun dipped below the horizon, drawing the curtain on the day, Me-Katilili, her co-wife Kavunje, and their children were steeped in the rhythm of their evening tasks within the confines of their homestead. The absence of Mulewa, their pillar, had compelled the family to adapt and weave a new tapestry of duties and roles amidst the void his departure had carved into their lives. Heavy and profound absence hung over them, a shadow that grew with each cycle of crops that sprouted and withered in the fields, each season passing without a trace of his return. Yet, as twilight cast its amber glow across the Mijikenda lands, a figure materialized on the horizon, his silhouette etching a stark line against the fiery earth beneath. Mulewa was returning, navigating the path back to the core of his family, his absence having stretched into what seemed an insufferable infinity. His arrival, both miraculous and wholly unforeseen, swept through the air, laden with the fragrance of night blooms, heralding his approach to the homestead, a flicker of hope in the dimming light.

Me-Katilili, Kavunje, and their children paused at the edge of their dwelling, the remnants of the day's labor slipping from their grasp as wonder and joy tangled in their gazes. There stood Mulewa, a breathing embodiment of their long-held prayers and the tender, secret hopes for a reunion. With hearts surging forward, they rushed to meet him, their steps a blend of haste and hesitance, casting playful shadows upon the earth as twilight embraced them. At this moment, under the watchful eye of the evening sky, the family was whole once more, their reunion a testament to enduring love and the unbreakable bonds of kinship.

Mulewa, once robust and full of life, now appeared frail, his body bearing the scars of enslavement and disease. Time and toil under the relentless sun of the Ramisi sugar plantations had weathered him, his skin etched with the dark patches of countless mosquito bites and the lingering frailty from battles with malaria and cholera.

This moment of reunion was a fragile bubble of joy in the harsh reality of their existence. Words were scarce as emotions overflowed, each touch and glance conveying the depth of their feelings more eloquently than any speech could. Mulewa's return was a personal victory and a symbol of defiance against the colonial forces that sought to break their spirits. Yet, even as they gathered around him, their laughter and tears a rare melody in the quiet of the evening, a shadow of fear lingered. The threat of informers, ever-present, cast a pall over their celebration. The joy of Mulewa's escape and return was tempered by the knowledge that their happiness could be swiftly crushed under the boot of colonial retribution. They celebrated in hushed tones, their happiness a secret kept close to their hearts, lest the winds carry their joy to the ears of those who would see them punished.

In the following days, the impact of Mulewa's ordeal and the resilience he demonstrated in returning to them ignited a renewed enthusiasm within Me-Katilili and the council of elders. They were reminded of the cruelty of their oppressors and the strength that lay within their people, a strength that no hardship could extinguish.

Together with the women's association *Mikushekushe* and the *Chifudu* dancers, Me-Katilili and Wanje resumed their mission with a passion that burned brighter against the backdrop of their triumphs and tragedies. They moved through the villages with a message of resistance, a call to arms against the colonial invaders who had taken so much from them. In hushed gatherings and through the power of dance and song, they spread the word, urging their people to stand up against the oppressors to reclaim their land and their dignity.

The journey was fraught with danger, the air thick with the tension of potential betrayal. Yet, amidst the fear and uncertainty, there was a glimmer of hope, a belief that together, united in their cause, they could overcome the shadows that sought to envelop them.

Relocation to Gede

Amidst the swirling mists of uncertainty and the palpable tension of potential treachery, Mulewa, alongside Me-Katilili, Kavunje - his second wife - and their unwed offspring, embarked on a cautious journey to the outskirts of Gede. Near the protective embrace of their eldest daughter's marital home, they sought refuge, a sanctuary against the looming threat of betrayal. This move, dictated by the stark necessity of safeguarding their family's welfare, underscored the precariousness of their existence in a world rife with distrust and hidden dangers. The specter of a traitor's whisper, potent enough to shatter the fragile peace they had reclaimed, loomed large over their heads, dictating their every decision with the weight of potential consequences.

In this new village, a beacon of hope and continuity emerged with the birth of a female child, a new link in the chain of their lineage. Me-Katilili, with a heart brimming with affection and memories of a bond forged in the fires of youth, bestowed upon her granddaughter the name Sayo in honor of her mother's cherished friend who was present during her birth and remained with her later, even after her mother's death. This act of naming was more than a tribute; it invoked the strength, resilience, and camaraderie that had defined her relationship with Sayo. The serendipity of resemblance between the young Sayo wa Kalama and Me-Katilili herself was striking, a mirror reflecting the physical attributes and the spirit of a lineage steeped in courage and wisdom.

From the tenderest of ages, Me-Katilili assumed the role of mentor and guide for Sayo, recognizing in her the spark of future leadership and the bearer of their ancestral legacies. Together, they ventured into the sacred depths of the sacred *Kaya* Forests, those hallowed grounds that held the secrets of their people. It was here, amidst the ancient trees and whispering spirits of the forest, that Me-Katilili imparted to Sayo the profound knowledge of their people's traditional medicine, the intricate heritage of their religion, and the rich heritage of their culture. These lessons, conveyed under the forest canopy, were not merely academic in nature but imbued with the essence of their ancestors' wisdom and the symbiotic relationship with the land that sustained them. Me-Katilili, with each word and gesture, wove the past with the present, instilling in Sayo a reverence for their traditions and an understanding of the interconnectedness of all life.

In Sayo, Me-Katilili saw the future - a continuation of a lineage that had weathered countless storms and emerged with the strength of the baobab. These teachings, passed from grandmother to granddaughter, were seeds planted in fertile soil, promising to blossom into a legacy of knowledge, resilience, and stewardship of their cultural heritage. Through Sayo, Me-Katilili's spirit and dedication to her people would continue to thrive, ensuring that the roots of their identity would stretch deep and unbroken into the generations to come.

Empowering speeches

Under the vast, open sky, where the whispers of the past meet the cries of the present, stood Me-Katilili, a figure of undeniable power and unwavering resolve. Her presence commanded attention, not merely for her physical strength, which spoke of years of toil and resilience, but for the fierce light of determination that blazed in her eyes. She was an upheaval of boldness, charisma, and unwavering conviction, her voice a clarion call that resonated across the lands, touching the hearts of her people with a fire that ignited their spirits and bound them in a shared purpose.

"As we stand upon this sacred ground, let it be known that beyond the divine - our God, our ancestors, and the spirits that guide us - nothing exists to instill fear in my heart. Not the might of man, nor the ferocity of beasts, nor the cold, unfeeling steel they wield," Me-Katilili proclaimed, her voice rising above the din of the gathering crowd, echoing off the trees and into the heavens. "With every ounce of my being, ancestors, I vow to safeguard this land. This land that nourishes us and holds our forebears' memories shall remain inviolate under my watch."

Her journey from village to village was not merely a series of rallies but a profound awakening, a revival of the spirit that had long defined her people. She laid bare the hidden, sinister intentions of the British colonizers; their guise of benevolence shattered by her words. "These foreigners, shrouded in their malevolence, seek to eradicate our essence, our culture and tradition, to uproot our faith, and to claim our sacred lands as their own. The blood of our brethren stains their hands, the innocence of our children defiled by their heinous acts," she cried out, her voice a meld of anguish and disgust.

"They come to us with tales of protection from foreign invaders, yet it is they who embody the greatest threat. And the religion they seek to impose upon us? Our hearts are already pledged to *Mulungu*, the supreme God who watches over us all. Their audacious claims of a singular God, as if it were their discovery, betray their ignorance. Even as they dispute with the Muslim Arabs, it becomes clear that at the heart of their faith lies a common belief. Yet, blinded by arrogance and greed, they remain embroiled in endless conflict," Me-Katilili declared, her insight piercing the veil of deception woven by the colonizers.

Her battle against the oppression wrought by the British was unyielding. She stood as an immovable force against the exploitation of her people, who were torn from their homes to toil in foreign lands, never to return. She railed against the taxation of their own soil, the seizure of their ancestral lands for the colonizers' plantations, and the erosion of their sovereignty. She spoke fervently of the need to reclaim their traditions, foster economic independence, and revive the rich heritage of African philosophy, culture, and spirituality.

"Our very existence is under siege by those who would see us stripped of our heritage, our lands, and our dignity. Yet within us lies the strength to rise, to reclaim that which is rightfully ours, and to restore the harmony of our world. We must protect the sanctity of our land, the purity of our water, and the myriad of lives that depend on us," she implored, her words resonating with the truth of her convictions.

She spoke of health, of protecting the young who are the future leaders of their land, and of the crucial role of women in guiding their families towards a path of resistance and empowerment. "We stand at a crossroads with the future of our people in our hands. It is up to us to shield our children, to nurture their spirits and minds, for they will carry the torch of our resistance, our hopes, and our dreams," Me-Katilili inspired, her message a beacon of hope in the shadow of oppression.

As her speeches spread from village to village, so did the spirit of defiance and unity she embodied. Men and women, young and old, took the oath of hyena 'Chiraho cha *Fisi*' and committed themselves to the struggle for freedom, empowered by Me-Katilili's indomitable will. Her vision of a people united in the face of tyranny, her dream of their land reclaimed and restored, became the rallying cry for a nation in the making. Me-Katilili, with her profound reverence for life, culture, and the divine, became not just a leader but a symbol of her people's enduring strength and resilience.

CHAPTER 13

A Traitor's Duty

As the sun dipped below the horizon, casting long shadows that danced upon the dusty earth, Ngonyo wa Mwavuo, his breaths quick and his purpose urgent, arrived at the doorstep of the British colonial administration's office. The knock that followed was not just a summons but the harbinger of a revelation that would ripple through the echelons of the colonial power structure. Inside, he was granted a private audience with Arthur Champion, the British assistant district commissioner, a meeting cloaked in secrecy and tension. Upon his departure, the news he bore set the stage for an encounter between Champion and his superior, Charles Hobley, who would seethe with disbelief and fury.

"That witch has returned! I've said it before; she's nothing short of a witch!" Arthur Champion, his voice a mixture of rage and disbelief, reported to Charles Hobley. Their offices, once halls of quiet bureaucracy, now echoed with the disruption of their discovery. A few months prior, a telegraph from Kisii detention camp had delivered the baffling news of Me-Katilili and Wanje wa Mwadorikola's mysterious disappearance from their cell. This cell remained locked before and after their disappearance, leaving no trace of their presence in Kisii or its environs. Given the daunting distance of over 900 kilometers from Kisii to Kilifi, the treacherous terrain, and the unforgiving wilderness, it had been naively assumed that a return to Kilifi was beyond the realm of possibility.

"How in the devil's name did she manage to return?" Hobley exclaimed, his words laced with a mix of astonishment and vexation.

"The means of their escape, it's beyond comprehension. And to think, they disappeared with that ... that diminutive sorcerer,"

Champion continued, his frustration boiling over as he recalled the humiliation he had suffered at the hands of Me-Katilili - his authority challenged, his pride wounded by her defiant act during a public confrontation that had led directly to her imprisonment.

"Wanje wa Madkoko...or whatever his name is," Hobley muttered, struggling with the unfamiliarity of the names that now symbolized an unprecedented challenge to their rule.

"And to hear them tell it, they flew here on a winnower! Such utter nonsense," Champion spat out, disbelief painting his features.

"Primitive idiocy," Hobley dismissed with a scoff, already considering their next move. "We must coordinate with the police to apprehend them once more."

"She ought to be executed, killed!" Champion suggested, the suggestion hanging in the air, heavy with the weight of its implications.

"No, Arthur. That course of action is off the table. Her death would incite her people to greater fury. They hold her in high esteem; killing her would only exacerbate our problems," Hobley reasoned, his mind already turning towards a solution that would neutralize the threat without martyring Me-Katilili. "We shall capture them again, but this time, we'll ensure their exile is to a place from which return is impossible. Kismayu in Somalia. Mmph... Nothing less than five years whatsoever. The conditions there are harsh and insurmountable. Survival is a rarity. And at their old age… I doubt they will ever come back."

With that, Hobley flipped through the pages of a file, his decision final. The fate of Me-Katilili and Wanje wa Mwadorikola was to be cast into the unforgiving landscape of Kismayu, a move they hoped would quell the rising tide of resistance.

Revolts of mid 1914

The Mijikenda lands, amidst the sacred groves of the *Kayas* and the vibrant tapestries of culture and tradition that defined their community, Me-Katilili's voice became the herald of a new dawn. With each rally she led, the ember of courage within the Agiriama was fanned into a blazing inferno of resolve and unity. Her return marked not just the resurgence of a leader, but the awakening of a collective spirit subdued under the weight of colonial oppression.

In the shadows, while they discreetly garnered intelligence from British administrators, likely via coerced laborers, a faction among their own betrayed their loyalty. These turncoats ferried secrets to the British, guided their strategies, and accepted bribes and allowances in exchange. A meeting was held late that evening.

Me-Katilili's voice, heavy with scorn, pierced the air, "Some among you have accepted a thousand rupees. For what purpose? To barter your souls? To trade the blood that runs through your veins? To betray your kin? To auction off the very land that sustains you? This is nothing short of blasphemy!"

Her tone hardened with conviction, "You traitors, we have not been blind to your treacherous plans - schemes to abduct our youth and consign them to chains far across the sea," she denounced, highlighting a grim reality of exploitation and deceit. "I repeat, I fear no man, weapon, or emperor. I only fear *Mulungu*, our supreme God." She affirmed.

The sacred *Kayas*, timeless sanctuaries nestled within the heart of ancient forests, pulsed with renewed vigor as Me-Katilili's impassioned words sparked a revival of the Mijikenda's sacred traditions and beliefs. Traditional education, which had dimmed under the oppressive shadow of colonial rule, now flared brightly once more, its embers stoked by the profound knowledge and insights Me-Katilili and Wanje wa

Mwadorikola brought back from their enigmatic odyssey from Kisii to Kilifi. They accounted lessons from diverse tribes, unveiling strategies, tactics, and armaments previously unknown to the Mijikenda, enriching their cultural bank. In turn, they had spread the wisdom of the Mijikenda everywhere, sowing seeds of unity and resilience against the harsh winds of adversity. Yet, the enigma of their escape was kept a fiercely guarded secret, a protective veil that shielded the community from the corrosive specter of treachery hiding in the penumbra.

Throughout their journey from Kisii, they learned the spirit of resistance was not unique to the Mijikenda. Across the lands, from the warlike Abagusii, renowned for their fierce protection of their cattle camps and autonomy, to the communities shadowed by the marvelous mountains - the Agikuyu, Embu, Meru, and Maasai - there stirred a collective defiance against the British yoke. Each community, though faced with the brutal realities of raids, imprisonment, and the theft of their lands and livestock, held fast to their heritage and their right to self-determination. In this crucible of colonial oppression, Me-Katilili emerged not just as a leader of the Mijikenda but as a symbol of unwavering resistance, her legacy a beacon for all those who dared to stand against the tyranny of conquest and to dream of freedom restored.

Recaptured

On 4th August 1914, beneath the relentless blaze of the sun, Me-Katilili and Wanje found themselves captured again in the meticulous plot woven by Hobley and Champion, their fate sealed as they were dispatched to a distant prison in Kismayu, Somalia. Their sentence was to span five long years, with freedom promised only as the late days of 1919 approached. The prison that awaited them was infamous for its cruel conditions and the mental anguish it inflicted upon its inmates. Positioned an arduous 900 kilometers away, their journey to captivity was a testament to human resilience against the stark backdrop of nature's extremes. The landscape transformed drastically beneath their weary feet, shifting from the lush greenery of their native land to a barren wasteland. Here, the sun's wrath was unrelenting, baking the earth to a crisp, while the nights offered scant respite from the sweltering days, weaving a tale of survival against the harshest of elements.

As they ventured further from Kilifi, the terrain became increasingly hostile - a vast canvas of sand dunes that shifted beneath the weight of their vehicle, challenging every mile they covered. The journey was fraught with obstacles; impassable paths choked with dust gave way to treacherous sands, their passage marked by frequent disputes between the driver and the soldier over the correct route and dwindling supplies. Water and food became scarce commodities, forcing them to resort to the meager sustenance of the cacti dotting the landscape. Mechanical failures plagued their vehicle, with flat tires halting their progress not once but twice and their equipment woefully inadequate for the repairs needed.

It was during one of these periods of enforced stillness, with the soldier struck down by illness, teetering on the brink of death, that Me-Katilili's compassion transcended the boundaries of captivity and enmity.

"My son, let me heal you. I am familiar with your affliction," she offered, her voice carrying the weight of empathy and wisdom honed through years of healing her people. The irony of addressing the foreign soldier as 'son' did not escape her, but her innate kindness overrode the strangeness of the situation. "But for my powers to work, you must free us from these bonds. Healing cannot flow through the shackled."

Reluctantly, driven by desperation, the soldier and the driver acquiesced, and together, Me-Katilili and Wanje, combining her ancestral knowledge with his medical expertise, pulled the soldier back from the clutches of death. This act of mercy, performed under the most improbable circumstances, not only saved a life but also forged a moment of human connection across the chasm of conflict and suspicion. Yet, their ordeal was far from over. The vehicle's fuel dwindled to nothing, stranding them in the desolate wilderness, miles from any sign of civilization. Days passed, each marked by the relentless sun by day and the cold embrace of the desert night until fate intervened in the form of Somali nomads. Initially hostile towards the British soldier and driver, the nomads were persuaded by Me-Katilili's pleas for mercy, her voice embodying the grace and dignity of her years and her cause.

Fortunately for Me-Katilili and Wanje, the nomads welcomed them into their fold. Fortunately, the nomads gave them water and sustenance, a kindness that felt like a balm to Me-Katilili and Wanje's weary spirits. It was here, amidst the nomads, that they shared the tale of their journey, their struggle for the freedom of their people, and the injustices visited upon their land. Wanje took the lead in these discussions, navigating the cultural norms that reserved public discourse for men. At the same time, Me-Katilili's presence - a matriarch of resilience and wisdom - lent silent support to their cause.

Their story, resonating with the nomads' own experiences of oppression, forged a bond of shared understanding and mutual respect. Me-Katilili, with her age-won wisdom and her capacity for empathy and healing, soon became a figure of reverence among the nomads, further cemented when she healed the chief's youngest child of a severe ailment, showcasing not just her knowledge but the depth of her compassion.

Recognizing the righteousness of their quest and moved by Me-Katilili's altruism, the nomads agreed to assist them in their return home. Under the cover of secrecy and with the chief's blessing, a plan was set in motion. A caravan was discreetly assembled, leading them to the port of Kismayu, where they were hidden aboard a fishing dhow. Under the cloak of night, they set sail, the waters carrying them closer to their homeland until, after several days and nights, they were safely disembarked near Malindi, their spirits buoyed by the unexpected kindness of strangers and the unbreakable resolve to continue their fight for freedom and justice.

Unbeknownst to Champion and Hobley, the spirit of defiance and the call for freedom that Me-Katilili embodied could not be easily extinguished, her influence reaching far beyond the confines of any cell or the harshness of any exile.

CHAPTER 14

Champion besieged

On 22nd and 23rd August 1914 the air was ecstatic as the horizon bled into shades of fiery orange and dusky purple in Kilifi. The Giriama warriors, embodying indomitable spirit and unyielding courage, stood poised on the brink of an epoch-defining confrontation. Their weapons, not mere tools of war but extensions of their will, gleamed under the fading light. Arrows honed to lethal points, sharp and precise daggers with edges, and spears that seemed to thirst for the fray were all meticulously prepared for the battle that loomed.

The warriors were the custodians of an ancient and mystical power, a sacred trust passed through generations. "Pufya" and "Bundugo," the mystical concoctions, were not merely potions but the essence of the earth's raw force, distilled into elixirs that could render their bodies impervious to the mortal instruments of their foes. Bullets, flames, and blades were said to shatter and dissolve upon their skin, forged in the crucible of their ancestral magic. This sorcery bestowed upon them not only the resilience of stone but the subtlety of shadows, allowing them to vanish from sight, to merge with the air itself when the need arose.

Among these titans of battle were figures of legend, warriors whose names were whispered with reverence and awe. Me-Katilili's sons, Dyeka, and the valiant Mwakidhuru led the vanguard, their presence an omen of the coming storm. Their comrades, the fearless Ngala, the swift Karabu, the stalwart Katana, and a host of others, were warriors of such prowess that they could fell a lion with nothing but the strength of their hands and the courage of their hearts. Adorned with hyena skulls, crowns that bore witness to their ferocity and adherence to the sacred *Fisi* (Hyena) oath, and faces painted with symbols of war and protection, they were a sight to behold - a tableau of power, of unity bound by a cause greater than any one man.

As night unfurled its dark canvas over the British station in Mwangea, the Giriama warriors, silent as the whispering wind, took their positions. Once a symbol of colonial imposition, the station was now encircled by the very essence of resistance. They had laid their plans with meticulous care, guided by information procured from an unwilling servant of the empire, now turned informant. Their approach was a study in caution and precision, moving through the underbrush with a silence that belied their numbers, every step bringing them closer to their objective.

Under the cloak of darkness, their movements were spectral, barely a rustle in the leaves, a shadow amongst shadows. They converged upon the jail, the heart of the British encampment, with a swiftness that belied the solemn gravity of their mission. Unaware and unprepared, the guards were swiftly and silently overcome, their fates sealed by the shadows they had dismissed. The prisoners, sensing the tide of their fortunes turning, greeted their liberators with a silence that was pregnant with unspoken vows of allegiance and gratitude.

The cells, symbols of oppression and subjugation, were flung open, the shackles of the imprisoned broken. Over thirty souls, once caged, now freed, stood at the brink of a new dawn, their liberation a testament to the unbreakable will of the Giriama warriors. This was not merely an assault; it was a declaration, a beacon of hope that burned fiercely in the night, heralding the beginning of a struggle for freedom, dignity, and the right to forge one's destiny.

In the thick of night, under a sky shrouded by the cloak of darkness, the air was charged with a palpable tension, a prelude to the unfolding drama. The Giriama warriors, emboldened by their initial success, turned their attention to a target of paramount importance: the quarters of Arthur Champion, the embodiment of colonial authority and oppression in their land. This strategic move was not merely an attack but a statement, a clarion call for freedom that resonated deep within the hearts of the freed prisoners who joined their ranks, their spirits ignited by the prospect of retribution and liberation.

The attempt to breach Champion's sanctum was met with an unexpected obstacle: the door, a formidable barrier, was securely locked from the inside. A testament to Champion's paranoia and fear of the uprising he now faced. All windows were securely shut. Yet the warriors, undeterred and adaptive, devised a cunning countermeasure. They sealed him within his own fortress, ensuring that escape was impossible. The silence of his guards, now mere memories in the night, served as a grim reminder of the warriors' resolve and prowess.

Inside, Arthur Champion, an once commanding and formidable figure, was reduced to a shadow of his former self. Clad in his pajamas, desperately reached out for a telephone, an artifact rendered useless. Its promise of salvation severed along with the 600 yards of wire cut by the natives. His heart pounded against his chest, a frenetic drumbeat echoing the tumult outside. The telegram, another beacon of hope, proved equally futile, its silence a stark testament to his isolation. Overcome by fear so potent it seemed to permeate the air he breathed, Champion's instincts propelled him beneath his bed - a pitiful attempt at concealment that he quickly deemed too conspicuous. In a frantic bid for survival, he sought refuge in a wooden chest, an ironic sanctuary amidst the spoils of his rule - half-filled with ivory, precious stones, and rupee coins, the tangible manifestations of exploitations - now companions in his confinement.

Meanwhile, the warriors, relentlessly pursuing justice, encircled the police quarters, and the air soon filled with the ominous crackle of flames. The voracious fire consumed the huts with a ferocity that mirrored the warriors' fervor. The once-imposing jail, a structure of despair and degradation, joined the conflagration, its destruction a symbol of the crumbling edifice of colonial dominion.

The night sky, a silent witness to the upheaval below, was illuminated by the fierce glow of the fires. The flames, dancing with reckless abandon, painted the darkness with hues of orange, red, and gold - a mesmerizing spectacle that belied the chaos it represented. The screams of the police officers, trapped in the inferno of their own making, pierced the night, a harrowing symphony of terror and despair. These sounds and sights reached the far villages, a beacon of both warning and hope, a testament to the indomitable spirit of the Giriama warriors and the inevitability of change.

Me-Katilili, alongside numerous village elders, observed the hues painting the night sky and nodded in silent pride.

This was more than an insurrection; it was a catharsis, a purging of years of subjugation and suffering through the transformative power of flame and resolve. Through their actions, the warriors were not just reclaiming their land; they were reasserting their very existence, their right to a future unmarred by the chains of oppression - a future forged in the fires of their courage and determination.

Amidst the turmoil unfurling across one of the Giriama villages, a cloak of panic enveloped Ngoyo wa Mwavuo and his spouse. Their son, Kingi, found himself entangled in a web of peril, serving within the quarters of Arthur Champion. This decision stood as a stark betrayal of the collective vow among the Giriama: no child should ever serve the colonialists. Yet, lured by substantial stipends, Ngoyo had broken this sacred pact, sending Kingi to the lion's den. Fear gnawed at his heart, the dread that his sole heir, the singular torchbearer of his lineage, might meet his demise within the walls of Champion's stronghold - a place now besieged.

From within the confines of his servitude, Kingi, gripped by a realization of the gravity of his predicament, peered through a slender gap in the kitchen window. The sight that met his eyes - a maelstrom of fire consuming the police quarters and jail - sparked a primal fear within him. His voice, laden with desperation, pierced the night, a plea for mercy to the encroaching warriors, "Help me, it's me, Kingi wa Ngonyo, spare me, I am your own flesh and blood, coerced into this, please let me live!"

The warriors, fueled by a quest for vengeance, called into the night for Champion, "Where is Chembe? His blood will quench our fury. Chembe, show yourself!" Their demands echoed ominously through the chaos.

Meanwhile, back in the village, Ngoyo and his wife, stricken with terror for their son's fate, sought the wisdom of the elders. They implored with heavy hearts and trembling voices, "Please, honored elders, dispatch messengers to beseech the warriors to spare Kingi, our son. He is the keeper of our future." The anguish of a mother's plea hung heavy in the air as Me-Katilili and the council of elders deliberated. Acknowledging the gravity of Ngoyo's transgression, they concurred on a resolution: Kingi would be spared, a decision rooted deeply in the tradition that no Mijikenda who sincerely seeks mercy should face death. Instead, such pleas were met with punitive measures - fines, exile, or other forms of reparation.

Emboldened by the maternal plea for clemency, village messengers, accompanied by Ngoyo's youngest sibling, hastened to Mwangea station. Their arrival, a race against time, bore the crucial message of mercy. They reached the brink of the moment, their words a shield against the imminent flames that threatened to engulf Champion's quarters. Their words were a testament to the profound bonds of kinship and the enduring power of compassion within the heart of turmoil. A vortex of rebellion and resolve surged like a relentless tide against the bastions of colonial power. The warriors, steadfast and unyielding, stood before Champion's quarters, a fortress symbolizing the very essence of their subjugation. Amidst this siege, a plea for mercy echoed through the tumult, the voice of Kingi wa Ngoyo, a son of the Giriama, caught in the whirlwind of his father's compromises and the colonial maelstrom.

Ngoyo wa Mwavuo and his wife, their hearts heavy with dread, hastened through the village under the cloak of night. Their desperate journey, a race against time, was fueled by the singular hope of saving their son, Kingi, from the wrath that engulfed Champion's quarters. Their plea to the village elders was a cacophony of anguish and desperation, a testament to the profound bonds of kinship and the crushing weight of choices made under the shadow of colonial dominion.

As the elders convened under the starlit sky, a solemn assembly marked by the gravity of the moment, Me-Katilili's wisdom shone like a beacon. The decision to spare Kingi, a concession to the sacred tenets of mercy and kinship, was intertwined with the stark reality of Ngoyo's transgression. The fine imposed was not merely a punishment but a reminder of the communal bonds the colonial yoke sought to sever.

Meanwhile, the warriors, their resolve as invincible as the ancient lands they sought to reclaim, issued their ultimatum. The demands were clear: the return of their lands in Sabaki, the release of their kin from the chains of forced labor, and the departure of the European settlers from their homeland. This decree, borne from the flames of resistance, was a clarion call for justice, a demand for the restoration of the dignity and autonomy stripped away by colonial greed.

The rebellion, now fully awakened across the Giriama territories, saw the burning of British shops and the expulsion of missionaries from their stations, a passionate rejection of the foreign presence that had sought to reshape their world. Villages of converts and the homes of those loyal to the colonial administration were consumed by flames, a purging fire that sought to reclaim the soul of the Agiriama from the clutches of colonial influence.

At Jilore, the confrontation between Captain Carew's police force and the Giriama warriors unfolded with brutal intensity. The battle, a vortex of violence that left both sides battered and bloodied, was emblematic of the fierce determination of the Giriama to resist their oppressors. Employing hit-and-run tactics, the warriors moved like shadows, striking with the precision and ferocity of the lion, their ancestral spirit. This guerrilla warfare, a dance of attack and evasion, became the rhythm of their resistance, a strategy that gradually eroded the invaders' grip on their lands.

Through the smoke of battle and the ashes of destruction, the spirit of the Agiriama burned brighter than ever. Their struggle, a testament to the unbreakable will, and the indomitable spirit of a people united in defense of their heritage and their right to self-determination, echoed across the hills and valleys of their ancestral lands. The rebellion, far more than a mere conflict, was a declaration of their existence, a war for the soul of their nation. The warriors fought with the courage and the wisdom of elders, under the guiding light of the stars that had watched over their land for generations.

In the besieged fortress that was once Arthur Champion's quarters, time seemed to stand still, each passing day marked by the growing desperation within its walls. With strategic acumen rivaling the greatest military minds, the Giriama warriors had effectively cut off all supplies to Champion, sealing his fate with each day that passed. Once a source of life, the water tank had been rendered useless, its contents tainted with the toxic branches of Euphorbia, a cruel but effective measure to ensure surrender. Within these confines, Champion's health spiraled downwards, a grim testament to the warriors' resolution and the harshness of their blockade.

Additionally, a state of emergency unfolded as German forces in Tanganyika and Uganda launched attacks on British colonies. Amidst this turmoil, Champion and his administration severely lacked support, facing shortages of troops and weapons and disrupted communications.

Meanwhile, the air in Charles Dundas's office in Malindi was thick with tension, starkly contrasting with the humid breeze that wafted through the coastal town. Dundas paced the floor, his mind a whirlwind of strategy and concern. The reports of the Giriama uprising had reached him, tales of a fury unleashed, a people reborn in defiance. The thought of engaging these well-organized and fiercely determined warriors filled him with deep-seated trepidation. Their armaments might not match the might of the British empire, but their sheer numbers and unbreakable spirit posed a threat no less formidable.

The arrival of an urgent dispatch from Mombasa only served to heighten the stakes. With Major G.M.P. Hawthorn, along with Captains Reynolds and Carew, pulled into the maelstrom of World War I in German East Africa, the British forces were stretched thin, and their resources diverted to a far larger conflict. Now, under the shadow of command from distant superiors, Dundas found himself in a dire predicament. The once robust ranks of the King's African Rifles had been reduced to a mere shadow of their former strength, leaving Dundas with only 25 armed police officers at his disposal.

Gathered in an enervate parade, the police officers stood before Dundas, a small band of men eclipsed by the enormity of the task ahead. Dundas, his voice imbued with a blend of resolve and an underlying current of desperation, addressed his makeshift squadron. "We may be few, but our ammunition surpasses theirs. This rebellion, this 'little war, as we might call it, shall be quelled with the might and discipline of the British Empire," he declared, his words an attempt to fan the flames of courage in the hearts of his men.

Dundas's plan unfolded with precision, a clear directive cutting through the moment's uncertainty. "Our first course of action is to extricate Arthur Champion from his quarters," he commanded, laying out a strategy aimed at striking at the heart of the rebellion and reclaiming the symbol of British authority from the clutches of the Giriama warriors. "From there, we move north to restore order village by village," he continued, his instructions painting a picture of a campaign designed to reassert control, one step at a time.

Yet, beneath the surface of Dundas's composed exterior lay a simmering cauldron of doubts and fears. The knowledge that the British forces were stretched thin, engaged in a global conflict that had drained their resources and workforce, hung over him like a shadow. The challenge before him was not merely a military engagement but a test of wills, a confrontation between the indomitable spirit of a people fighting for their land and the crumbling façade of colonial dominance.

As Dundas rallied his men, the air was charged with a turmoil of determination and the palpable sense of an impending clash. The stage was set for a confrontation that would test the limits of loyalty, strategy, and the essence of courage, a battle not just for territory but for the hearts and minds of those caught in the crossfire of history.

As the early morning mist clung to the lush landscape of Mwangea, the sun's rays began their slow dance across the sky, casting long shadows that seemed to herald the arrival of an uncertain dawn. Charles Dundas, his face etched with lines of worry and contemplation, led his small force of 25 armed police officers through the terrain that had become the epicenter of an uprising that would forever alter the course of colonial history.

The air was heavy, charged with an energy that seemed to pulse with the land's heartbeat. The vibrant chorus of the African wilderness, usually a testament to the unyielding spirit of life, now carried a different message - one of impending confrontation, of an inevitable clash between the old world and the new.

As Dundas and his men neared Mwangea station, the silence was palpable, a suffocating blanket that muffled every step, every breath. Once confident in their supremacy, the British contingent found themselves enveloped by an atmosphere of foreboding, their earlier assurances of dominance now haunting echoes in the vast expanse of the Giriama lands.

Dundas paused to survey the scene before him and realized the magnitude of their underestimation. Before them, the Giriama warriors stood arrayed, a formidable force that seemed to emerge from the very earth. Their numbers were staggering, their resolve unbreakable. With their modern weapons and ranks, the British were but a drop in the ocean of spirited defiance that faced them.

"Men," Dundas began, his voice betraying the gravity of their situation. " We stand on the precipice of history. Before us lies not merely a military engagement but a testament to the enduring spirit of a people yearning for their rightful place in the annals of time." His words, meant to still the resolve of his men, hung in the air, a poignant reminder of the futility of their mission. The realization that brute force and superior arms could not quell the fire of freedom burning in the hearts of the Giriama was a bitter pill to swallow.

It was then that Dundas, a man of action now cornered by the inevitable tide of change, made the decision that would mark a turning point in the conflict. "We have but one course of action," he declared, his voice resonant with the weight of command yet softened by the acknowledgment of their predicament. "We shall seek parley with the warriors. We will promise to vacate their lands in hopes that this gesture will secure the release of Arthur Champion."

The air was tense as Dundas approached the Giriama lines, a white flag held aloft to symbolize their willingness to negotiate. The silent and imposing warriors critically listened as Dundas conveyed his message with a humility born of necessity.

"We, the representatives of the British Crown, have underestimated both your resolve and your right to this land," Dundas admitted, his voice steady yet laced with the unspoken tension of the moment. "In recognition of your valiant struggle, we pledge to leave your lands, to return to you what is rightfully yours, in exchange for the safe release of Arthur Champion."

The warriors, unmoved yet considering the proposition, exchanged glances, their faces stoic masks that belied the tumult of emotions within. The silence that followed was a testament to the gravity of Dundas's offer, a moment suspended in time where the future of the Giriama lands hung in the balance.

It was a moment that would be recounted in tales and songs, a pivotal point where the course of history was irrevocably altered not by the clash of weapons but by the power of words and the promise of peace. For Dundas and his men, it was a retreat from the brink, a concession to the indomitable will of a people united in their quest for freedom. It was a hard-won and dearly cherished victory for the Giriama, a testament to the enduring spirit of resistance that would echo through generations.

The weight of a crown

On 31st August 1914, Arthur Champion stood amidst Malindi's colonial architecture, his silhouette hardening against the backdrop of the setting sun. Having been extracted from the besieged quarters at Mwangea station, his rescue, far from being a moment of relief, only served to stoke the fires of retribution burning within him. The ordeal had left its mark, not just on his body, worn from days of deprivation and fear, but on his spirit, now fueled by a desire for vengeance. The air in Malindi was thick with the heavy scent of the ocean mixed with a growing sense of unease.

Champion's orders, issued with a cold, steely resolve, set into motion a series of "precautionary patrolling" operations. These were not mere patrols, but a scorched earth campaign aimed at breaking the will of the Agiriama. British forces, acting under Champion's directives, began their relentless assault on the villages, a destructive march through the heart of Giriama lands.

"Let them feel the weight of the Crown," Champion declared, his voice devoid of remorse. "Burn their villages, lay waste to their crops, and seize their livestock. We shall leave them with nothing," he commanded, his words echoing colonial power's ruthlessness.

The countryside soon bore the scars of this punitive expedition. Flames devoured thatched roofs and granaries, leaving behind a trail of smoke that rose like dark pillars against the cloudless sky. The crackling of fire mingled with the distant cries of despair as the British forces methodically destroyed the sustenance and shelter of the Agiriama. Livestock, the wealth of the villages and precious lives, were rounded up, spoils of war to be claimed by the conquerors.

As weeks turned into a relentless campaign, the promised withdrawal of British forces from Giriama land became a distant memory. This broken promise faded against the backdrop of continued oppression. Instead, a new wave of colonial power arrived in the form of the King's African Rifles (KAR) reinforcements meant to quell any remnants of resistance and to assert, with unequivocal force, the dominion of the British Empire over the defiant heart of Giriama lands.

The arrival of these forces marked a new chapter in the struggle. It was a punitive expedition that sought to punish, subjugate, and erase the Giriama's fierce spirit of defiance. The landscape, once vibrant with its people's life and culture, became a testament to the cruelty of colonial ambition, a harsh reminder of the price of resistance in the face of overwhelming power.

Yet, within the ashes of devastation, the spirit of the Agiriama endured. A flickering flame of resilience and hope that no campaign of retribution could extinguish. The punitive patrols, though they sought to crush, unwittingly sowed the seeds of unity and determination, a collective resolve to reclaim their land, dignity, and future from the clutches of an empire that sought to define their destiny. This struggle, marked by the scars of battle and the ashes of lost homes, would forever stand as a monument to their unconquerable will, a beacon of resistance in the dark days of colonial oppression.

As the British campaign of "precautionary patrolling" scorched the earth of Giriama lands, the resolve of the Agiriama, rather than wilting, flourished with an intensity that the colonial forces had grossly underestimated. The rebellion, now etched in the annals of Mijikenda history as "*Kondo ya Chembe*" - the battle against Champion - grew in strength and scope, a testament to a people united in their defiance against an oppressor whose might was matched only by their unyielding spirit.

The echoes of Me-Katilili's impassioned rallies reverberated through the hearts and souls of the Agiriama, igniting a vigor that transcended the mere act of resistance. This was a holistic rebellion. Giriama force that rejected not only the physical presence of the British but the ideological and cultural hegemony they sought to impose. The Giriama became bastions of resistance, their hostility extending beyond colonial governance to encompass foreign religions such as Islam and Christianity, as well as those among their own who, fearing the specter of re-enslavement, clung to the foreign influences that promised safety but at the cost of their cultural identity. Traitors, perceived as betrayers of their heritage, faced stringent punishments, a clear message that the integrity of their traditions would be preserved at all costs.

In this climate of relentless resistance, the refusal to pay hut taxes and labor for the British were acts of defiance as potent as any armed engagement. These were statements of sovereignty, declarations that the Agiriama would not be subjugated, not in spirit, culture, or labor.

The Mijikenda, united in their struggle, fortified their warriors with better weapons and the potent mystical energies of "*bundugo*" and "*pufya*." These magical forces, steeped in the ancient wisdom of the Mijikenda, endowed the warriors with abilities that bordered on the supernatural. Bodies impervious to bullets, the capacity to vanish from sight and reappear at will, and the endurance to withstand the most grueling conditions were the gifts of their ancestors, a legacy of strength that turned the tide of battles and frightened the hearts of their enemies.

The warriors' tactics evolved, with traps and ambushes that utilized the terrain to their advantage, making each engagement a nightmare for the British forces. Despite its superior firepower, the British army was outmaneuvered and outwitted at every turn, a testament to the Giriama's intimate knowledge of their land and clever strategies.

Amidst this physical and spiritual warfare, the " *Chiraho cha Fisi*" - the hyena oath - emerged as a symbol of unbreakable unity and commitment to the cause. The fear and respect for this oath among the Giriama far surpassed any fear of the British government. It was more than a pledge; it was a binding force connecting every warrior to their community, ancestors, and land, imbuing them with an invincible sense of purpose. This era of the Giriama uprising against Champion and the British colonial forces was marked by a resurgence of cultural identity, a reclamation of autonomy, and an indomitable will to resist. Through the smoke of battle and the shadow of oppression, the Agiriama, supported by the broader Mijikenda community, forged a legacy of resistance that would be remembered not as a footnote of colonial history but as a testament to the enduring power of the human spirit to fight for freedom, dignity, and the sanctity of its cultural heritage.

The upper hand

22. Sept 1914. A meeting was held at *Kaya* Mudzi Muvya in Rabai by the Council of Elders and the Traditional Court.

"Similani, atumia similani." Pembe wa Bembere, a highly respected council of elders and close associate of Me-Katilili, sent greetings to the living and the dead, his stick, crowned with a leopard's head, hitting the earth next to his feet. His voice was deep and powerful. "First, I commend our courageous warriors for the incredible fight against our enemies." There was a bout of jubilation in the sacred *Kaya* forest, drums, whistles, and flutes. "We now want to regain our fertile ancestral land, our rich economy, and everything that is rightfully ours. In doing so, however, we want to be sure that we will not lose any more of our people. For these reasons, we shall send a delegate issuing a peace treaty to the British." Pembe wa Bembere announced.

Bogosho wa Biryaa cleared his throat and spoke, "We have shown Chembe what he is; he is just a crumb. This is what unity can achieve. We shall never deter, never give up! Alume huwooo (traditional empowering calling for men crowd)

"Huwooo," the men answered with vigor, making masculine sounds afterward to reinforce their strength and masculinity.

"Acheee" (a traditional empowering calling for a women crowd) is a female elder called from the group.

"heeeee," replied all the women present, following up with high-pitched jubilation sounds.

The meeting concluded with the council of elders and the traditional court agreeing to send a peace treaty through a delegate, a senior respected Arab intermediary, Sheikh Fathili bin Omar, who worked as an Islamic teacher in Arabuko.

A bull was then slaughtered, the meat roasted, and a feast was held.

At the British Post on weekly reports,

Lt P. F. Carew recorded:

- 26th September, 220 sheep and goats captured
- 27th September, patrolled as far as north Mombasa
- Burnt all villages in the locality, captured 30 sheep and goats, 1 native killed.
- 29th September, all villages around Mugadini burnt, also villages at Shakadulu. 145 sheep and goats captured.
- 1st October. Finished burning villages at Bungale. Some natives had fled … 1 native killed, 200 sheep and goats near Garashi and a large amount of property hidden in the bush was found and destroyed.

Lt. A.A Hughes recorded:

- Have been on going on these lines, i.e. burning villages and trying to capture stocks.
- 14th September I burnet villages close to the mission.
- 15th moved at 2:00 p.m. and burnt 5 villages. On the return journey we were followed by a number of natives, some of these were killed before they left us.

Amidst the tumult and devastation that marked the nadir of the struggle for Giriama independence, a startling admission emerged from the British government: it had never truly conquered the Agiriama. Throughout the conflict, the Giriama's battle strategies evolved with cunning ingenuity, incorporating more sophisticated weapons and traps, a testament to their resilience and adaptability. This escalation compelled the

British to seek a ceasefire, especially during the height of World War I, as the King's African Rifles were requisitioned for duty in German East Africa. Driven by a pragmatic desire to safeguard their lands and livestock from further ravages and loss, the Agiriama, too, were inclined to negotiate peace. This convergence of interests, born out of necessity and the weariness of conflict, paved the way for discussions that promised a cessation of hostilities, albeit under the shadow of a world at war and a community determined to preserve its essence against imperial designs.

The peace agreement

On the rain-soaked morning of September 30, 1914, Sheikh Fathili bin Omar, entrusted with the Giriama's hopes for peace, made his way towards the British administrative stronghold. Accompanied by two of his Islamic students, members of the Duruma subtribe of the Mijikenda, they braved the relentless downpour that greeted them at the dawn of this pivotal day. As they advanced, one student held an umbrella high above Sheikh Fathili's head, a shield against the relentless rain, while the other carried his belongings. Both students were drenched to their core. The deluge turned the hem of Sheikh Fathili's white thobe a muddy red, each step they took splashing the vibrant earth of the Mijikenda homeland onto the fabric.

The guards at the entrance, cloaked in their preconceptions, greeted them with eyes narrowed by distrust. Yet, undeterred by their frosty reception, Sheikh Fathili, embodying the serene resolve of his mission, sought an audience with Hobley. After a moment's hesitation, the guards revealed that Hobley was not present. Nonetheless, they suggested that Sheikh Fathili could meet with Champion instead, offering a glimmer of hope in the midst of a stormy encounter.

Moments later, the rain had taken a break. Champion and Sheikh Fathili sat on his terrace. "Hah! Now the hooligans want peace, huh? Let's see what it will cost them," Champion arrogantly scoffed. Lighting his pipe conceitedly, he said, "I will speak with the head offices ..." He blew a heavy puff of smoke.

"When will they get an answer?" questioned Sheikh Fathili.

"In a week or so. Come back with the native elders and their people."

Under terms and conditions

Early October 1914. A few days later, the peace conference took place in Sabaki. This meeting, however, seemed designed to belittle and humiliate the native populace, as it was conducted strictly according to the British's predefined terms and conditions. Arthur Champion, taking center stage, unfolded a telegram paper and declared in a loud voice,

"We shall agree to your plea for peace," signifying the British's conditional acceptance of the peace overtures, underscored by condescending toward the native participants.

Champion spread out the telegram paper and read aloud, "... on the following conditions:

(1) A fine of two goats or six rupees is to be levied on each male; a total of 100,000 rupees must be paid.

(2) The 1914 tax collection is to be observed keenly.

(3) Raise 1000 laborers to be sent to Mombasa to work at the water project and as carrier corps for the world war.

(4) Leaders, and any person opposing us, are to be handed over, and weapons, all bows and arrows, swords surrendered.

(5) Government headmen we appoint are to submit to our demand; and

(6) All natives to move to the south of the Sabaki immediately.

All conditions were to be fulfilled within ten days. ..."

Under the guise of these terms and conditions, the Mijikenda were starkly reminded that the sequence of their historical oppressors had merely transitioned from Arab to British control. The latter, having established the East African Protectorate under the pretense of offering "protection" and putting an end to the slave trade, had now revealed themselves as colonial rulers' intent on governing with an iron fist. This realization underscored a bitter truth: their presence was not for the benefit of the indigenous people. Still, it was driven purely by self-interest and the pursuit of profit, completely sidelining the well-being and interests of the natives.

The Giriama's resistance was unwavering and resolute. They refused to pay hut taxes, fines, or provide laborers. Weapons remained in their hands, elders stood firm in defiance, and no concessions were made to British demands. This steadfast opposition left the British administration depleted, visibly outnumbered, and without the means to enforce their stipulated conditions. The local headsmen, appointed by the British, found no legitimacy among the natives; they were outright rejected and even targeted, with some losing their lives to acts of defiance. This atmosphere of hostility and fear deterred other headsmen from cooperating with the British, regardless of the stipends offered to them. These appointed leaders deserted British official council meetings, betraying the colonial administration's faltering grip on authority.

Treason within the Giriama ranks was not tolerated; known traitors faced severe repercussions. The community's collective actions spoke volumes:

Not a single tax was paid.

Collaboration with the Imperial British East Africa Company (IBEAC) by providing labor was strictly prohibited.

The supply of food to the British administration was effectively boycotted.

Through these measures, the Giriama showcased a powerful
and coordinated resistance, undermining the colonial structure
imposed upon them and asserting their refusal to acquiesce to
foreign domination.

CHAPTER 15

Back from second imprisonment

As the twilight hues of dusk wrapped the village of Mkange in a cloak of melancholy beauty, Me-Katilili wa Menza, weary yet unbowed, stepped across the threshold of her homestead. It was a quiet return, a homecoming shadowed by the specter of past incarcerations and the ever-present threat of renewed captivity. Her family - spanning generations from the stoic presence of her husband, Mulewa, to the innocent gazes of great-grandchildren - gathered in a silent embrace. Their celebration was a muted affair. Their joyous hearts were tempered by the chilling fear of loss. Time had etched its tales upon Me-Katilili's visage, yet her spirit, that indomitable force, blazed with a passion undimmed by age or ordeal.

In the wake of her return, Me-Katilili reignited the flames of her cause with a fervor that belied her years. She became the architect of revival, weaving the threads of resistance and empowerment into the very fabric of her community. Her wisdom flowed like a river, nurturing young and old with lessons of resilience and heritage. Days melded into nights as she traversed the landscape of healing and spiritual solace, a beacon of hope amidst the tumult of colonial strife.

Tragedy struck in the stillness before dawn, a moment suspended between night's ebb and day's birth. Mulewa, her companion through decades of struggle and joy, slipped silently from this world. Me-Katilili's lamentation tore through the veil of the morning, a heartrending cry of loss that echoed the depths of her soul's despair. The mournful call of a gemshorn pierced the air, a herald of sorrow that resonated through the village, announcing the departure of a man whose life had been a pillar of strength and dignity.

As the first light of dawn touched the earth, the village elders gathered, their voices weaving prayers into the morning breeze, a sacred rite that escorted Mulewa's spirit on its journey to the ancestors. A goat, symbolic of passage and sacrifice, was offered at the doorstep of their home, its blood a testament to the cycle of life and death. The solemn procession from Mkange to Musoloni, where Mulewa would join the lineage of his forebears, was a web of grief and reverence, the *Chifudu* group's mournful songs a haunting farewell melody.

In the following days, Mkange transformed into a sanctuary of collective mourning. The tradition of *hanga,* a funeral, drew a reunion of souls. The community united in its tribute to Mulewa's legacy. The nights came alive with the rhythmic grace of the *Chifudu* dancers, whose movements poignantly reflected the transient nature of existence. The closure of the mourning period heralded a ritual of renewal and protection, a cleansing that stripped away the remnants of sorrow, preparing the path for a new beginning. Yet, for Me-Katilili, the loss of Mulewa was a chasm that plunged deep, unearthing a well of grief that spanned the breadth of her people's suffering. Her tears became the voice of the voiceless, mourning the warriors, the violated, the butchered elders, and the disrupted families - a litany of loss that bled into the very soil of her homeland.

Yet, beneath the surface of communal support and ritual healing, Me-Katilili's heart bore the scars of a grief that spanned beyond the personal. Her lamentation was a dirge for the lost: her son Katilili, whose spirit had joined the ancestors; her brother Kithi, taken before his time; the warriors and elders slaughtered in the sanctity of the *Kayas*; the young men of Mwangea, their potential extinguished by colonial brutality; the innocent girls of Vitengeni and many other villages, their purity violated. Her tears were a river of mourning for the lives torn asunder by the ravages of injustice, for the countless village raids that had severed the threads of countless destinies, and for the motherland besieged by sorrow.

In this crucible of loss, Me-Katilili's once indomitable strength waned, her vitality dimming under the weight of collective sorrow. Her mourning transcended the personal, becoming a reflection of a people's anguish, a mirror of the suffering that had permeated the fabric of her community. Through her tears, Me-Katilili grieved not just for Mulewa but for every soul that had been swept away by the storm of colonial oppression, her spirit a beacon of resilience and remembrance in the face of overwhelming darkness.

Continuity of life

In the twilight of her years, surrounded by the encroaching shadows of loss and grief, Me-Katilili found a flicker of hope in the bright eyes of her grandchildren. They were the living testament to the resilience of her people, the assurance that the spirit of resistance and the essence of their culture would persevere through the ages. In these moments, with the innocence and curiosity of youth gathered around her, Me-Katilili would wipe away the tears that clung to her lashes, her voice adopting a tone of enthusiasm as she delved into the lore of their ancestors.

"Behold, Sayo, my dear grandchild," Me-Katilili began, her words carrying the wisdom of their history under the canopy of stars, "the prophetesses Mepoho, Nimahongo, and Nimunyumba foresaw the turmoil that clouds our lands today. They spoke of vessels cresting the ocean waves, iron birds slicing through the sky, and the iron serpent crawling across the land. They warned of invaders, their skin pal, hair fine as sisal fiber, drawing puffs from alien plants, foretelling a time when our young girls would cradle babies born of turmoil."

Sayo, her young mind teeming with questions, inquired with the innocence of one untouched by puberty's scars, "Why didn't our people drive these invaders away before their shadow spread across our land? Such an act would have spared us so much suffering!"

Me-Katilili sighed, the weight of centuries heavy in her gaze. "You see, there's wisdom in the proverb "do not look where you feel. Look where you slipped." Generations before us saw the arrival of the Portuguese, the Arabs, the Persians, and others. They came and, for a time, coexisted with us in peace. We, a community that cherishes harmony, saw no harm in their presence, provided they respected our ways. Trade and interaction blossomed between us," she recounted, the sorrow in her voice a mirror to the sorrow in her heart. "But slowly, insidiously, they began to kill, capture and enslave our people, dragging them into the abyss of slavery."

With a shake of her head, she continued, "Oh, the countless souls lost to their greed... Your uncle Katilili, he'd be a full-grown man by now, perhaps with his own children. My brother Kithi would now have been a respected elder by now... Karisa, and many, many others..." The names fell from her lips like leaves from a dying tree, each a symbol of a life interrupted, a future stolen.

Then, young Chengo, a spark of defiance in his great-grandmother's sea of sorrow, declared with youthful bravado, "Grandma, don't cry. If I were there, I would have fought them off, boom, boom!" His small fists danced in the air, and his legs kicked at invisible foes.

Touched by his spirited display, Me-Katilili gently touched his bare chest. "I have no doubt you would have, Chengo. And you would carry *'pufya'*, the magical energy that makes your body as impervious as a rock." His broad smile, punctuated by gaps where milk teeth once resided, was a beacon of innocence and unspoiled courage.

"Will you take us to see where Mepoho vanished? I want to see it to believe," Sayo implored, her young mind alight with wonder and skepticism.

"When I have regained my strength, I promise we will visit," Me-Katilili assured her. "It is said that Mepoho, witnessing the impending doom brought by these foreigners, chose not to endure their injustices. Summoning her last ounce of power, she danced with such intensity that the earth opened to embrace her, leaving behind nothing but a mound of earth as a testament to her departure. That place, now known as Kaloleni, beckons all to bear witness to her resolve. That is where it got its name from, Kaloneni; go and see."

Turning her gaze to her family, her voice steady and imbued with solemnity, Me-Katilili declared, "When my time comes, lay me to rest in the sacred embrace of *Kaya* Fungo." Her eyes sought out Kavumbi and Mlamu, her daughter and son-in-law, ensuring her final wish resonated in the hearts of her kin. "Hear me well. Upon my death, I wish to be buried in *Kaya* Fungo," she reiterated, her words a covenant between the present and the eternal, a final request from a matriarch whose life had been a testament to the enduring spirit of her people.

As the relentless march of seasons bore witness to the inexorable decline of Me-Katilili's health, the vibrant matriarch who once stood as a bastion of strength and resilience for her people succumbed to the ravages of time. No longer able to fend for herself, the mantle of her care was passed to Sayo wa Kalama. Sayo now blossomed into a young woman of keen intellect and striking resemblance to the fiery spirit of Munyazi - the youthful embodiment of Me-Katilili herself, was bestowed the solemn duty of caregiver by her parents, in adherence to the time-honored traditions that guided their community.

In the waning chapters of Me-Katilili's storied life, the relentless passage of time whispered promises of an end. With her once formidable strength now a memory whispered on the winds, her days were cradled in the arms of Sayo wa Kalama. Sayo, whose youth blossomed under the shadow of her grandmother's legacy, mirrored Me-Katilili's fierce spirit and intellect in her prime. Entrusted with the sacred duty of caregiving, Sayo upheld the traditions of their ancestors, tending to Me-Katilili with a devotion that transcended the mere passage of blood through veins - it was a testament to the enduring bond of family and legacy.

The resolution to embrace the guidance of traditional healers catalyzed Me-Katilili's journey back to Bungale, the haven of her matrimonial years - a place interlaced with the memories of her adult life. This familiar terrain was not only steeped in her personal history but also home to her offspring and extended kin, all of whom stood ready to envelop her in their embrace of care and comfort. Bungale, cradling the echoes of her most cherished moments, was to become a sanctuary where she would be enfolded in the wisdom and ministrations of those skilled in the time-honored healing practices. However, the unpredictable currents of fate had mapped out a divergent path, steering her story towards unforeseen horizons.

Passage of spirit

Mid 1920s. On a day scorched by the relentless embrace of the sun, Sayo returned from the stream, her footsteps echoing the rhythm of simpler times. However, the home that greeted her was draped in silence - a silence too profound to be anything but ominous. There, in the stillness of her room, lay Me-Katilili, her spirit having taken flight on the gentle breeze of Sayo's absence. The shock of discovery sent waves of panic and disbelief crashing through Sayo, who quickly rallied the community to their side.

As the '*hanga*' (funeral) rituals unfolded, the air was thick with the scent of mourning and the murmured respects of a community united in grief. Yet, beneath this veneer of communal sorrow, a disruption of dissent brewed. Elders and family alike were caught in a quiet dispute, the core of which lay in Me-Katilili's final resting place. Some elders shared a profound revelation: the religion was at odds with Me-Katilili's expressed desire to find her final resting place in *Kaya* Fungo. They elaborated on this contention, explaining that according to Giriama religious dictates, only those who pass away within the sacred confines of a *Kaya* are eligible for burial there. Moreover, the heat of the coastal climate posed a challenge to preserving the body for any extended period. Thus, the practical considerations of a burial in Bungale stood in contrast to her wish to be interred in *Kaya* Fungo.

The divine energy chose to make its presence known amidst these turbulent waters of contention. As the women tasked with preparing Me-Katilili's body for its journey engaged in their solemn duties, a phenomenon as mysterious as it was awe-inspiring unfolded - a shroud of black ants enveloped her, sending a ripple of shock and disbelief through the household. This inexplicable sign brought the preparations to a standstill, compelling the elders to seek communion with Me-Katilili's spirit, entreating her understanding and blessing for the path chosen in her honor. The ritual sacrifice of a goat at her doorstep served as a bridge between the realms, a blood offering to herald Me-Katilili's ascension to the ancestors. A final homage to a woman whose life was a beacon of resistance, wisdom, and unyielding love for her people.

As the community grappled with the manifestations of her will and the dictates of tradition, it became clear that Me-Katilili's legacy was not bound to the earth upon which she walked; it was etched in the hearts of those she touched, a living testament to the power of one woman's spirit to inspire generations. Whether cradled by the sacred earth of *Kaya* Fungo or nestled in the embrace of Bungale, Me-Katilili's essence would forever permeate the land she loved, her story a guiding light for all who dare to dream of freedom and fight for justice in the face of adversity.

Port of Charleston, South Carolina, USA, mid 1870s

The day was waning as The Queen's Endeavor made its solemn procession into the Port of Charleston, its sails heavy with the weight of a journey that had stretched across the merciless expanse of the Atlantic. Captain Theodore, a man whose face was etched with the lines of countless voyages, stood steadfast at the helm, his gaze fixed on the horizon. Beside him, Sir Herbert, whose reputation as a trader and explorer was known in many a distant land, surveyed the bustling port with an air of finality. Both men, seasoned by the trials of the sea, had silently agreed that this passage would be their last; the perils they had faced on the transatlantic route had burgeoned beyond their wildest reckonings.

Beneath the oppressive confines of the deck, the air was suffocating, heavy with the mingled odors of saltwater and despair. In the dim glow of what remained of a once robust people, Kithi stood among the dwindling survivors. Their numbers now reduced to a mere fraction of their former strength. They clustered together in the feeble light, their weary bodies and downtrodden spirits reflecting the toll of their harrowing journey. The brutality they had faced left visible marks on them, both physically and emotionally, as they grappled with the harsh realities of their plight.

A pall of mourning enveloped them, the loss of more than half their number to the ocean's insatiable depths casting a shadow that felt almost tangible, a silent witness to their grueling journey. Kithi's own odyssey had its genesis amidst the chaos of the Mtsanganyiko market, weaving its way through Malindi, reaching the shores of Zanzibar, before pressing on to Bagamoyo (Tanzania). Their numbers, already thinned by hardship, were sorrowfully bolstered there, swelling the ranks of those bound for unimaginable fates. Their voyage stretched across the unforgiving expanse of the transatlantic, touching down briefly in the West Indies, where some amongst them were disembarked, their fates sealed far from home.

The Queen's Endeavor, a vessel now synonymous with the loss and despair of its human cargo, charted its final course for South Carolina. Each leg of their journey was steeped in sorrow, marked by the silent disappearance of lives swallowed by the oceans, or left behind in distant lands. For Kithi and her fellow prisoners, the journey they were compelled to embark upon was more than a mere passage; it was an inscription carved deep within the essence of their beings. Each step, akin to the stroke of a blade, left behind a profound scar, a permanent emblem of the anguish and loss they bore together. This path was not simply a route they traveled; it was a silent witness to their communal tribulation, a somber homage to the resilience of their spirits in the face of relentless adversity. Through this shared odyssey, their souls were bound together, each carrying the weight of an unspoken narrative, a testament to their collective endurance and the indelible mark of their united plight.

As the ship docked, the captives were ushered onto the deck, their eyes squinting against the harsh glare of the setting sun. The air suffused with the tang of salt, the earthy musk of tar, and the cries of seabirds mingled with the docks' raucous din. The heat enveloped them like a thick blanket, the humidity clinging to their skin, a cruel reminder of the oppressive hold they had just left.

The bustling port market lay ahead, a cacophony of sights, sounds, and smells. The cries of auctioneers cut through the air like a discordant melody against the backdrop of clinking chains and hushed whispers. Kithi, his gaze lowered, was acutely aware of the myriad strange faces that surveyed him and his companions, their eyes appraising, calculating their worth.

Sir Herbert's rich and commanding voice rose above the din as he began the auction. "Gentlemen, behold the prime selection of labor, hailing directly from the heart of Africa!" he declared, gesturing grandly towards Kithi and the others.

Captain Theodore remained silent, his expression unreadable, as he watched the proceedings from the sidelines. His thoughts were a tumultuous sea, reflecting the myriad emotions that battled within him - a sense of relief at the end of the voyage, tinged with a deep-seated unease at his role in it.

Standing amidst the crowd, Kithi felt the weight of countless eyes upon him. Despite not understanding the words, the intent was evident as he was prodded forward, the object of eager bidding. His heart raced, a tumult of fear and defiance swirling within him. The touch of the sun on his skin, the distant call of the sea -they spoke to him of freedom, a concept that seemed as distant now as his home on the East Coast of Africa.

Throughout the journey, Kithi's heart was a silent chapel of prayer, his thoughts quietly swirling in dimming hope and lucid despair. Yet, with each step taken under the shadow of captivity, a shroud of disappointment settled over him. "Where is *Mulungu*? Where have my ancestors gone? Where are the spirits that once guided us?" he pondered, his soul echoing questions that seemed to vanish into the void. Within the hidden chambers of his heart, a flicker of rebellion sparked; he began to craft a secret blueprint, almost conspiring with his own spirit on how he might weave through the unseen threads of fate to find his way back to the familiarity of his village in Bungale. This clandestine plot was not only a plan of escape but also a pilgrimage towards reclaiming his freedom, his heritage, and the whispers of the land that called him home. The possibility of reuniting with well-known faces from Bungale flickered through Kithi's mind. 'Had Karisa and the rest of our people, seized from our soil, been brought here? If we met, would we recognize each other after all that has happened? Could there be a chance to devise a covert plan, to escape and return to our cherished homeland?' These questions, heavy with longing and speculation, nestled deeply in Kithi's thoughts, a private trove of secrets he carried within himself.

Finally, a voice cut through the clamor, signaling the end of his auction. George Richmond, a man with a countenance that bore the marks of both hardness and a peculiar curiosity, had claimed him. Kithi, unable to comprehend the words exchanged, could only follow as George led him away from the market, his future uncertain, his past a distant memory.

As they departed, Captain Theodore and Sir Herbert exchanged glances, silently acknowledging the end of an era. "We have made great fortunes and a lot of wealth. We have made our last journey," Theodore stated, his voice barely above a whisper.

"Aye," Herbert replied, his gaze lingering on the fading light of the day. "The world is changing, and so are we."

In the days that followed, Kithi would come to know the harsh reality of his new existence, yet within him burned the indomitable spirit of a man who had faced the darkest depths of despair and survived. The Queen's Endeavour's journey had ended, but for Kithi, this was the beginning of a new chapter that would test his strength, will, and heart in ways he could never have imagined.

…… THE END ……

SOURCES / REFERENCES

Some of numerous References

http://www.standardmedia.co.ke/?articleID=2000020686&story_title=Mekatilili%E2%80%99s-braveresistance-against-British-rule24
http://www.open.ac.uk/Arts/fergusoncentre/memorialisation/gallery/mekatilili-index.shtml;
http://www.africareview.com/Special-Reports/The–mad-Kenyan-woman-who-rattled-the-British/-/979182/1876464/-/x2seyf/-/index.html;
http://www.sourcememory.net/veleda/?p=28;
http://www.nation.co.ke/News/regional/-/1070/641820/-/7lmwal/-/index.html;
http://thabalance.wordpress.com/2011/12/21/mekatilili-wa-menza/;
http://www.standardmedia.co.ke/?articleID=2000020686&story_title=mekatilili-s-brave-resistance-against-british-rule&pageNo=3; Mekatilili wa: She Feared No Man

http://www.standardmedia.co.ke/?articleID=2000065265&story_title=women-who-stood-where-men-trembled;
http://www.open.ac.uk/Arts/ferguson-centre/memorialisation/events/london-symposium2011/Celia_Neil_Mekatilili.pdf;
http://www.academia.edu/5017110/Ikonya_Philo_The_Woman_Question_
http://www.standardmedia.co.ke/article/2000016796/honouring-a-woman-of-war;

"Shujaa Me Katilili Wa Menza – Her legacy in independent Africa" (Book written by Dr. Tsawe-Munga wa Chidongo, 2018)